MASHED UP

A volume in the series

Science/Technology/Culture
Edited by Carolyn de la Peña
and Siva Vaidhyanathan

MASHED UP

Music, Technology, and the Rise of Configurable Culture

Aram Sinnreich

University of Massachusetts Press

AMHERST AND BOSTON

LC 2010008989
ISBN 978-1-55849-829-7 (paper); 828-0 (library cloth)

Designed by Dennis Anderson
Set in Chaparral Pro by Westchester Book, Inc.
Printed and bound by Thomson-Shore, Inc.

Library of Congress Cataloging-in-Publication Data

Sinnreich, Aram.
    Mashed up : music, technology, and the rise of configurable culture /
Aram Sinnreich.
        p.   cm. — (Science/technology/culture)
    Includes bibliographical references and index.
    ISBN 978-1-55849-829-7 (pbk. : alk. paper)—ISBN 978-1-55849-828-0
(library cloth : alk. paper)
    1. Popular music—Social aspects.   2. Music and technology
    3. Mashups (Music)—History and criticism.   4. Remixes—History
and criticism.   5. Turntablism.   I. Title.
    ML3918.P67S56 2010
    306.4'842—dc22

                                                          2010008989

British Library Cataloguing in Publication data are available.

This book is for Listening and Hope.

This shit is not about me, it's about all of us,
'cause we're the same motherfuckin' person.
So take a picture of your goddamn self,
'cause we're all the same dude!

—Girl Talk

Contents

List of Illustrations

Preface

Confessions of a (Reformed) Musical Reactionary

It is both fitting and ironic that I have written this book. Fitting, because I have been obsessed with both music in general and the expressive potential of recording technology in particular for as long as I can remember, and because my entire professional career to date has been dedicated to exploring the intersection between music, technology, and society. Ironic because, while many or most other members of my generation happily embraced what I have come to call "configurable" music styles such as hip-hop, house, and techno[1] as both we and they reached adolescence in the 1980s, I actively resisted these innovations, and only grudgingly came to accept and finally to love them a decade later.

I still remember the wonder and amazement I felt when I first heard my own voice recorded and played back to me. It was the late 1970s, I was four or five years old, and my father, an attorney, brought home a battery-powered Dictaphone with an internal condenser mic. He held the small black box in front of me while we talked, then pressed a button. All of a sudden, my own voice came out, repeating the words I had just spoken. I was shocked; he hadn't told me what the box was for, and I had never dreamed that such a thing was possible.

Even at this young age, I was already quite familiar with sound recording technology. I had been requesting to hear albums by my favorite musicians—the Beatles, the Rolling Stones, and the Everly Brothers—since I could first speak, and by four or five I was very comfortable with the mechanics of the turntable and the amplifier, and happy to raid my parents' record collection whenever I had the opportunity. I had even come to view the stereo with a kind of familiar reverence, often running my fingers over the knobs on the receiver or the fabric covering the boxy Advent floor speakers as I listened to music, and wondering how it all worked.

Thus, my sense of awe on encountering the Dictaphone had nothing to do with the technology per se. What shocked me, though of course I could never have put it in words at the time, was that the device allowed me to *produce* recorded sound, and not just to *consume* it. The thought had literally never occurred to me. Although we had a beautiful Steinway baby grand piano in our home, it was rarely used; in my family, music was something that you primarily listened to, rather than made.[2] We could listen appreciatively—even passionately—but the notion that we'd make it for ourselves was as absurd as the notion of making our own butter, or shoes. That was a job for experts, whose work we acquired at a store and brought into our home to enjoy.

Nonetheless, over the ensuing years, I developed a passion both for making music and for recording sound. I begged my parents for piano lessons, but they demurred, believing (perhaps accurately) that I lacked the requisite attention span, and that forcing me to practice would quickly become a chore for them. I would not receive my first formal music instruction—on guitar—until I was thirteen. Much earlier on, however, I acquired my first tape deck, and by the age of eight, I was recording my own "radio show" (call letters WARAM) from the dining room table.

A few years later, my parents bought me a RadioShack integrated stereo system, which included both a turntable and a dual-deck cassette recorder. Most important, it had a headphone jack and a microphone jack. It didn't take me long to figure out that a set of headphones could serve as an improvised microphone if plugged into the "wrong" jack, and by the time I was twelve or so, I had upped the ante on my recorded radio show, creating tapes on which I alternated songs from my parents' record collection and my own patter. From there, I made the obvious leap, to talking and singing while the record was playing, rather than waiting for the interstitial silences between songs. To this day, one of my most treasured relics is a tape I made at the age of fifteen with my three-year-old brother, on which I cajole him to sing along with songs such as the Rolling Stones' "You Can't Always Get What You Want," and to chant slogans such as "LSD, LSD, LSD is the thing for me" (never mind that I had never tried LSD—it just seemed to go with the territory).

Toward the end of my teens, I actually fulfilled my childhood ambitions and became a disc jockey (for three years on my college radio station) and a semi-professional musician, writing songs and playing guitar and bass first in college bands, and then in gigging and recording bands in New York and elsewhere.

None of this is extraordinary. In fact, as I will argue throughout this work, I believe that my own relationship to recording technology is indicative of a much larger cultural shift, a redefinition of our relationship to media production and consumption. My generation was the first to have cheap, accessible, and even disposable audio recording equipment in the home from early childhood, and in the decades since then, both audio and video production have become increasingly accessible in many senses, including affordability, ubiquity, and ease of use. And, because technology and culture coevolve, continually nudging one another in new directions, we have seen drastic changes in our aesthetic and symbolic environments in these years as well, many of which I will describe in greater detail in the pages that follow.

What *is* extraordinary is that, despite my practical enthusiasm for recording (and rerecording) music and sound from earliest childhood, I was not only blind to the merits of configurable culture for many years, but actively hostile as well. As I have mentioned, I was reared on the rock-and-roll of the 1960s, and throughout my childhood, that music remained my gold standard, even as popular idioms moved further and further away from it. Even the most mainstream pop acts of my adolescence—Prince, Madonna, Michael Jackson—felt somewhat foreign to me. The big, gated drum sound, tinny synthesizer patches, and electronic percussion that pervaded nearly every popular recording of that era sounded like music from another planet; it just didn't fit into my aesthetic at all.

Far more foreign, and even threatening, were the musical styles of the '80s that dispensed with the fig leaves of guitars, chord charts, and vocal melodies retained by the pop stars I mentioned above. Emerging styles such as hip-hop (which was suddenly everywhere in my Brooklyn neighborhood), house, and techno were unapologetically mechanical in their aesthetic, and though I didn't fully understand it at the time, Afrocentric in their structural logics. In a sense, then, I understood the message of the music intuitively—these recordings were hostile to the music I held most dear, and to what I refer to in this book as the modern discursive framework.

What I didn't understand yet was how these musical innovations related to me, and to my own life experiences and social position. My aesthetic antipathies to these new musical styles were consciously and unequivocally moral—I viewed them as a kind of commercial bamboozlement, a bait-and-switch operation in which the human soul was being replaced with a robotic facsimile, and I believed myself to be uniquely conscious of this tragedy among my unthinking peers. In short, I felt about hip-hop the way that Theodore Adorno did about jazz.

This continued even into my early college years, during which I remained a musical reactionary, believing myself to be a revolutionary: strumming my acoustic guitar, playing only "live" recorded tracks on my radio show, and condescendingly insulting the tastes of my friends and acquaintances. I remember many conversations with my friend Henry, around the age of nineteen, during which he tried fruitlessly to convince me that sampling was a legitimate art form, and just as creative as sitting down and playing a piano. I rejected his arguments out of hand; in my mind, sampling was *copying*, it was *unoriginal*. How could Run DMC or Public Enemy ever approach the *genius* of the Beatles if they didn't even know how to play their own instruments?

Then something changed, around the time I turned twenty. Suddenly, I could hear hip-hop. I could appreciate the brilliance of a well-flipped sample, the ingenuity of an unexpected remix. I began, for the first time, to feel that configurable music was *my* music, my generation's music, in a way that the rock I had formerly cherished and the jazz I had come to adore could never be. Almost overnight, I became an enthusiast, blasting KRS-One, De La Soul and Negativland from my stereo. I had arrived, late, to the configurability party.

What precipitated this change of heart, this change of ear? I'm not completely sure myself. It may be that, as I entered adulthood and roamed ever farther from my home, I paradoxically came to see myself ever more as a New Yorker, and to immerse myself nostalgically in its culture. Or it could be that, as the miles and the years separating me from Brooklyn widened, the palpable threat contained in hip-hop waned, and I was better able to appreciate what was left over.

Or maybe the change had nothing at all to do with *leaving*. Maybe it had to do with *arriving*. Halfway through my college career, I transferred to Wesleyan University, where I instantly immersed myself in its stellar music and ethnomusicology programs. There, I was exposed for the first time to innovative music theorists such as Anthony Braxton and Alvin Lucier, and to new (for me) musical traditions, from locales as diverse as Ghana, South India, and Indonesia. Also, during these years, I developed a deeper cultural competency in the African American musical styles of the 1970s and 1980s (my parents had stopped collecting soul and R&B records around the time I was born, at the beginning of the '70s), as well as in dub and dancehall reggae. Given how deeply the hip-hop of the 1980s and 1990s drew on these traditions, it makes sense that I would gain a fuller appreciation of this newer music only once I had further developed my historical musical lexicon.

It is also possible, of course, that my change in tastes reflected an actual change in the form of the music itself. The early 1990s witnessed a blossoming of new hip-hop subspecies, many of which seemed tailored to appeal as much (or more) to middle class white kids as to the inner city black kids who comprised much of the form's original audience. Some of my earliest and most enduring loves included groups like De La Soul and A Tribe Called Quest, whose "Native Tongues" ethic included a style that sampled a broader range of musics (some of which I actually knew), rapped more melodically, and used more "sophisticated" language in its lyrics. Also, at this time, there was conscious emphasis among some DJs to integrate jazz into a new hip-hop "fusion" style— and my preexisting love of bop and post-bop made me a natural candidate to appreciate these efforts.

Most likely, my conversion to the cause of configurability was a result of all these factors and more. Along with effecting a change in my musical tastes, they also helped to spur in me a dawning recognition that music is intrinsically political, and that my intransigence on the subject of sampling was therefore evidence of some reflexive social conservativism that didn't jibe with either my progressive politics or my own cultural practices and predilections (e.g., tape recording accompaniments to vinyl records).

This realization, and my musical conversion, were the true genesis of this work. In the decade and a half since my about-face, I have had the opportunity to explore the questions surrounding musical taste and meaning, and the complex relationship of music to both social organization and communication technologies, from a variety of angles. As a musical composer, performer, and sonic experimenter, I have progressed from recording with bands on two-inch magnetic tape in recording studios to recording and sequencing tracks on my own laptop at home, and assembling them in "virtual" space with other musicians via the Internet. As a digital music industry analyst, I have been privileged to meet and speak with many of the executives, policymakers, journalists, and musicians working in this sector, and to contribute my own questions, opinions, and expertise to the field as the need has arisen. Finally, as an academic, I have discovered many rich veins of discourse and debate over these issues in a broad range of disciplines, including media studies, communication, cultural studies, psychology, sociology, anthropology, science, technology, and society (STS), art history, musicology, and others—many of which I will explicitly reference and address in the course of this book.

The ethic of configurability has informed not only the substance of my work, but also its style. I view this book as something of a mash-up in itself: an improvised amalgam of theories, methodologies, and writing styles, loosely harnessed together to suit my own idiosyncratic purpose—namely, to address the questions that have interested me most throughout my life. Ironically, however, I am still a reactionary in some ways; although the book emulates the structural *logic* of configurability to a certain degree, it still takes on the *form* of traditional scholarship—not just at the superficial level of footnotes and formatting, but at the deeper level of linear argumentation and the written word. Therefore, I am quite aware that, although I am relatively new to academia, I am already a member of the old guard. As the ethic of configurability increasingly comes to full fruition, and the modern framework that dominated the nineteenth and twentieth centuries recedes into intellectual and cultural history, I consider it likely that scholarship will change as well. Most likely, it will come to resemble increasingly the musical principles I describe in this book, in both its material aspects (e.g., the use of configurable technologies rather than paper and ink) and its formal ones (e.g., the use of recursive argumentation).

This idea is not so far off, or so absurd, as it may seem. I believe that, in many ways, the spirit of configurability and the spirit of scholarship have always been one and the same: both are communitarian enterprises, emphasizing the benefits of collective ideation, and yet both recognize and celebrate the needs and contributions of individual participants. Both ethics relentlessly reexamine their own origins, continually seeking to recast old assumptions in a new light, and to challenge dominant and ossified ideas. Finally, both ethics explicitly acknowledge that the last word has never been spoken, and that no project is ever complete. There is always another stone left to turn, another perspective to add to the mix. As you read this book, I encourage you to keep this in mind. Even for me, these pages are no more than a snapshot capturing a few years of my own intellectual evolution, and the moment I finish writing, it will be obsolete. I look forward to editing, abridging, and augmenting it in the future, and I look forward to your remixes, as well.

Acknowledgments

Much of this work centers around the subject of collaborative authorship and the blurring of the lines between the individual and the collective. It is therefore essential that I emphasize my own indebtedness to several individuals and communities, without whose contributions this book could not exist.

I would first like to thank my professors, colleagues, and the staff at USC Annenberg School for Communication and the Annenberg Center for Communication, where I developed the theoretical underpinnings of this book and conducted many of the interviews. Larry Gross, Doug Thomas, and Joanna Demers were my guiding lights, but I also received significant support and/or feedback from Jonathan Aronson, Johanna Blakley, Francois Bar, Manuel Castells, Peter Monge, Howard Rheingold, Cory Doctorow, danah boyd, Mimi Ito, and Jennifer Urban.

I would also like to thank my colleagues at NYU Steinhardt's Department of Media, Culture, and Communication, where I was given the time and resources to transform early versions into the more compact, readable, and well-structured text you now hold. Specifically, I owe a great deal of gratitude to Ted Magder, Biella Coleman, and Marita Sturken. I will always treasure the time I spent in your department.

I owe a significant debt to those who read and commented on my many drafts, manuscripts, and ravings, without any academic or professional obligation and with a degree of faith and credence that I probably didn't deserve. Your numbers are legion, but the greatest thanks go to Marissa Gluck, Mark Latonero, Alissa Quart, Noah Shachtman, Harry Bruinius, and Sarah Banet-Weiser. I also humbly thank my copy editor,

Paul Berk, and my editors and series editors at University of Massachusetts Press—especially Siva Vaidhyanathan, who brought me into the fold, and Clark Dougan, who kept me here.

I would also like to acknowledge the many individuals who contributed directly to this book as sources. These include the 1,779 anonymous survey respondents whose opinions I cite frequently in these pages, and the dozens of interviewees I spoke with, each of whom contributed hours of time and serious thought and energy to addressing the questions that interest me most. Your expertise and observations are the "heart" of this work.

Finally, I would like to extend my boundless and undying gratitude to the many healers, friends, and family members who sustained me throughout the five-year period between this book's genesis and its publication. Those years brought many joys, but also included some of the most difficult months of my life, during which I could neither walk nor read nor write, and genuinely feared that I would not live to complete this work.

I have already named some of you above. The rest, in no particular order, include Dr. Peter Goldman, Dr. Robert Baloh, Dr. Nerses Sanossian, Stephanie Cushna, Miriam Gerace, Arul Chib, Li Ying, Richard Hodkinson, Jake Myers, Henry Myers, Jessica Ritz, David Ritz, Roberta Ritz, Elizabeth Visceglia, Nikki Lewis, Gail Shand, Eric Pakula, Mollie McQuarrie, Matt Urbania, Julie Thaxter-Gourlay, Jesse Gilbert, Dan Heller, Kathy Dong, Michael Heller, Debora Cahn, Ahmed Best, Raquel Horsford, Bahati Best, Ahmondylla Best, Nancy Zager, Bob Zager, Kim Graves, Emily Pines, Rachel Cleves, Tim Cleves, Dan Sinnreich, Masha Zager, Jonathan Sinnreich, my beautiful and musical son, Simon Sinnreich, my sweet and sonorous daughter, Asha Sinnreich, and my wonderful and patient wife, Dunia Best Sinnreich. I love you all, and am truly fortunate to have you in my life.

MASHED UP

Introduction

The Bust

On a gray, windy afternoon in January 2007, on a quiet street in downtown Atlanta, a team of thirty or forty law enforcement officers, dressed in S.W.A.T. gear, armed with assault rifles, and accompanied by drug-sniffing dogs, burst through an unmarked door. After arresting their two targets, they confiscated several items, including cars, computers, bank statements, and electronic equipment. Most important, they found the contraband they'd been looking for: tens of thousands of "mixtape" CDs, none of them officially licensed by the recording industry.

This was hardly a back-alley counterfeiting operation. For one thing, the CDs in the studio, though slated for retail distribution, contained material that can't be found on the shelves of Wal-Mart or in the catalog of the iTunes Music Store. For another thing, the targets of the raid were two of the most famous names in hip-hop. The suspects, Tyree "DJ Drama" Simmons and Donald "Don" Cannon, were partners in the Atlanta-based Aphilliates Music Group, co-owners of the raided recording studio, and producers of the wildly successful Gangsta Grillz mixtape franchise—a CD series on which songs by new and established hip-hop performers were remixed, assembled in a playlist, and rapped over by guest vocalists. After being charged with felony violations of Georgia's Racketeering Influenced Corruption (RICO) law—typically used to fight organized crime—each suspect was released on $100,000 bail.

The raid was organized and overseen by members of the Recording Industry Association of America (RIAA), a trade group that represents the interests of record labels. The 81,000 CDs seized at the Aphilliates studios[1] were only a tiny fraction of the millions of unlicensed mixtapes confiscated each year; however, due to the high profile of this raid's targets, it became national news, and sparked nationwide debate and protest. Brad Buckles, the executive vice president of the RIAA's antipiracy division, explained that it was a cut-and-dry matter of crime and punishment. As he told an MTV reporter shortly after the raid, "We enforce our rights civilly or work with police against those who violate state law. . . . If it's a product that's violating the law, it becomes a target."[2]

Many fans and commentators questioned the logic of this argument. After all, the Aphilliates had been working with the blessings of their accusers. The RIAA's member labels were some of their biggest customers, often paying $10,000 to $25,000 just to have the company produce a single mixtape for one of their artists—largely for the sheen of authenticity it provided, but also for the additional marketing and distribution clout represented by Atlanta's mixtape network. Major hip-hop acts like T.I., 50 Cent, Jay-Z, and Sean "Diddy" Combs gained early prominence on mixtapes, and continued to rely on them heavily even after achieving mainstream success. True, it was a legal "gray area," as DJ Drama acknowledged when we spoke,[3] but up until then, the record labels had been equal partners in the affair.

Why would the recording industry organize a felony bust of their own business partners, for manufacturing the very products they'd been paid to produce? Why risk alienating the same fans and communities that they'd paid so handsomely to court? Why demonize some of the industry's most successful producers, among the few who reliably bring new acts to national prominence, as record sales continue to slide precipitously? As Ted Cohen, a music industry consultant and former major label executive, told the New York Times, it was just a matter of the music industry being "schizophrenic"—of the "right hand not knowing what the left hand is doing."[4] Ultimately, however, this is more of a description than an explanation. What caused this "schizophrenia?" Why can't the recording industry decide whether DJ Drama is its savior or its nemesis?

These questions lie at the heart of this book. We are living in times of ambiguity, confusion, and contradiction that reach far beyond the boundaries of the music industry. On the battlefields of Iraq and Afghanistan, traditional warfare between standing armies has been supplanted by clashes between military contractors and "enemy combatants." On the trading floors of New York and London, traditional stocks and bonds have been joined by increasingly esoteric securities comprised of repackaged debt. In America's corporate headquarters, factories buy and sell the rights to dump carbon dioxide and other pollutants into our atmosphere. We no longer have a clear notion of where the lines may be drawn between soldier and civilian, asset and liability, consumption and conservation. And the price of this uncertainty is mounting crisis—political, economic, and ecological.

This is a moment of profound change, a moment when the old definitions no longer apply, and when the new definitions have yet to be written. Although the change is fueled by such forces as accelerating technological innovation and globalization, these terms don't tell us much about either its causes or its potential effects. I argue in this book that we may gain a wider understanding of the situation, and even glimpse the grains of the emerging social order, by examining a smaller discursive crisis and its emerging resolution: namely, the struggle over musical culture and practice in the age of sampling and file sharing.

Throughout history, musical aesthetics, practices, and technologies have been at the center of countless battles and debates over the shape of society. This is because music possesses a unique power to reflect, transmit, and amplify what Cornelius Castoriadis[5] (echoing Lacan) calls the "social imaginary"—even when it is devoid of explicit lyrical or symbolic denotation. Some acts of musical regulation and resistance—such as the prohibition, preservation, and transformation of African musical forms in the antebellum American South—have carried explicit political connotations for all parties concerned. The great bulk of battles, though, have taken place without any conscious acknowledgment of their larger significance. When a shopkeeper plays classical music to keep teens from hanging out in his parking lot, or when those teens bring a boom box to counter his sonic claim over the space, neither action is taken as anything more than instrumental. Yet the consequences of these actions, especially in aggregate, ripple throughout the larger geographical, economic, and political landscapes.

Clearly, my definition of "resistance" differs somewhat from the standard Gramscian model. Far from being "organic intellectuals," fighting hegemonic power in the interest of class-consciousness, the resisters I describe in this book are mostly interested in circumventing regulatory hurdles for practical purposes. A DJ would never get any work done if he had to clear the copyrights for every sample he used; far better just to make the music, and hope to fly under the radar of the recording industry's legal departments. Nonetheless, the impact of the DJ on today's hegemonic institutions couldn't be more destabilizing if it had been plotted in the back room of a smoky café by a cabal of wild-eyed insurrectionists.

My argument is framed in terms of cultural production and its relationship to power and material production; this fact would appear to locate my work squarely within the field of cultural studies. However, I believe a more appropriate philosophical home for this book lies within an emerging interdisciplinary field that Siva Vaidhyanathan[6] has recently dubbed "critical information studies," or CIS. Like me, scholars in this field are concerned with "the ways in which culture and information are regulated, and thus the relationships among regulation and commerce, creativity, science, technology, politics and other human affairs."[7]

I am attracted to this field for a variety of reasons. First, it is inherently, enthusiastically multidisciplinary. I have brought many theories and perspectives to bear on the questions I raise, from disciplines as diverse and far afield as political economy, musicology, and personality psychology. No other academic field I know of could so easily assimilate these into a single analytical framework.

The second reason I have adopted a CIS approach is because it best fits my philosophy regarding the relationship between a scholar and his or her subject(s). I am keenly aware that I lack a clinical detachment from my work, and I would never expect or attempt to gain such a vantage point. I have written this book because I care deeply about music, about society, and about the complex interrelations between the two. Not only are my preexisting biases and beliefs integral to my understanding of the phenomena I discuss, but I fully hope and expect that my own analytical contributions will, in some small way, change the very subject of study—not simply by informing future scholarly analysis, but also by influencing the behaviors and beliefs of the actors themselves. Research, analysis, and advocacy are messy, and deeply intertwined; CIS gives me the freedom to turn this weakness into a strength, by employing "multiple complementary methodologies," and by striving for "influence far beyond the gates of the university."[8]

My primary reason for taking a CIS approach, however, is a sense of shared purpose with other authors and theorists in this discipline. Research and theorization, like other forms of cultural production, are collective endeavors, and the work I've relied on most crucially has been in this field. Not only have scholars such as Siva Vaidhyanathan, Lawrence Lessig, Henry Jenkins, Biella Coleman, Yochai Benkler, Kembrew McLeod, danah boyd, Mark Latonero, Jesse Gilbert, and Marissa

Gluck[9] provided vital theoretical foundations for my entire frame of analysis, but many have also been my friends and peers for years, actively providing me with feedback and challenges as I researched and wrote this book, and participating in the development of our shared endeavor via conferences and symposia, publications, creative endeavors, blogs, Facebook, Twitter, cups of coffee, and pints of beer.

Finally, I have to confess to another motivation: the thrill of being part of something new, and of having the opportunity to contribute significantly to an emerging field before it has developed its canon. I began researching the social and economic ramifications of music and technology during the "dot-com" boom of the mid-to-late '90s, and continued to build on this body of work once I began my doctoral studies in communication in 2002. During this time, I never felt a dedicated kinship to any given doctrine, and believed myself to be at best a reluctant fellow traveler with the true believers in fields such as cultural studies (CS), science and technology studies (STS), and information sciences (IS). Only years later did I come to realize that the hodgepodge of theoretical and methodological perspectives I'd assembled amounted to something more than the idiosyncratic interests of a lone scholar; with CIS, I believe I've found my intellectual home.

Given the newness and interdisciplinarity of my field, it should come as no surprise that most of the texts, theories, and methodologies I draw from in this book belonged first to other disciplines. Chief among these, as I have indicated, is cultural studies; not only are the foundational premises and questions of this discipline vitally relevant to the project at hand, but dozens of contemporary scholars have helped me to refine my approach to the subject. If my definition of resistance diverges from Gramsci, it owes much to R. D. G. Kelley's argument that "politics comprises the many battles to roll back constraints and exercise some power over, or create some space within, the institutions and social relationships that dominate our lives"[10]—a formulation that Kelly himself says he adapted from Geoff Eley.[11]

Cultural studies has contributed to the methodology of this book, as well. My method of acquiring interviewees largely through "snowballing"—contacting an initial source, and then mining his or her network for additional sources—is similar to that employed by Eva Illouz.[12] Like her, I acknowledge that this method is flawed in that it produces a "more homogeneous"[13] sample than some other techniques. As Illouz also observes, however, the benefit of this method is in the depth to which the interviewer can explore the shared meanings circulated among the group under examination. The result isn't necessarily generalizable to the population as a whole, but it says more about the symbolic system of a given social network than would a random sampling technique. In this book, I have attempted to account for this imbalance by relying on a second qualitative data source as well—the self-described attitudes and opinions of hundreds of American adults from diverse backgrounds, culled from the write-in responses to a national survey I fielded while I was conducting interviews.

Of course, the specific subjects I address in this book have been a matter of curiosity and concern to scholars for time immemorial. I cite both Plato and Confucius in chapter 1, and throughout the book I draw on the domain expertise of many scholars both within and without my field. I am hardly the first to suggest a relationship between musical and macrosocial structures; in addition to the ancients, theorists as diverse as Alan Lomax,[14] Jacques Attali,[15] and Simon Frith[16] have all contributed heavily to my thinking on the subject. Nor am I the first to discuss music as a site of contestation between and among institutions and communities; in addition to Kelley, I could point to dozens of other excellent works on the subject, by authors such as Josh Kun,[17] Lawrence Grossberg,[18] and George Lipsitz.[19] Similarly, scholars from Lawrence Lessig[20] to Joanna Demers[21] to J. G. Schloss[22] have written eloquently on the role that new communication technologies are playing in reshaping musical aesthetics and practice, and in transforming the legal and economic institutions that enable and exploit music.

What I hope to contribute to the discussion in this book is a sinew of argumentation connecting these three strands of inquiry. While I don't document specific structural correlations between musical and social forms, I do propose a theoretical mechanism connecting the cognitive and affective dimensions of musical experience with the macrosocial structures surrounding musical practice. While I don't explore the role of music within and between specific ethnic, geographical, or political groups, I do examine the discursive process that links music and identity, and document confrontations between rival epistemologies, rather than rival social groups. And, while I don't discuss any specific legal cases in great depth, I do analyze many laws and judicial decisions discursively, and demonstrate the ways in which our legal system often serves as an institutional bulwark against cultural innovation and social change. In short, my work strives to extend and connect, rather than to duplicate, the work of the scholars I have mentioned here and throughout the book.

This book is intended for multiple audiences: scholars in the fields I have cited above, musicians and entrepreneurs interested in the role that new technologies play in their livelihood, and informed readers seeking a greater understanding of the social and cultural disruptions we are currently witnessing and are bound to witness for years to come. As with any such broadly targeted work, I have achieved an uneasy peace at best; those outside academia will no doubt find some of my language and theorization a bit too arcane for their taste, while those within might balk at my lack of critical distance or my willingness to engage in abstract leaps of extrapolation and association. I acknowledge these flaws, but can't apologize—I have always balanced precipitously on the seams between scholarship, art, and industry, and could not have produced any other kind of book. I hope that the story I tell in the following pages—liberally enhanced by the fascinating and perceptive contributions of my many interviewees and survey respondents—will be compelling enough to compensate. Below is an abbreviated summary of the book's contents, which you may use for clarification as you read, or just as a way to skip ahead to the good stuff.

The first section of this book is about music's power to help shape our social and political environments, about the historical regulation of (and resistance to) this power, and about the ways in which new and emerging technologies are requiring us to confront our long-held assumptions about this process.

Chapter 1 begins with Plato's claim that "the musical modes are never changed without change in the most important of a city's laws,"[23] and examines both its veracity and its social historical consequences. States and other powerful institutions have often exerted regulatory controls over musical aesthetics and practices, in an ever-evolving dialectical relationship with communities of resistance to these strictures. While this process has contributed to musical innovation, it has also constituted something of a détente between regulators and resisters. The overarching timbre of the debate—what I call the "discursive framework"—survives the more minute day-to-day battles, and actually helps to support the foundational institutional principles of a given society over the longer term. Significant changes to the technological or social environment can dislodge this framework, however, and in so doing, open the door to new macrosocial ideas and formations— represented in part by new musical aesthetics and practices.

Chapter 2 maps out the "modern discursive framework," a system of definitive assertions about art and music that have set the terms for debate in Western society for the past two centuries. Although the framework is defined broadly, in terms of six fundamental binaries (e.g., artist vs. audience, composition vs. performance, and figure vs. ground), its foundational principles map clearly onto many more specific political, economic, and organizational precepts of modernity (e.g., complex class structure, the division of labor, and the elevation of the "Romantic" individual to social primacy, respectively). Thus, not only is the modern framework institutionally supported (legally, educationally, and so forth), it also serves to support these institutions in return, by naturalizing the underlying principles that justify their continued existence.

Chapter 3 chronicles recent changes to our cultural infrastructure that may pose significant challenges to the modern discursive framework. "Configurable" technologies, constituted by global, digital, networked communications systems, contribute to qualitative changes in the nature of human consciousness and commerce, allowing us to explore modes of expression, collaboration, and creativity that were not only impractical, but unimaginable, in the past. Myriad examples of "configurable culture," from mash-ups to remixes to machinima, problematize the traditional producer/consumer dichotomy (although distinctions do remain between what I term "consumption-adjacent" and "production-adjacent" practices), and expose an ever-growing sea of "gray area" between the modern framework's black and white polar binaries. Who is the author of a mash-up, and who is its audience? Are DJs composers, or performers? Is a digital music file source material or finished product? Clearly, there can be no definitive answer to these questions; however, the practical solutions emerging from configurable culture both prefigure and influence the decisions we will make about how to rebuild and reshape our social institutions as the modern framework continues to erode.

The second section of this book combines interview and survey data to chart the specific ways in which DJs, music industry executives, and Americans in general are attempting to reconcile the discursive foundations of modernity with their direct experiences of configurable culture. Rather than grappling explicitly with the larger and more daunting questions of our age, these explorations and conversations focus on the constituent elements of the modern framework, asking smaller questions about musical ethics, aesthetics, and economics in specific contexts and situations.

Chapters 4 and 5 discuss the changing definitions of "art" and "artistry" in today's musical environment, and show that within mash-up, techno, and hip-hop communities, reputation, pride, and professionalism can exist without recourse to traditional concepts of creative genius or absolute authorial power. They also deconstruct the commonly invoked trope of "some kid in his bedroom," analyzing this straw man nonartist as both a projection of DJs' fears of illegitimacy and a mascot of group pride for adherents of a "DIY" (do-it-yourself) creative ethic.

Chapter 6 explores the ways in which configurable musicians are problematizing the distinction between "original" and "copy," identifying the emerging conventions of personal style, derivativeness, homage, and theft within a sample-based aesthetic. This chapter also contrasts legal definitions of creativity and originality—rooted in the modern framework—with these newer definitions, and analyzes recent court cases and legal disputes in light of this disjuncture. Finally, the chapter discusses the concept of "uniqueness," the fetishization of the art object discussed by Walter Benjamin,[24] in light of the infinite, global reproducibility of information presented by a configurable communications infrastructure.

Chapter 7 examines the role of configurability in realigning the musical distribution of labor and in blurring the lines between categories such as "performance" and "composition." Traditional categories have become increasingly inadequate to the task of describing emerging musical behaviors, problematizing entrenched economic, legal, and organizational systems finely tuned to the power balances (and imbalances) of the modern framework. While a new category, "DJing," appears to have emerged in the gray area between performance and composition, in practice it functions more as a negative category, meaningful only in opposition to established ontologies.

Chapter 8 explores the formalistic disruptions presented by sampling, layering, and other cut-and-paste musical techniques, and discusses the epistemological significance of the blurring between "figure" and "ground." If the elevation of the melodic figure to aesthetic primacy is a symbolic, organizational, and economic instrument of the elevation of the Romantic individual, what does its displacement in configurable music portend for modern, atomistic social institutions? Moreover, if the aesthetic boundaries of a modern composition demarcate social boundaries separating public and private, what can we make of their interpenetration within configurable aesthetics?

Chapter 9 discusses the ways in which new musical practices and techniques undermine the distinction between categories of production such as "materials" and "tools," and in so doing, present larger challenges to the fundamental principles of today's music industry—and of our economy at large. If we can no longer distinguish between a raw material and a finished product, or between the chaos of our natural environment and the order of our industrial apparatus, then we can no longer have any confidence in traditional "value chains," or, indeed, in the linear logic of our production process as a whole.

The final section of this book examines the lessons learned from the interview and survey data presented in the second section, and applies them to the larger social questions raised in the first section. If the challenges and solutions presented to today's musical regulators and resisters are a foretaste of the uncertainties facing society in the network age, then configurable culture may provide us with some valuable indications of how best to prepare for these disruptions.

Chapter 10 explores the degree to which we can understand configurable music as a genuinely "resistant" or "critical" movement, using the same taxonomic matrix of regulation and resistance introduced in the first chapter. It also addresses the question of co-optation, and discusses the potential for the modern institutional framework to absorb and exploit the transformational capacity represented by configurable technology and culture. In simple terms: is configurability just another subcultural trend, to be exploited and appropriated by the gatekeepers of culture, or is it a more resistant strain, with the potential to uproot centuries-old traditions and institutions?

The final chapter begins with the premise that configurability does, indeed, offer the potential for social and epistemological change, and sketches out five basic principles that may come to define a configurable discursive framework. These principles are: Configurable Collectivism (a reorientation of the relationship between the individual and the collective); the Reunion of Labor (an economic principle based on greater free agency and modularity); the Collision of Public and Private (a response to the growing surveillance and "transparency" of network society); the Shift from Linearity to Recursion (a transformation in the logical and epistemological foundations of social reality); and DJ Consciousness (a widespread fracturing of identity, and strategic accommodation thereof, analogous to W. E. B. Du Bois's[25] concept of "double-consciousness"). The net effect of these principles, I argue, suggests a roadmap for the emergence of new social forms and institutions in the networked age. The chapter concludes, however, with the acknowledgment that these premises are neither utopian nor dystopian; some form of social order will be maintained, and it will almost certainly retain some historical social inequities, while eradicating others and producing yet more.

Despite the final caveats, this is an optimistic book. Times of crisis and change can be terrifying, and are often violent in one way or another. But the inescapable conclusion I have reached through this research is that, no matter the challenges we face, we can weather the storm. As in countless other historical epochs, we have reached the end of our collective tether; our principles have helped us to shape a reality that belies its own foundations, and the development of a new social imaginary (or, in "geek speak," the switch to a new social operating system) will naturally entail a period of turmoil and insecurity. But we will not be operating in the dark; music has always been available to us as a staging ground for new social ideas, and the thoughts and opinions of the people I have interviewed for this book contain many seeds of insight regarding the potential solutions to today's seemingly intractable problems. I recommend we listen to them.

I

WHEN THE MODE OF THE MUSIC CHANGES

Although the subject of this book is newness—
new music, new technologies, new forms of social
organization—I will begin with the ancients. Despite
the millennia separating us from Plato and Confucius,
their insights about music's role in shaping the way
we think, feel, behave, and govern remain as true
today as ever, and their warnings about the dangers of
musical innovation still reverberate in the ears of our
leaders.

It is fascinating how frequently, and to what degree,
musical aesthetics, practices, and technologies have
been sanctioned and proscribed by hegemonic institutions in so many societies spanning the globe and the
centuries. Even more surprising, perhaps, is that after
all this time, we still tend to view music as something
innocuous—a form of entertainment, a pastime, a
disposable commodity.

In the following chapters, I attempt to unify many
historical examples of musical regulation into one
consistent theoretical thread, and to argue that music
is anything but innocuous. It has been the site of

countless contestations, and each battle large and small has contributed in some way to our evolving social imaginary.

I will also argue that new technologies such as the Internet-connected laptop, and new cultural forms such as the mash-up, are posing a significant challenge to modern social institutions, and to the hegemonic order. They are not simply doing this by enabling people to communicate, educate, and organize on a scale heretofore impossible—although this is certainly the case. They are also demanding that we reevaluate our deepest beliefs about music and society, and in so doing, are threatening to dislodge the discursive foundations on which our institutions are built.

1

Music as a Controlled Substance

> Those in charge . . . must guard as carefully as they can against
> any innovation in music and poetry or in physical training that is
> counter to the established order . . . for the guardians must beware
> of changing to a new form of music, since it threatens the whole
> system. As Damon says, and I am convinced, the musical modes are
> never changed without change in the most important of a city's laws.
> Plato, *Republic*

> The Meanies captured everything that maketh music.
> Lord Mayor, *Yellow Submarine*

Since the beginning of recorded history, and perhaps longer, human beings have wondered and argued about the meaning, the power, and the
beauty of music. There is a remarkable passage in Plato's *Republic*, written over 2,300 years ago, in which the philosopher Socrates debates
these issues with the sophists Adeimantus and Glaucon. After much
deliberation, he comes to the conclusion that a nation's rulers must
"guard carefully as they can against any innovation in music," because
"musical modes are never changed without change in the most important of a city's laws." Socrates advocates for censorship, therefore, out
of concern that music's unique capacity to "permeate the inner part of
the soul" threatens the political stability of Athens—indeed, of any state
or institution. This is because the state's citizens, especially its leaders,
are at risk of being unwittingly corrupted by any music that produces
antisocial or undesirable tendencies in its listeners.

Socrates and the sophists go on to review a laundry list of musical elements, examining the worthiness of each rhythm, harmony, and musical instrument. The mixo-Lydian and syntono-Lydian harmonic modes, which express sorrow, must be "excluded" because "they're useless even to decent women, let alone to men." The Ionian and Lydian modes must be prohibited as well, for by virtue of their "relaxed" sound they encourage "drunkenness, softness and idleness" in listeners, undermining the state's military preparedness.

Ultimately, Socrates and company agree that only two harmonic modes are of any use to the state: the Dorian, valuable in wartime for building courage in its listeners, and the Phrygian, valuable in peacetime for encouraging obedience. Similar proscriptions are made against inappropriate rhythms (specifically those "suited to slavishness, insolence, madness and the other vices") and instrumentation (only "the lyre and the cithara are left, then, as useful in the city, while in the country, there'd be some sort of pipe for the shepherds to play").

As dangerous as these rogue aesthetics are to the state, in Plato's estimation, at least they are known quantities. Far more dangerous, as the quote suggests, are innovative musical structures and practices. Musical innovation, Adeimantus tells Socrates, is the gateway to lawlessness. He describes a process whereby minor aesthetic changes can have major social effects: "When lawlessness has established itself [in music], it flows over little by little into characters and ways of life. Then, greatly increased, it steps out into private contracts, and from private contracts, Socrates, it makes its insolent way into the laws and government, until in the end it overthrows everything, public and private." Consequently, Socrates holds that the guardians of the state must be vigilant against even seemingly inconsequential musical aesthetic changes; to give way even slightly would jeopardize the very foundations of society.[1]

It may be tempting to dismiss the conclusions of Socrates in this case as merely another example of Platonic hyperbole, or a quaint notion more suited to the magical thinking of classical antiquity than to an era of scientific empiricism. The fundamental premise, though—that musical aesthetics reflect and influence sociopolitical structures, and that innovative or challenging aesthetics pose a consequent threat to powerful institutions—has been remarkably popular across a broad range of cultures and eras, and still holds sway in some circles today.

In fact, musical regulation by powerful social institutions—political, religious, commercial, and otherwise—has been a frequent theme

throughout much of recorded history, in a broad range of societies spanning the globe. While a comprehensive catalog of musical regulation is
beyond the scope of this book, I will begin by discussing some historical examples, and by attempting to connect the dots between them. In
this way, I hope to reveal a consistent pattern uniting the isolated inci-
dents and anecdotes that have often been consigned to the footnotes of
musical and social history.

Matrix of Musical Regulation

Plato's list of musical do's and don'ts is both long and thorough; in his
ideal state, the vast majority of harmonic modes, rhythms, and instrumental timbres known to contemporary Athenian society would have
been censored. Yet all of these prohibitions operate according to a single premise: the legal prohibition of aesthetic codes. In reviewing many
other historical examples of musical regulation, it becomes apparent
that this premise is only one category in a broad matrix of regulatory
practices, which may be organized along two axes: *methods* of regulation and *sites* of regulation.

The *Republic* suggests that music should be regulated legally, codified through political mandates and policed by the state. As Foucault
argues, however, institutional regulation of individual behavior may
occur in ways more subtle than the direct physical threat and intervention that Plato advocates. In the case of music, there are at least two
other methods of regulation that often come into play: ideological regulation, in which one set of ideas about music is given primacy over another; and commercial regulation, in which companies such as broad-
casters or record labels serve as "gateways" between musical producers
and consumers. Thus, the first axis of our matrix contains *three methods of musical regulation:* legal, ideological, and commercial.

If the *Republic* focuses on a single method of musical regulation, it
focuses on a single site, as well. For all his many mandates, Plato seems
primarily concerned with controlling the aesthetic codes—harmonic,
rhythmic, and timbral—that circulate within the state's borders. Actual historical instances of musical regulation have focused on at least
two other sites: praxis, which concerns the behaviors and practices surrounding the composition, performance, and reception of music; and
technology, which concerns the mechanisms by which music is composed, performed, distributed, and audited. Thus, the second axis of our
matrix contains *three sites of musical regulation:* aesthetic, praxis, and

Table 1: Taxonomy of Musical Regulation

Legal/Aesthetic	Legal/Praxis	Legal/Technology
Ideological/Aesthetic	Ideological/Praxis	Ideological/Technology
Commercial/Aesthetic	Commercial/Praxis	Commercial/Technology

technology. In all, our matrix describes nine different categories of musical regulation, which are arranged in Table 1.

Historical Examples of Musical Regulation

As with all methods of categorization, this model no doubt suffers from being at once too detailed and too vague. There are almost certainly historical examples of musical regulation that may not find easy classification according to my scheme, and even the examples I do use are not clean-cut—the lines between aesthetics and praxis, or between law and ideology, are seldom sharply drawn. The examples below should, I believe, both indicate the general truth of musical regulation as a historically prevalent practice and illustrate the categories well enough to validate my system of analysis.

The first category of musical regulation, Legal Regulation of Aesthetic Codes, has appeared in ancient, classical, and modern times alike. Fabre D'Olivet[2] cites the public exhibition of state-mandated diagrams of permitted melodic and harmonic codes (aesthetic pronouncements literally written in stone) in ancient Egypt as the inspiration for Plato's recommendations in the *Republic*. Similarly, in 1725, the Yongzheng Emperor of China's Manchu Qing Dynasty established an Office to Harmonize Sounds within a newly appointed Music Ministry. By doing so, M. H. Sommer writes, he "replaced the 'licentious music' of a morally debased caste with 'harmonized sounds,' to conform with the Confucian vision of music as a tool for moral order in the hands of a sage ruler."[3] The Confucian texts that bear on this matter are strikingly similar to Plato's. Confucius is quoted in *The Classic of Filial Piety* as saying that "for the reform of customs and mores, there is nothing better than music." Similarly, in his "Discourse on Music," Confucian sage Xunzi wrote that "when correct sounds move a man, they cause a spirit of obedience to rise, and when such a spirit has arisen, good order results. As singers blend their voices with that of the leader, so good or evil arise in response to the force that calls them forth."[4]

More recent (and more local) examples abound as well. Consider, for instance, the explicit legal prohibition against African musical codes and instruments in the American South prior to the Civil War. This censorship served two purposes, one immediate and one general. Slaveholders, who were "well aware of the African tradition for 'talking instruments',"[5] realized correctly that African music could serve as a secret mode of communication between African Americans and as a vital instrument in slave rebellion. More generally, the prohibition was intended to sever the cultural ties between Africa and the diaspora. By extinguishing the slaves' cultural memory of their origins, slaveholders hoped they could also extinguish any hope or even desire for repatriation.

The second category in our matrix, Legal Regulation of Musical Praxis, applies to the widespread practice of officially licensing or sanctioning musicians and musical performance. An excellent example, chronicled extensively by Paul Chevigny,[6] is the eighty-four-year-old New York City institution of the cabaret license, which dictates such practical matters as who can play music, in which venues, at what times, and even whether audience members are allowed to dance. Although cabaret laws have their origins in the Prohibition era, and perhaps reached their prosecutorial apogee in the postwar period, they continue in diminished form today. Following a successful public interest campaign to reduce their scope in the 1980s, the laws' remaining statutes (which prevent customers at unlicensed venues from dancing, even if music is permitted) were exploited by Mayor Giuliani in the mid-to-late 1990s as a vital tool in his controversial "Quality of Life" campaign.

As Chevigny argues, the complexity and breadth of the cabaret laws served to mask an inherent bias in their function. In his words, the laws "expressed the view of the NYC lawmakers—rooted ultimately in racism as well as fear of bohemian mores." Additionally, he argues, the cabaret license functioned as an institutional bulwark against musical innovation, "calculated to favor chiefly those with considerable staying power,"[7] at the expense of newer and less established acts. Given that such innovative black performers and composers as Charlie Parker, Billie Holiday, and Thelonious Monk were each subject to cabaret license revocation at various points in their careers (all as a result of drug charges), Chevigny's argument carries some weight. It is no small irony that half a century later, even as the Giuliani administration was being widely criticized for bias and abuse of power in its use of the cabaret law, all three of these musicians, safely enshrined as geniuses in posterity, were featured on United States postage stamps.

The third category of musical regulation, Legal Regulation of Music Technology, has increased in prevalence as new production, recording, distribution, and playback technologies have become increasingly central to both innovative and established musical practices. In a general sense, many of these technologies have been regulated since they first emerged. The use of the electromagnetic spectrum for radio broadcasts, for instance, has been regulated by the U.S. government since Congress established the Federal Radio Commission (FRC) in 1927.

However, neither the FRC nor its descendant, the Federal Communications Commission (FCC), ever exerted the kind of sweeping control over consumer technologies that has been exhibited in recent legislation, such as the Audio Home Recording Act (AHRA, 1992), or the Digital Millennium Copyright Act (DMCA, 1998). Among its many provisions, the DMCA makes it a crime for music listeners to bypass the copy protection or other "antipiracy" technology that may accompany recorded music, *even if this is the only way for listeners to engage in legal behaviors* such as making backup copies of their music collections, or reselling their property to new buyers. As authors such as Lawrence Lessig[8] and Siva Vaidhyanathan[9] persuasively argue, such legal provisions regarding music technology constitute an unprecedented incursion of corporate and governmental power into the individual rights of musicians and music listeners, and threaten to undermine the very social practices that give music its power and meaning.

The examples of legal musical regulation I have cited thus far are fairly cut-and-dry; although we may argue about a given law's implications, there can be little argument about its existence. The next set of examples, which focus on the ideological regulation of music, are far more difficult to document conclusively, although I would argue these methods exert an even greater degree of influence over musical codes, practices, and technologies than the legal methods cited above.

I should mention here that the term "ideology" seems to have as many definitions as there are social theorists, and I must confess to using it in my own way, as well. My use of the term comes close to Anthony Giddens's textbook definition of "shared ideas or beliefs which serve to justify the interests of dominant groups";[10] however, I must emphasize that I believe these "groups" are better understood as transient, fluid, and contingent amalgams of social power, rather than fixed and unchanging social edifices. Put another way, the construction of ideology is a site-specific process in which we each have a small but significant voice, yet to which we each are largely bound. Similarly, though I share the Birmingham school's interest in music as a site of social contestation, I view music as a discrete target of ideological intervention, rather than merely one of many vectors of ideological hegemony.

Thus, in this portion of the matrix, I am concerned with the efforts by individuals and institutions to regulate music by influencing standards and opinions, as an operational alternative (or analog) to the rule of law. In short, these examples suggest coercion, rather than compulsion.

Although Plato's *Republic* advocated legal regulation, the text itself arguably served as a form of Ideological Regulation of Aesthetic Codes, explicitly politicizing music to a degree unrivalled by previous and contemporary Greek philosophers.

Ideological regulation of musical aesthetics has been a prominent element in modern American social thought and political strategy as well, from the Civil War through the Cold War and the Culture Wars. Above, I described the legal prohibitions against African music and dance in the antebellum South. By the time of the Civil War, many black churches in the South had absorbed these aesthetic proscriptions into their own doctrines, discouraging both dance and African-derived work songs as sinful and irreligious. In other words, what had begun as externally imposed legal regulation became an internally imposed ideological regulation. As D. J. Epstein writes, the provenance of these self-imposed aesthetic strictures can only originate within European American culture: "The prejudice against secular music, and especially against dancing, has not been traced to Africa, where such distinctions between sacred and secular cannot be said to have existed. This is one case where the blacks appear to have been influenced by the whites."[11]

In the period following World War II, as tensions between the United States and the Soviet Union escalated sharply into a global war of ideas, aesthetics became a prime target for ideological regulation on both sides of the great divide. The role of abstract expressionist painting as a badge of American liberty and individualism, and the role of the CIA in surreptitiously sponsoring its promotion at home and abroad, is perhaps the best known example of this practice. However, music also played a vital role. As Penny von Eschen recounts in her recent book *Satchmo Blows Up the World*,[12] top-tier American musicians including Dave Brubeck, Duke Ellington, and Louis Armstrong were routinely dispatched as "jazz ambassadors" to Eastern Bloc countries throughout the Cold War's most virulent decades. Although the intention of the

U.S. government was to demonstrate American racial equality and personal liberty in action, von Eschen describes some unintended consequences of these tours: the globalization of jazz and other regional musics, and the growing resolution among the American musical community to fight for real equality on the home front, even as they promoted its fictitious existence abroad.

Clearly, the examples I have just cited entail the regulation of musical practice (e.g., dancing) in addition to musical aesthetics. In addition, it is worth citing a few examples specifically related to the Ideological Regulation of Musical Praxis for the sake of our matrix. An excellent—if relatively idiosyncratic—historical example is the interdict imposed on the twelfth-century German abbess and composer Hildegard von Bingen by her church superiors, the prelates of Mainz.

The prelates, ostensibly upset about Hildegard's willingness to bury a nobleman who had once been excommunicated in the consecrated ground of her monastery, commanded that she be punished unless and until the body was exhumed—a demand she resisted until the interdict was lifted, shortly before her death. In addition to provisionally excommunicating Hildegard, the interdict called for mass at her monastery, usually celebrated musically, to be performed without musical accompaniment of any sort. Given that Hildegard was eighty years old and quite famous as a musician, scholar, and religious figure, this was a severe sentence. J. L. Baird and R. K. Ehrman argue that the prelates' motives in imposing the musical ban were "suspect,"[13] and Fiona Maddock directly attributes the move to "jealous spite."[14] Both analyses suggest that the nobleman's burial was a pretext, and that the true ambition of the prelates was to put Hildegard, one of the few powerful women of her era, back in her place by banning the very musical practices that had marked her ascent.

A more recent (and general) example can be found in the contemporary American debates over music education. E. R. Jorgensen, in her call for sweeping changes to the organization and practice of music education, argues that "musicians and educators are engaged in a fundamentally social, political, and cultural enterprise."[15] She argues that music education, by virtue of its power to influence children's values and behaviors, has become a battleground for wars between different cultural, religious, and political interest groups. Thus, seemingly academic debates over the relative importance of music appreciation and musical performance in the classroom, theoretical arguments over whether music should be interpreted structurally, symbolically, or aesthetically, and efforts to strike the proper balance between the Western classical canon and multicultural and popular music traditions are freighted with a far greater burden of significance than may at first be apparent. For Jorgensen, then, ideological regulation of musical praxis amounts to ideological regulation, period. This is an argument I examine in greater depth later in this chapter.

The next category in our matrix, Ideological Regulation of Music Technology, has an obvious contemporary example: the vilification of digital music encoding and distribution technologies—specifically, the MP3 encoding format and peer-to-peer (P2P) file sharing software. These technologies, due to their contentious role in the growth of new music distribution paradigms that have momentarily tipped the scales of power away from the corporate sector and toward consumers, have arguably become more rapidly and thoroughly politicized than any other music technologies in modern history.

Largely powerless to halt the spread and use of these technologies by their standard means (legal regulation) and unwilling to undertake the risk and expense of neutralizing their threat through market competition (commercial regulation), the music industry has relied primarily on threats and propaganda (ideological regulation) to achieve these ends.

Perhaps the most important achievement of the music industry along these lines has been in persuading people to adopt language that frames the debate in industry-friendly terms. It has become commonplace to describe P2P in terms of "piracy" and "theft." These terms are typically used to refer to the commercial distribution of what economists call "rivalrous goods," meaning objects that can only be used by a single person or group at any given moment. Songs shared on a P2P network are neither rivalrous nor commercially distributed—no one is deprived of a digital music file when it is copied, and no one profits commercially from sharing songs on a network (although participants profit in the sense of gaining access to the libraries of other users). Thus, the relationship of P2P to our conventional understanding of the terms "piracy" and "theft" is ambiguous, at best. Despite—or because—of this ambiguity, these pejoratives have been aggressively promoted as the terms of choice by proindustry organizations like the Recording Industry Association of America (RIAA) and the International Federation of the Phonographic Industry (IFPI). Hilary Rosen, when head of the RIAA, was frequently quoted using moralistic terms to discuss the issue—arguing, for instance, that P2P services like the original Napster were "morally and legally wrong."[16]

This choice of words was hardly accidental. According to a recent IFPI publication, the music industry is explicitly hoping to influence behavior and policy by framing the debate in this way: "The recording industry launched four targeted international education campaigns in 2005, by far the biggest expansion of its public information activities in this area. Each campaign . . . aims to help change attitudes to online music, improve understanding of copyright and promote the legitimate services."[17]

The final set of categories in our matrix involves capital as the musical regulatory mechanism. Although businesses are usually considered objects of regulation rather than as regulators themselves, we must also acknowledge the central role they play in inhibiting and enabling the flow of information and culture throughout society. Thus, we can say they serve a regulatory function, especially if we consider the organic connotations of the term (e.g., the circulatory system regulating the flow of blood throughout the body).

The first category concerning capital's relationship to music, Commercial Regulation of Aesthetic Codes, can be traced back at least as far as Europe's feudal era. Liturgical music became increasingly secularized during the fourteenth century, as feudal courts began to offer permanent positions to church-trained musicians. This development led to the establishment of a new professional class—salaried career musicians in the modern sense of the term, suddenly reined in from itinerancy and "bound to a single master." Of course, the security and prestige that came with professionalization carried a price as well; these court musicians were required to obey the aesthetic dictates of their patrons—arbitrary, stultifying, and self-serving as they may have seemed. The French music theorist Jacques Attali quotes an official reprimand levied against J. S. Bach, for "having hitherto made many curious variations in the chorale, and mingled many strange tones in it," and laying out a number of permissible melodic alternatives, as but a single example of the aesthetic micromanagement faced by court musicians every day of their professional careers.[18]

As modern capitalism and industrialization emerged, music's role in society, and its relationship to capital, changed with the times. The professionalization of musicians was followed first by the commercialization of musical performance and composition and then by the mass production and distribution of recordings. During this process, businesses continued to exert an ever-greater regulatory force on musical aesthetics. Today, one of the most contentious issues in cultural policy is the overwhelming degree of power exerted by oligarchic organizations in highly consolidated music industry sectors such as broadcasting, record distribution, and music retail. Large corporations in these sectors are routinely referred to as either "gatekeepers" or "bottlenecks" for their ability to dictate the tenor of the mainstream music marketplace by including or excluding music that meets their favor or disfavor.

Because I have written at length about this subject in other research focusing on the structural role of independent promoters[19] and the origins of the mash-up phenomenon,[20] I will not expand on it here. I will close, however, by saying that the argument that consolidated media companies are simply "giving people what they want" and obeying no ideology but the quest for profit when they exert regulatory control over musical aesthetics is patent nonsense. This "myth" has been thoroughly debunked by media critic Robert McChesney, who compellingly argues that "the commercial media system has generated a hyper-commercial carpet-bombing of our culture that is decidedly unwelcome by much of the population."[21]

This argument is also belied by the media oligarchs themselves; Wal-Mart, which is America's second-largest music retailer, accounting for roughly 15 percent of all sales in this country,[22] has repeatedly come under fire for censoring or altering the music it carries. The company makes these decisions based not on the anticipated popularity of a given artist or title, but rather on the socially conservative ideologies of the company's founding family, the Waltons. The consequences of these decisions are severe and far-reaching. As Neil Strauss writes, "because of Wal-Mart's clout, record labels and bands will . . . omit songs from their albums, electronically mask objectionable words and even change lyrics in order to gain a place on Wal-Mart's shelves."[23] In other words, these decisions amount to unilateral aesthetic regulation by a powerful corporation, not the democratic choice of an empowered consumer base acting through the mechanism of the marketplace.

The next category in our matrix, Commercial Regulation of Musical Praxis, has also become more prevalent as culture and capitalism have grown more intertwined. There is no clearer example of this than in the licensing of copyrighted musical compositions and performances.

The application of copyright to music has expanded significantly since its first appearance in American law at the dawn of the republic. Printed material, such as scores, were first covered in 1790. Public performances were not covered until 1889. Mechanical reproduction, a right currently applied to songs on CDs, was first introduced in 1909 to cover piano rolls. In 1972, nearly a century after the invention of recorded sound, a new kind of copyright was developed to describe the performances (rather than the compositions) embodied on records. Television broadcasts and jukebox playback were first added in 1976. Online radio performances were added with the DMCA in 1998, and other, new forms of protection are currently being explored through proposed legislation, contractual innovation, and case law.

Even as the range of behaviors and technologies subject to copyright has expanded, "fair use" restrictions on the scope of copyright and time limits on copyright's applicability have been scaled back. In recent decades, powerful media and software companies have successfully lobbied Congress to push back expiration terms,[24] limit fair use in new legislation, and include a growing range of categories as "works" that can be protected under copyright.

These commercial developments have impacted cultural praxis to an extensive, and sometimes absurd degree. David Bollier,[25] in his excellent *Brand Name Bullies,* recounts a particularly ridiculous episode involving music royalty collection society ASCAP[26] and the Girl Scouts of America. In 1996, ASCAP sent letters to 288 summer camps, 16 of them run by Boy Scouts or Girl Scouts, demanding hundreds or thousands of dollars per camp for the right to allow campers to sing ASCAP-controlled songs such as "This Land Is Your Land" around the campfire. The San Francisco Bay Girl Scout Council, unable to pay tens of thousands of dollars in licensing fees for its twenty chapters and unwilling to face far steeper fines and possible jail time for violating ASCAP's demands, was forced to ban the singing of such songs in its camps. The Girl Scouts' plight ignited a media furor over the issue, and a week after the matter became public ASCAP waived its demands. Despite the waiver, the organization has made it clear that "the free singing of songs by the Girl Scouts remains an ASCAP-granted indulgence, not a legal entitlement."[27]

The final category in our matrix, Commercial Regulation of Music Technology, can be observed in the century-old tug-of-war between the music industry, who generally would prefer that music production and playback technologies be separated; music lovers, who generally would prefer the technologies be integrated; and technology manufacturers, who must please both factions to successfully sell their products.

This question matters because technology has the power not only to limit behavior (people can't easily do what their machines won't let them) but also to help set cultural boundaries (people tend to base their decisions and expectations on concrete options, rather than abstract ideals). Thus, a technical decision today can become a cultural norm tomorrow and a legal axiom the next day.

Consequently, although the music industry has consistently argued for the separation of music production and playback technologies on the grounds of protection against piracy and lost sales,[28] another, broader agenda may be inferred from their arguments. The ongoing growth of the industry is predicated on encouraging values and behaviors that follow the logic of mass production: a handful of manufacturers produce music, and the great bulk of consumers—unable, unwilling, or unaware of their capacity to produce it for themselves—purchase music. This producer/consumer dichotomy is reified through the technological separation of production and consumption technologies, and undermined by their technical union. This relationship between economic, ideological, and technological logics deserves greater attention, and I return to it in chapter 2.

For now, I will simply observe that the history of recorded music, even in its simplest, most reductive form, reveals a startling pattern of alternating union and disunion of production and consumption capabilities.[29] The phonograph was initially conceived and marketed as a device that would both record and play back sound. This changed as the recording industry grew and the phonograph's many possible uses crystallized around music in the home; record players became playback-only devices. The next dominant music storage medium, the cassette tape,[30] developed in 1963 but gaining mainstream adoption only in the 1970s, allowed users to record as well as play back. Perhaps this shift back toward a union of functions was due, at least in part, to the emergence of mainstream pastiche-based musics (from the Beatles' *Sgt. Pepper's Lonely Hearts Club Band* to Lee "Scratch" Perry's dub reggae innovations), and to the burgeoning efforts of record DJs, first in Jamaica, then in New York and throughout the world, to reclaim the turntable as a means of musical production through aesthetic innovation.

The cassette gave way to the CD, which became the dominant recorded music medium for over a decade beginning in 1992—and remains so, depending on one's measuring stick. During the 1980s and 1990s, commercially available CD players were playback-only devices. The situation changed with the rapid proliferation of digital music technology, including the MP3, the Internet-connected personal computer, and affordable CD-writable drives around the turn of the twenty-first century, which once again reunited music production and consumption technologies.

During the last decade, the entertainment industry's embrace of digital rights management (DRM) technology—digital padlocks that prevent people from copying or editing songs—again threatened to sever music production and playback. After protest from retailers and indifference from consumers, however, the pendulum swung back, and today a variety of online music stores offer MP3 files of major label music without DRM. This technological cycle and the underlying tensions behind it show no signs of abating any time in the foreseeable future.

Resistance to Regulation

In Michel Foucault's famous formulation, "there are no relations of power without resistance."[31] This is certainly the case when it comes to musical regulation. In each of the examples I have cited above, the exercise of regulatory power was in some way met with resistance from the subjects of regulation, and this resistance served both to reify the regulatory power and to mitigate its effects. For instance, M. Sullivan writes that African slaves in the antebellum South responded to the "void left by the ban on drums . . . by contriving new means of creating rhythm" using European instruments, household objects such as spoons and washboards, and even their own bodies.[32] These tactics of resistance, which reinforced the diasporic bond to African culture through the very act of transforming it, contributed to the development of new, fundamentally subversive African American musical forms, such as "patting juba" and the spiritual. These new musical practices managed to use the "double-consciousness" of the African American experience to the slaves' advantage, presenting one set of meanings (carefree, nonsensical fun; Christian theology) to white audiences while simultaneously communicating altogether different messages (armed insurrection; prophecies of liberation) to black listeners and participants.

There is an odd symmetry between government prohibition of African musical codes in the eighteenth and nineteenth centuries, and government exploitation and amplification of African American musical codes in the twentieth century. Above, I described the State Department's role in exporting American musicians as "jazz ambassadors" to the world at large (especially Eastern Europe and the Middle East) during the height of the Cold War, and noted the program's galvanizing effect on African American musicians to fight for equality on the home front after advertising it (falsely) abroad.

The most visible example of resistance against the jazz ambassador program within the American musical community came in the form of a musical revue called *The Real Ambassadors,* created by Dave and Iola Brubeck and Louis Armstrong, and staged at the 1962 Monterey Jazz Festival.

The show, which explicitly "satirized State Department objectives, personnel and protocol and voiced a powerful and unequivocal indictment of Jim Crow America," represented a significant political and professional risk for its contributors and participants. Brubeck and Armstrong had both been staples of the State Department program a few years earlier, but had grown disenchanted with it after witnessing the ugly side of American geopolitics abroad and federal ambivalence about segregation and civil rights at home. At a time when the public demand for jazz was starting to wane, outspoken opposition to the government's Cold War policy was broadly considered tantamount to treason, and the battle over civil rights was escalating toward riot and bloodshed, *The Real Ambassadors* was anything but an empty gesture: lives and livelihoods were at stake.

The show was so volatile, in fact, that despite its political relevance, aesthetic appeal, and superstar provenance, it was never performed publicly again, despite attempts to bring it to Broadway. Its effects reverberated for decades, however, in the increasing autonomy and militancy of jazz musicians on and off the State Department circuit, and in the burgeoning political and aesthetic alignment between musicians in America and around the world. This process, in turn, contributed to a new, globalized jazz aesthetic, reflected in the work of American musicians such as John Coltrane, Charlie Haden, and Don Cherry, and foreign musicians such as Hugh Masekela, Shobha Gurtu, and Yolande Bavan. Through this process, the very notion of diplomacy through jazz was recuperated. Instead of promoting a propagandist vision of American freedom to strategically chosen target audiences, jazz musicians at home and abroad negotiated a new vision of freedom based on the premise of global struggle against oppressive use of force—a vision in which the American government was as much aggressor as liberator. As von Eschen writes: "The jazz ambassador, epitomized by Louis Armstrong, conveyed through his horn and voice hopes and aspirations for freedom in a world where he, like so many of the audiences for whom he played, was still waiting for the day when he was 'really free.'"[33]

Another excellent example of resistance to musical regulation, which I touch on above, is the repurposing of the turntable from a playback-only consumption instrument to a creative production instrument. As other scholars have argued, the creative innovations that led to the genesis of rap music were fundamentally resistant acts, even if the innovators themselves—inner-city New York DJs such as Kool Herc, Grand Wizard Theodore and Grand Master Flash—were primarily concerned with starting parties and building their careers.

Arguably, the repurposing of the turntable signified an act of resistance on at least two distinct (if interconnected) levels. First, the disruption of the technologically imposed separation of production and consumption can be understood as an attempt to disembed musical codes and practices from the logics of capitalism and mass production. If the implicit message of the playback-only musical device is that production is something best left to the professional elite, while the masses must find pleasure only in listening, then hip-hop turntable techniques such as looping, scratching, and beat juggling amount to a simple and resounding "au contraire" from the erstwhile masses.

There is a more subtle dimension of resistance implicit in turntablism—namely, the assertion of the dominance and validity of an Afro-diasporic musical paradigm over European or Euro-American source material. As J. G. Schloss writes, "there is clearly a political valence to the act of taking a record that was created according to European musical standards and, through the act of DJing, physically forcing it to conform to an African American compositional aesthetic."[34] This ongoing tension between African and European compositional aesthetics and performative ethics, and its enactment and transformation through new music technology, is a theme I will touch on again later in this book.

Resistance and Innovation

Each example I have just cited of resistance to musical regulation suggests an important secondary effect: through the process of resistance, the musical codes, practices, and technologies themselves are transformed. Thus, by applying proscribed African aesthetic logic to European instruments, scales and subject matter, African American music was created. By turning the apparatus of American cultural imperialism against itself, jazz was newly politicized and globalized. By transforming a playback-only entertainment device into a viable and accessible musical instrument for the masses, the hip-hop era was born. In short, resistance to musical regulation becomes an engine of aesthetic innovation. This process is dialectical in nature: the opposing forces of musical regulation and resistance combine to alter the very codes and practices under dispute; the resulting new codes and practices themselves become subject to regulation, and the cycle repeats ad infinitum (fig. 1).

I am hardly describing a Marxist dialectic; this process can better be described as a war between ethics than as a war between social groups or classes. The institutional ethic embraces a centralization of power over cultural production, while the communal ethic seeks to decentralize such cultural power. The constituents of these warring ethics are always fluid and contingent—a single individual may (and often will) support both ethics in different ways, in his roles as consumer, employee, artist, citizen, or parishioner.

It is also important to recognize that neither regulators nor resisters are necessarily aware of the larger process of cultural innovation that they are helping to constitute. To the contrary, as I have discussed, regulatory institutions seem more dedicated to halting or controlling the spread of existing musical codes, practices, and technologies than to contributing to the birth of new ones. And resistant individuals and groups often seem to rely on innovation more as a tactical workaround in the face of regulatory obstacles than as a strategic end in itself.

This may help to explain why innovation so often springs from creative environments where it is least expected and least sought after as

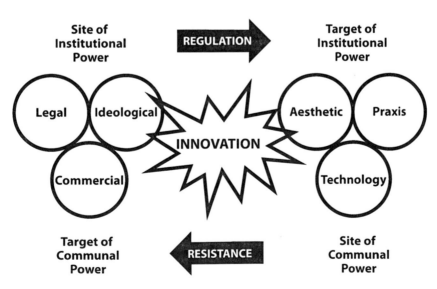

Figure 1: Musical regulation, resistance, and innovation.

an abstract ideal. John Cage, for example, accurately predicted in the 1940s that samples of recorded sound would become widely used as the constituent elements for new compositions, and that the resulting aesthetic codes would contribute to dominant cultural forms in the second half of the twentieth century.[35] And yet, despite the self-conscious efforts of academic "avant-garde" composers throughout the Western world in the ensuing decades to define this new aesthetic, it was the youth culture of an urban American ghetto that ultimately provided the blueprint for the cultural phenomenon currently known as hip-hop.

Clearly, this process fuels innovation in realms of cultural production beyond music, as well. Jeff Chang, in describing the evolution of modern graffiti, makes it clear that regulation was essential to the form's development: "Politicians and bureaucrats played an unwitting role in the development of style. . . . [G]raffiti's inherent risk and its perpetual removal catalyzed innovation and ingenuity; its countless deaths generated countless, more magnificent rebirths."[36] Similarly, Douglas Thomas argues that computer hackers are continually driven to create innovative new software in response to the information barricades erected by network systems operators and other regulatory entities. As he writes, the desire to confront regulatory authority surpasses any more instrumental desires regarding the forbidden files themselves: "what defines the value of the information is not necessarily how useful the information is but, rather, how secret the information is."[37]

Changing Modes, Changing Codes

As I have shown, musical codes, practices, and technologies have been subject to legal, ideological, and commercial regulation across a broad range of societies and epochs. This has spurred both organized and spontaneous resistance among groups and individuals, and the resulting tension between regulation and resistance has contributed to a dialectical process of aesthetic innovation.

Underpinning this entire process is a remarkably durable idea, so pervasive that it often becomes a tacit element in struggles over musical regulation: namely, Plato's claim that "the musical modes are never changed without change in the most important of a city's laws." In other words, musical regulation would not be such a pervasive cultural practice if the regulatory institutions (and those resisting them) did not believe in the power of music to reflect, amplify, and influence the human psyche, the social ideas we embrace, and the organization of society itself.

For such a durable, widespread, and powerful idea, there is very little conclusive evidence to support or reject it. What mechanism could possibly allow an ordered series of sounds, or the practices and technologies that produce and reproduce these sounds, to exert such influence over the course of our lives, and over the shape of our world?

In addition to the ancient philosophers I have mentioned, contemporary scholars in fields as diverse as musicology, cultural studies, ethnomusicology, sociology, psychology, neurobiology, and economics have addressed this question in recent decades. While this is not the place to discuss each scholar's work in detail, it is worth describing the problems they have grappled with. These can be boiled down to three fundamental questions: directionality, structure versus agency, and levels of meaning.

The question of directionality is fairly straightforward. If we accept the premise that social change and musical change historically have been correlated, we must ask which came first, the chicken or the egg. Does musical change effect social change, or vice versa? Do music and society change in tandem, as reciprocals in a cyclical relationship, or as equally dependent factors of yet another, larger process?

Likewise, the question of structure and agency seems deceptively simple. To what degree are musical and social change the result of individual efforts and intentions, and to what degree are they guided by macrolevel forces, sweeping us along in the tide of history? The answer is elusive, to say the least. In its broadest terms, this debate has always been, and remains, one of the most troublesome questions in social theory, from St. Augustine's reflections on the nature of "free will" to Giddens's "structuration theory."[38]

I believe both these questions can be addressed through a model that understands the relationship between musical and social codes as coefficient—not only are the processes of change in each sphere interrelated, they are intimately linked. I would go so far as to suggest that one of music's primary functions is to serve as a vector of communication between individuals and society. The act of encoding, decoding, or recoding organized sound, then, is a facet of the act of social orientation, and vice versa. This doesn't mean that we can read music the way we would tea leaves, identifying one-to-one correlations between specific musical and social developments. Social orientation and cultural change are ongoing processes of negotiation between countless individuals, alliances, groups, and ideas, and neither society nor musical culture can or should be viewed univocally.

Finally, there is the question of levels of meaning: how does music's meaning on a small scale (e.g., for individuals) translate into meaning at the large scale (e.g., for society), and vice versa? This question, like the previous one, has been the subject of countless books and articles over the years, focusing on somatic, spiritual, emotional, cognitive, psychological, metaphorical, semantic, and semiotic processes (and no doubt many others as well). While each of these approaches has merit, no theory of musical meaning would be complete without proposing a mechanism that can encompass each of these dimensions.

In order for music to act as a vector of orientation and communication between the individual and society, it must somehow retain its capacity to *mean*, from the most fundamental microlevel to the most sophisticated macrolevel. This means that, in order to see the whole picture, we must combine a "bottom-up" model emphasizing cognitive and psychological processes with a "top-down" model emphasizing cultural and social ones. One way in which to view this multilevel mechanism is to understand it as a complex system of *nested networks-within-networks*.

At the smaller end of the spectrum, the human cognitive–affective system itself can be understood as a network of networks—whether viewed at the molecular, cellular, or systemic scale, the organization of the constituent elements produces emergent, and often unpredictable, effects at the next scalar level. As J. D. Mayer, a scholar in the emerging field of "systems framework" personality psychology, argues: "The biological, psychological, and social systems are connected, in part, along a continuum called the molecular-molar dimension. The molecular end of the dimension refers to smaller systems of interest—at its extremes, subatomic particles. The molar end refers to larger systems—at its extremes, the entire universe as a system."[39]

Between the molecular and the molar scales, in Mayer's schema, we find several distinct levels of organization (fig. 2).[40] The molecular level emerges into the level of "brain processes," which comprises a multitude of separate neurological subsystems. This level, in turn, emerges into a level of "psychological processes," which comprises internal psychological subsystems as well as interpersonal relationships and shared social meanings.[41]

Above the psychological level, according to the systems framework, we emerge into the realm of the cultural and the social. Although Mayer, who is primarily concerned with the scalar level describing psychological processes, declines to extend his analysis beyond this horizon, his theoretical framework dovetails well with the work of network-oriented social and cultural theorists.

If the individual cognitive–affective system itself can be understood as a series of nested subsystems (the term "nested" in this context means that "lower levels are at least partially included in higher levels"),[42] social network analysts offer a similar vision of society as a whole. As P. M. Monge and Noshir Contractor argue, quantitative analysis of social organization requires a multilevel, multitheoretical analytical framework. From a methodological standpoint, this means that any model of social organization must simultaneously account for the processes governing relationships between individuals, groups, organizations, cities,

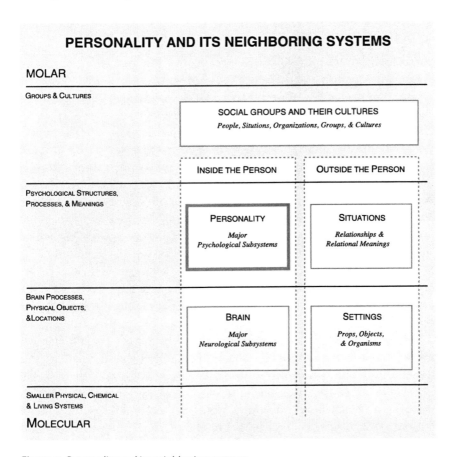

Figure 2: Personality and its neighboring systems.

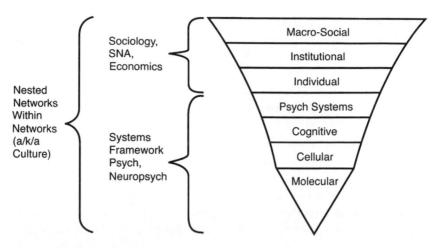

Figure 3: Levels of meaning production.

and countries, each of which emerges from the other and yet may be driven by a unique and different set of organizing principles. In their terms, "the exigencies of nonindependence in relational data preclude the use of standard statistical testing procedures."[43]

From a theoretical standpoint, this means that society both reflects and extends the multiplicity and interdependence of organizational scale found within the individual cognitive–affective system. Thus, if individuals and society can each be viewed in terms of "networks-within-networks," then any model seeking to understand how changes to the cognitive–affective system ramify throughout society as a whole (and vice versa) must understand the bigger picture as a nested set of "networks-within-networks-within-networks-within-networks . . ." nearly ad infinitum. This also means that changes at any level of organization—from the microcellular to the macrosocial—can have emergent and often unpredictable effects that ripple throughout the scalar chain (fig. 3).

While some cultural scholars may balk at the use of psychobiological mechanisms to model phenomena traditionally treated solely at the level of individuals and institutions, I believe the marriage of fields makes perfect sense. First, social theory has never treated the human mind as a "black box." Although biological explanations have been treated with justifiable skepticism in the wake of the essentializing rationales for social doctrine embodied in the work of eugenicists, social Darwinists, and more recent scholars such as R. J. Herrstein and

Charles Murray,[44] psychological theorists from Freud to Lacan are still considered canonical social texts, and are routinely included in the core curriculum of cultural studies and related fields.

More important, we are currently witnessing a renewed interest in cultural phenomena—especially music—among members of the neuroscience community, several of whom (such as D. J. Levitin[45] and Oliver Sacks[46]) have recently published popular books on the subject. It would be absurd for a social theorist with a subject such as mine to ignore Sacks's claim that "just as rapid neuronal oscillations bind together different functional parts within the brain and nervous system, so rhythm binds together the individual nervous systems of a human community,"[47] simply because his work is rooted in biological rather than social science.

But it is not enough simply to say that changes at the biological or cognitive level have effects at the social level. What do these "changes" and "effects" consist of, and how can we know them when we see them? I argue that both micro- and macrolevel structural change can be understood in terms of organizational patterns. Inside the individual cognitive–affective system, organizational patterns of relationship among or within neurological and psychological subsystems are typically described in terms of emotions, thoughts, or associations. Within the broader social system, they are described in terms of ideas, styles, and cultures.

These patterns change as they travel. Like the nested levels of culture and cognition, the organizational patterns that constitute meaningful information at each scale emerge unpredictably into different (if related) patterns at a larger scale. Similarly, it is not especially useful to think of single patterns working their ways up the scalar chain as separate phenomena; like waves on the surface of a windy lake, the myriad patterns that populate our minds and societies must constantly intersect, amplifying and disrupting one another in equally unpredictable ways. Finally, changes in these patterns over time and across scalar levels are not simply the result of blind mutation or poor copy fidelity. By virtue of our self-awareness, we have an active and agentic role in the process at every scale, from meditation to mood management to mimicry to mass media.

This schema helps to illuminate two of the central conundrums that echo throughout music scholarship. First, music appears to be both a universal human behavior and yet so polysemic and so culturally specific in its details as to confound any attempt at identifying universal elements in its codes and praxes. As Ian Cross writes, "it can be *about* something, but its *aboutness* can vary from context to context and even within context."[48] Second, although music plays a vital role in countless rituals, ceremonies, and social functions across countless cultures, it has neither a fixed reference point nor an identifiable function pertaining to our material condition.

I believe that the answers to these two conundrums are one and the same: namely, that music's reference point is the human cognitive–affective system itself, that its function is the psychological and social maintenance of the cognitive–affective system, and that our universal capacity for cognitive–affective adaptability is the source of our musical aesthetic polymorphism and the polysemy of our musical codes and practices.

In other words, we can view our cognitive–affective systems as cultural filters, which change as a result of the cultural information flowing through them, altering the information flows in the process. This process is both agentic and constrained; we have some degree of self-awareness and control over our own filters, but none save perhaps an enlightened few (monks? yogis?) possess full awareness or autonomy. Society, in turn, can be understood as a vast network of filters, and the cultural information that flows through it has the capacity to effect change at the macrolevel by virtue of its individual interactions at the microlevel. Music is a uniquely effective form of cultural information, because it addresses the filter mechanism itself, without recourse to linguistic or representational abstractions. Or, in Sacks's words, "music has the power to embed sequences and to do this when other forms of organization (including verbal forms) fail."[49]

Thus, we may draw relationships between musical phenomena at different scalar levels that have been traditionally treated as separate and unrelated: music's role in cognitive development and in the evolution of the human mind itself; music's role in psychological processes, such as mood management and self-identification; music's role in social processes like group identification and religious ritual. Each level of meaning I alluded to above can be viewed as one of the many interrelated tiers in this nested network model. In other words, music's psychological functions are predicated on its cognitive functions, its social functions are predicated on its psychological functions, and so on.

This capacity of music to contribute to macrolevel changes without necessarily conveying explicitly referential social information helps to explain why it has been so often regulated across such a broad range of societies. Its power can be viewed as a kind of *cognitive–affective capital* (which contributes emergently to the "cultural capital" that Pierre Bourdieu[50] ascribes to music and other cultural forms). This capital, like any other, is coveted, collected, and exploited by individuals and institutions who are invested in promoting or inhibiting a given social agenda or organizational ethic. Each of the powerful institutions I alluded to in my discussion of musical regulation, and each of the individuals and groups who resist against this regulation, can be seen as warring over cognitive–affective capital, whether their explicit focus of these battles is intellectual property, religious dogma, or political affiliation.

Music's Discursive Framework

The unpredictability stemming from music's emergent nature and the organizational complexity of society's nested networks would seem to make it very difficult for any individual, group, or institution to effectively leverage music's cognitive–affective capital toward a specific end. This unpredictability, however, is mitigated by the *discursive framework* a given culture develops to understand and define the role that music

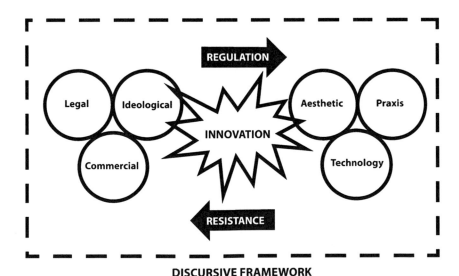

DISCURSIVE FRAMEWORK

Figure 4: Musical meaning production bounded by discursive framework.

plays in society. This framework serves as a kind of cement, binding together ideas and assumptions about how music operates, and what it means, at the various scalar levels of society's nested network. In so doing, the framework encourages us to view and hear music in certain ways, and precludes us from viewing and hearing it in other ways, serving as a discursive boundary and constraining the process of dialectical innovation I describe above (fig. 4).

For instance, a framework defining a musical composition as a piece of "intellectual property" owned by an individual composer will support a very different set of beliefs and associations than one defining musical compositions as conscious and autonomous supernatural entities. Both frameworks are perfectly justifiable in their own ways, and both have been embraced by large cultures comprised of millions of individuals.

Because of its power to overdetermine the application of music's cognitive–affective capital at various scalar levels of society, the ability to influence the discursive framework is of great interest for any individual or group with a stake in social organization. And the framework is such a ponderous edifice, and so deeply entrenched in every aspect of social practice, that it does not change easily. It is instantiated in our laws, our customs, and our ideologies, to the point of near-invisibility: of *course* music is X; how could it *possibly* be Y? And yet, arguably, the battles between musical regulation and resistance represent the frayed edge of the social fabric, and every tiny victory and defeat constitutes an act of renegotiation, a minor revision to the overarching structure.

On rare occasions, however, the discursive framework undergoes a serious revision within a relatively short span of time. Usually, this is precipitated by some sea change in either the social or the technological landscape. In the first instance, political revolution may bring a new party or group to power, which may demand that all frameworks be revised to suit its philosophies. In the second, technological development may so drastically change the locus of possible codes and praxes that the old discourse becomes nakedly obsolete, jutting out for all to see like the foundations of some long-buried city suddenly regurgitated by the Earth. I argue that we are in the midst of exactly such a sea change today, a development I explore further in the following chapters.

2
The Modern
Framework

In the course of history, the various arts change not only their content and style, but also their relations to each other, and their place in the general system of culture, as do religion, philosophy or science. Our familiar system of the five fine arts not merely originated in the eighteenth century, but it also reflects the particular cultural and social conditions of that time.

Paul Oskar Kristeller

In 1830, Hector Berlioz was a young Parisian composer with a growing reputation and a promising career. Even then, however, he was embroiled in the financial difficulties that would dog him for the rest of his life. To help make ends meet, he accepted a simple job, far beneath the capabilities and stature of a composer whose grand orchestral work *Symphonie Fantastique* had premiered earlier in the same year, to both fanfare and controversy. As he relates in his memoirs, Berlioz was given the task of correcting proofs of musical scores for local music publisher Eugène-Théodore Troupenas. Some of the scores, including works by Beethoven, had been edited by François-Joseph Fétis, a professor at the prestigious Paris Conservatory, a stalwart member of the French musical establishment, and a sometime mentor to the younger composer.

Berlioz worshipped the recently deceased (and not yet canonized) Beethoven as a "modern master," the "king of kings," and a "great Homeric mind,"[1] and modeled aspects of his life, his compositions, and (apparently) even his hair style after the elder composer's. When he discovered that Fétis, in editing Beethoven's work, had "corrected" some of the notes to suit his own harmonic principles, he was appalled at the "incredible audacity" of these "insolent modifications." As Berlioz later wrote, he instantly resolved to prevent Troupenas from ever publishing the offending scores: "'What?' said I to myself; 'they are making a French edition of the most marvelous instrumental works ever brought forth by human genius, and because the publisher has called in the aid of a professor who is drunk on his own vanity . . . therefore these monumental works are to be mutilated, and Beethoven is to submit to *corrections* like the veriest pupil in a harmony class. No, indeed, that shall never be.'"[2]

True to his word, Berlioz spread the news about the forthcoming publication and its revisions throughout the Parisian music community, from the Société des Concerts to the Opéra. Eventually, he raised such a furor that Troupenas was forced to withdraw Fétis's revised score, and to publish "the original text." Not content to celebrate his victory in private, Berlioz composed a monologue in his subsequent work, *Lélio*, in which the title character excoriates "the desecrators who dare to attack original works," equating their "ridiculous outrage to art" with the actions of pigeons who defecate on public sculptures and then "strut about with as much pride and satisfaction as if they had laid a golden egg."

This incident drove a wedge between Berlioz and the French musical establishment that would undermine his career for the rest of his life (it wasn't until 1850 that he was finally awarded his first and only institutional sinecure, as Librarian at the Paris Conservatory). Later, however, Berlioz wrote that he didn't regret the consequences of his attack on Fétis, because "I was even more his enemy than he was mine, and I could never think of his attempt on Beethoven without quivering with anger."[3]

Despite the many difficult years he had spent between authoring *Lélio* and his memoirs, Berlioz was probably telling the truth when he wrote that he had no regrets. By the time he completed the book, in 1854, he could be confident that history would vindicate him. Not only was his place in the French musical pantheon securely established, the rest of the world had come around to seeing things his way.

The model of music and society that Berlioz had embraced in his youth, premised on the supremacy of genius and the inviolability of artistic vision, was still relatively new. Although many elements of this discursive framework had their origins in Enlightenment-era philosophy, they only began to crystallize into a coherent worldview around the turn of the nineteenth century. The Parisian musical establishment of Berlioz' youth had come of age before this crystallization.

Berlioz was among the first to come of age after it. But by the middle of the century, the Romantic era was in full swing and the new paradigm was ascendant. Berlioz could rest assured that most, if not all, of his readers would view his "defense" of Beethoven (himself well-enshrined in the canon by this point) as both principled and reasoned.

Many readers of Berlioz's memoirs today no doubt feel just as sympathetic to his cause as did his contemporary readers. In the century and a half since the memoirs were published, the notions he fought so fiercely to defend have become thoroughly enmeshed in our system of thought, and in the institutions that govern art in society, to the point that we have come to take them for granted. As I argue in this chapter, I believe this era may be nearing its end. The rapid pace of technological development in the past three decades has helped to effect paradigmatic changes in the way we make and experience music, forcing us to reevaluate our most fundamental assumptions and bringing theory increasingly into conflict with practice. I consider it entirely likely that, a generation from now, readers of Berlioz's memoirs will have to struggle to understand what motivated his vitriol against Fétis, and, finally understanding, will marvel at the quaintness of his ideas.

The Modern Discursive Framework

In order to discuss how things are changing, we must first establish what they are changing from. The discursive framework that Berlioz embraced, which we may as well call, for lack of a better term, the "modern" framework, consisted of far more than simply rushing to the defense of genius. This elaborate and robust system of thought, which has remained dominant during the last two centuries, was the first to elevate art above other fields of human endeavor, the first to recognize the artist as a separate class of individual, and the first to place such a premium on originality. In fact, the entire framework as it existed by the end of the twentieth century can be understood in terms of a series of binary distinctions, including:

An art as opposed to a craft
An artist as opposed to an audience
An original as opposed to a copy
A performance as opposed to a composition
A figure as opposed to a ground
Materials as opposed to tools.

As I discuss in the following pages, each of these distinctions has its own philosophical origins, serves its own social functions, and is perpetuated through its own set of institutional foundations. Collectively, they have amounted to a remarkably durable and flexible system that has survived centuries of social and technological upheaval.

Origins of the Modern Framework: Art vs. Craft

The elevation of Art-with-a-capital-A to its own stratum of human endeavor is the most essential defining characteristic of the modern discursive framework. As philosopher and historian Paul Oskar Kristeller demonstrates, ancient and medieval societies did not distinguish between the categories we now refer to as art, craft, and science; nor did they distinguish between aesthetic beauty and moral good as independent concepts or frames of reference. In his words, writers in these periods "were neither able nor eager to detach the aesthetic quality of . . . works of art from their intellectual, moral, religious and practical function or content, or to use such an aesthetic quality as a standard for grouping the fine arts together or for making them the subject of a comprehensive philosophical interpretation."[4]

Thus, the ancient Greek term for art, *tekhne*, may also be translated into English as "skill," "craft," "method," or "system," and applied to shoemaking or shipbuilding as easily as to painting and sculpting. A similar breadth of interpretation may be applied to the equivalent Roman term, *ars*. Classificatory systems such as the seven "liberal arts" and the nine muses only began to crystallize during later antiquity, and as Kristeller argues, these systems were fluid and ever changing, consistent only insofar as "poetry and music are grouped with some of the sciences, whereas the visual arts are omitted."[5] In the late middle ages, seven "mechanical arts" were added to match the liberal arts, introducing a rudimentary distinction between intellectual and practical pursuits, but even within this schema, painting and sculpture remained relegated to the (inferior) mechanical sphere, while mathematics and astronomy remained in the (superior) liberal sphere.

Only at the end of the eighteenth century, coincidental with the 1790 publication of Immanuel Kant's *Critique of Judgment*, did Western culture begin to crystallize the definitive understanding of art that we have taken for granted in the two intervening centuries. Kant is an emblematic figure in modern aesthetics, not because he was the first to propose that diverse arts may share traits in common, or that they may collectively constitute a discrete field of human endeavor, but because he was one of the first to integrate the many elements of Enlightenment-era aesthetics into a single, coherent philosophy, thus paving the way for their institutional adoption.

Kant's schema distinguishes the experience of gratification (getting what we want) and the experience of goodness (getting what we expect) from the aesthetic experience of beauty, which he argues is fundamentally "disinterested" pleasure.[6] In other words, our aesthetic response to a beautiful object exists regardless of our relationship to or desires surrounding that object. This is because aesthetic judgments are based on pure intuition, which exists prior to practical or conceptual understanding. Thus, we may find people, places, or works of art beautiful regardless of other negative associations we attach to them. For instance, I may reprehend Wagner's anti-Semitic mythologizing, but I'll happily sit through a live performance of the entire Ring Cycle as often as I can.

This last point suggests another important facet of Kantian aesthetic philosophy: namely, that beauty can inhere both to the natural world and to human-made objects. Within the modern framework, the notion that beauty can be simultaneously man-made and prior to logical categorization allows for the emergence of a vital distinction: among man-made objects, those which serve no function other than their inherent beauty are classified, definitively, as art. Mere functional objects, regardless of the skill involved in their production or the beauty of their form, are relegated to the category of craft. As art historian James Trilling put it in a recent lecture: "Unlike the arts that we call art, the arts we call craft have a built-in standard, a test of practicality to pass."[7]

If the general concept of art as we now understand it is a fairly recent invention, the categorical status of music and its relationship to other arts has also been fluid throughout most of history, crystallizing only in the modern era. In the ancient world, music was not initially understood as a discrete practice; what we would today consider musical performance was traditionally grouped, along with dance, as a constituent element of poetry. As with the terms *tekhne* and *ars*, the ancient Greek term *mousike* "was not confined to music; it encompassed euphony in poetry and rhythm in gymnastics," and could even be used to describe "the spiritual harmony of a soul in balance."[8] After Pythagoras's investigation of music's relationship to mathematics, however, this began to change. By late antiquity, and into the Renaissance, music (more specifically, music theory) was widely considered one of the liberal arts—the only one of today's "fine arts" to hold that distinction. Thus, throughout much of history, music has teetered on the brink between its roots in poetical praxis and its Pythagorean elevation to the realm of mathematical theory.

As art and science increasingly diverged during the Enlightenment, and disciplines such as painting and poetry became definitively classified as fine arts, music faced something of an identity crisis. On the one hand, the rise of opera recemented music's relationship to poetry and theater. On the other, the rekindled interest in Pythagorean notions of "music of the spheres" after the Baroque period, and the increasing scientific fascination with musical prodigy, reinforced its ties to mathematics. Music's unique ability to straddle this divide has only been achieved through the somewhat artificial separation of musical composition as a creative act (i.e., art) from music theory as an analytical practice (i.e., science), a distinction first proposed by the Bohemian Jesuit Jacobus Pontanus in 1600 and well enshrined in the philosophy of art by Kant's time.

Origins of the Modern Framework: Artist vs. Audience

The distinction of the artist as a separate class of individual, and the simultaneous reification of the audience, closely parallel the elevation of art to a discrete class of human endeavor. The relationship is not interdependent; although the category of the artist would be meaningless without the category of art, the reverse does not apply: the concept of art could easily exist without requiring the existence of artists. Thus, we must understand this philosophical development on its own terms.

Throughout both ancient and medieval history, art was considered to be fundamentally teachable. Skill, it was assumed, was transmissible from teacher to student, cemented through practice, and passed on again to the next generation, along with any functional refinements that may have been developed along the way. In this respect, portraiture, sculpture, and music were understood to operate in much the same way as blacksmithing, masonry, or any other skilled trade.

The rise of scientific discipline and the simultaneous elevation of the arts to a putatively higher sphere of human endeavor at the outset of the Enlightenment produced some unanticipated consequences. Scholars began to realize that, although the scientific revolution was propelling the technological knowledge and capacity of contemporary Europeans far beyond the achievements of antiquity, aesthetic achievement appeared to be at best consistent with, and by some opinions, inferior to,[9] the work of ancient artists. Clearly, these scholars reasoned, there must be some functional difference between scientific and artistic capacity behind this growing achievement gap. One logical answer to this conundrum was that, while scientific expertise was completely transmissible, allowing consecutive generations of scholars to build cumulatively on one another's work, artistic skill must be somehow inherent to the individual, and therefore both unteachable and noncumulative.[10]

Thus were born two enduring ideas that have gained much currency within the modern discursive framework: *talent* and *genius*. These two interrelated concepts are often difficult to distinguish from one another, and some may argue that they differ only in terms of scale. The *Oxford English Dictionary*, for instance, offers a definition of talent as "a special natural ability or aptitude, usually for something expressed or implied," while its definitions of genius include "natural ability or capacity; quality of mind" and "native intellectual power of an exalted type, such as is attributed to those who are esteemed greatest in any department of art, speculation, or practice." I would argue that there is actually a functional difference between the common uses of the two terms, reflecting two variant philosophies of art, or two classes of artist, that both compete with and reinforce one another within the modern framework.

Talent, as the dictionary definition suggests, reflects a greater-than-usual innate capacity for artistic accomplishment. The logic of the concept of talent suggests that while art is teachable, it may be taught more easily and effectively to some than to others. An artist, therefore, is someone who has taken advantage of his or her native talent to become proficient in a given artistic discipline. Art, in this model, becomes merely a craft without a practical function, and the role of an artist is to become proficient at the production of beauty.

The concept of genius suggests a different approach to art and artistry. Although the term dates back to antiquity (the *OED* cites Roman mythology's use of the word to describe a "tutelary god or attendant spirit"), our modern use of the term only appeared during the eighteenth century, in England, Germany, and France. Thus, this definition was still relatively new when Kant argued, in the *Critique of Judgment*, that artistic geniuses are those who do not simply follow the aesthetic codes of their times; rather, by producing innovative work, they change the codes themselves. This innate capacity for aesthetic innovation, which is called *imagination*, allows geniuses to translate their own aesthetic experience to other individuals, through the medium of art. Thus, in post-Kantian aesthetic theory, the terms "genius" and "artist" are often treated as virtually synonymous. In this model, the role of a true artist is simply to innovate. Self-styled artists who fail to innovate or to communicate their aesthetic visions effectively are simply pretenders to the throne; called to greatness, perhaps, but not chosen.

Art theorist Larry Gross[11] describes a gradual shift in the definition of artistry, analogous to my distinction between talent and genius. The earlier definition, he writes, emphasizes virtuosity in execution, measuring the ability of the artist in terms of fidelity to an idealized form.[12] By contrast, the newer definition is predicated not on the *skill* evident in the artist's *work*, but rather on the *innovation* evident in the artist's *ideas*. The sincerity and therefore the quality of an artist, according to this definition, could be inferred not from the *objective faithfulness* of his work to its subject or its style, but rather from his idiosyncratic *subjective distortion* of the subject or style.

This new definition, along with the image of the artist as the innovative and exceptional genius and the necessary relegation of the remainder of society to a role of mere appreciation (or worse, lack of appreciation), came to dominate the discourse of art by the early-to-mid nineteenth century. As Gross observes, this concept grew in prevalence and power as both a result and a contributory factor of the increasing Western preoccupation with the individual, beginning in the Renaissance but achieving dominance in the Romantic era.

The social category of "musician" appears to have existed in many cultures throughout human history. As with the broader category of "artist," however, its definition within the modern framework differs drastically from those of other times and places. In many traditional and preindustrial societies, music was integrated into the fabric of life and shared among the community in a way many people in our society would find it difficult to imagine. As Jacques Attali writes of music in Europe's Middle Ages, "The circulation of music was neither elitist nor monopolistic of creativity . . . music in daily life was inseparable from lived time, in which it was active and not something to be watched."[13] Historian Eileen Southern describes a similar dynamic in West Africa during the slave trade years of the seventeenth through the nineteenth centuries, writing that "for every activity in the life of the individual or the community there was an appropriate music; it was an integral part of life from the hour of birth to beyond the grave."[14]

Thus, while jongleurs, minstrels, or griots may have inhabited the specialized social role of musician in these societies, they were not nearly as removed from quotidian social practice as they are within the modern framework. These musicians served something akin to a shamanistic function, officiating and organizing musical events in which every member of society was a vital participant—whether by singing, dancing, or simply clapping hands. Only after musicians were professionalized, becoming "bound to a single master"[15] during the late Renaissance era, did a greater gulf emerge between musicians and other members of society, whose role eventually crystallized under the more passive rubric of "audience." The Kantian concept of genius, then, can be understood as the final step in this process, affirming the separation of artist from audience as both natural and inevitable.

The ethnomusicologist John Blacking[16] provides additional evidence that the category of the musician as we understand it within the modern framework is highly idiosyncratic, and that our concept of musical genius is a social construction. In the course of his fieldwork among the Venda people of the Northern Transvaal, Blacking came to wonder how it was that every individual he encountered had a degree of musical competence observed only among a special few in Western culture. Rejecting localized biological anomaly as an explanation, Blacking concluded that all humans have an innate capacity for a highly sophisticated level of musical accomplishment, but that most cultures, including our own, tragically fail to nourish this capacity.

The editors of the *Cambridge Handbook of Expertise and Expert Performance* have provided a great deal of support for Blacking's argument. Their book offers a broad survey of recent psychological research suggesting that, for highly accomplished individuals (in music as well as other fields), the influence of native "talent" is dwarfed by the influence of "deliberate practice" (self-directed and strategically planned skill acquisition).[17] Journalist Malcolm Gladwell makes a similar argument as well, in his book *Outliers: The Story of Success*. As he summarizes recent research: "The closer psychologists look at the careers of the gifted, the smaller the role innate talent seems to play and the bigger the role preparation seems to play."[18]

In other words, although we may differ from one another to a limited degree in our native capacity to produce music, the cultural concept of musical exceptionality suggested by the terms "talent," "genius," and "musician," and taken for granted within the modern discursive framework, are largely the products of social construction.

Origins of the Modern Framework: Original vs. Copy

The idea that an artist's work occupies a place of distinction, apart from all other objects both natural and manufactured, is closely tied to the philosophical notions of art and artistry described above. If art is a discrete category of human endeavor, and an artist is an exceptional member of society, then the work he or she produces must necessarily be equally distinct from all that surrounds it. This distinction is evident in two defining features that are ascribed to a work of art in the modern discursive framework: its *originality* and its *uniqueness*.

The concept of originality applies to the artist as much as to the work of art itself. In essence, the logic of this concept suggests that *no other individual could have produced this work of art*. As Kristeller observes, the idea shares its Enlightenment-era provenance with the others I have discussed: "such dominating concepts of modern aesthetics as taste and sentiment, genius, originality and creative imagination did not assume their definite modern meaning before the eighteenth century."[19]

The definition of originality evolved in subtle ways along with the definition of artistry. During the formative years of the modern framework, when artistry was defined in terms of virtuosity, originality was more of a functional constraint than an ideal. Only Bach could have produced Toccata and Fugue in D Minor, this logic holds, because he alone possessed the mastery of both the instrument and the aesthetic codes. As the badge of artistry moved from virtuosity to innovation, and from objective fidelity to subjective distortion, the definition of originality necessarily changed as well. Only Van Gogh could have produced *Starry Night*, this newer logic holds, because only his personal vision could have translated a normal landscape into such an idiosyncratic image.

The concept of uniqueness offers a different form of distinction than the concept of originality. According to the logic of this concept, *a given work of art is unlike any other object in the world*. As Walter Benjamin famously observed, this logic can be traced back much further than the modern framework: "The uniqueness of a work of art is inseparable from its being imbedded in the fabric of tradition."[20] This uniqueness, he argues, has traditionally engendered an "aura" around works of art, tying them to the unique cultural circumstances that produced them and to the unique cultural interpretations of their local and contemporary audiences.

However, Benjamin argues, industrialization ushered in an era of "mechanical reproduction," which fundamentally changed the ways in which we understand a work's uniqueness and authenticity. In an age when industrial processes can produce a painting or sculpture more flawless than the "original" it is based on, and when emerging creative media (such as film, photography, and sound recording) are made explicitly for mass production, the aura surrounding a work of art withers and dies.

Despite (or because of) the death of aura, Benjamin continues, the importance of authenticity has only increased—to religious proportions. "The function of the concept of authenticity remains determinate in the evaluation of art," he writes. "With the secularization of art, authenticity displaces the cult value of the work." This shift from aura to authenticity is effected through an evolution in the definition of uniqueness, similar to the shift in the definition of originality I discussed above. In Benjamin's words, the "uniqueness of the phenomena" that possessed aura in traditional society is "displaced by the empirical uniqueness of the creator or of his creative achievement." Again, the locus of distinction within the framework shifts away from the work itself, and toward the artist, whose vision and genius cannot be reproduced.

The distinction afforded to a work of art by virtue of its originality or uniqueness is matched by the lack of distinction attributed to a *copy* of such a work. Originality and uniqueness each suggest a different definition for this term. According to the logic of originality, a copy is a work of art that attempts to replicate either the style or the actual form of another work. Put in other terms, a copy may be described as a work lacking originality, and therefore undeserving of distinction. Given a definition of artistry and originality based on virtuosity, copying is more likely to be explicitly acknowledged, as when a student of Rembrandt signs his master's name to his own work. Given a definition of artistry and originality based on innovation, the definition of copying is more likely to be subjective, as when an art critic or historian avers that Picasso copied Braque, or vice versa.

According to the logic of uniqueness, the term "copy" suggests either forgery or mechanical reproduction. In both cases, the uniqueness of a work is challenged by the existence of another, seemingly identical (and, therefore, interchangeable) work. If, as Benjamin observes, the age of mechanical reproduction (and the modern framework) increasingly requires that uniqueness be defined in terms of the artist rather than the work, we may infer that copies are increasingly defined (and thereby deprived of distinction) by their lack of authorization—quite literally, by their theoretical distance from the author (fig. 5).

Figure 5: An "authentic reproduction" available at a retail store.

Thus, a *hierarchy of uniqueness* begins to emerge. At the top of the pyramid are theoretically unreplicable works, such as signed paintings, live performances, and handwritten manuscripts. Although the phenomenological experience of these works may be reproduced through industrial processes, their verifiable connection to the artist cannot survive the journey. Next in the hierarchy come the constituent elements of the industrial process, such as animation cells, photo negatives, musical instruments, or "master" tapes, which are typically accorded the same assiduously documented provenance as a "unique" work of art. Next come industrial products bearing the unique imprimatur of the artist, such as signed or "limited edition" photographic prints, books, or recordings. Near the bottom of the pyramid are standard mass-produced commercial fare, such as posters, prints, books, recordings, and films. Finally, at the very bottom of the pyramid are the unauthorized "pirated" copies of such works, reproduced without the legal permission, let alone the imprimatur, of the artist.

The modern framework offers fairly fixed interpretations of concepts such as originality, uniqueness, authenticity, and copying as they apply to the field of music. As the Berlioz–Fétis imbroglio demonstrates, one of the foundational premises of this framework is that an artist's authority (in every sense of the word) extends across the gulf introduced by mechanical reproduction. Put another way, Berlioz emphasized that the physical act of copying or reproducing a score does not give the copyist any right to alter its contents—the originality and uniqueness of the underlying composition are preserved regardless of the mode of expression of that composition. This remarkably durable idea, which denies even the possibility of originality or uniqueness (and, therefore, of artistic expression) being introduced in the act of reproduction, was applied to sound recording as well, when it emerged around the turn of the twentieth century. As I discuss at greater length throughout this book, it has also become one of the primary assumptions in which intellectual property law is currently rooted.

Origins of the Modern Framework: Performance vs. Composition

The modern framework's emphasis on the inviolability of an artist's vision, when applied to music, tacitly relies on another relatively new idea: namely, that music exists both prior to and independently of its expression. This distinction is typically represented in terms of the composition/performance dichotomy, although "expression" can certainly refer to recordings and printed scores as well.

Kristeller argues that the concept of the musical composition as an independent work of art was introduced to Western philosophy in 1600 by Jacobus Pontanus, who placed it on a plane of aesthetic achievement equivalent to poetry and painting. The musicologist Edward E. Lowinsky demonstrates that Swiss poet and scholar Glareanus emphasized the primacy of composition over interpretation a half-century earlier, in his *Dodekachordon*: "Shall we not consider him who invented the melody of the *Te Deum* or the *Pange lingua* a greater genius than him who later composed a whole Mass on it?"[21]

Regardless of its precise origins, most scholars agree that the concept of the musical composition as a discrete artistic enterprise appears to have emerged toward the end of the Renaissance period, on the cusp of the modern era.[22] The timing of this shift can be correlated to many of the philosophical developments outlined above, such as the professionalization of musicianship and the elevation of art to its own sphere of human endeavor. The reification of musical composition can also be understood as a factor (both dependent and contributory) of two more or less contemporary technical innovations: standardized musical notation, which allowed composition to be expressed independently of performance, and movable type, which allowed musical notation to be produced and distributed on a massive scale.

One of the many results of the reification of composition was the consequent relegation of performance to a lesser sphere of artistic achievement. Before the development of printing and notation, music was orally (and aurally) transmitted, and performance was everything; without audible expression, music could not exist. From antiquity through the Renaissance, music represented one of the last bastions of orality in an increasingly literate society. The liberation of composition from performance reversed the logic of musical expression. No longer did composition comprise a mere *element of* performance; it became something necessarily *prior to* performance, and thus more essential.

This process parallels the rise of the composer to the pinnacle of the musical labor hierarchy, as evidenced in Berlioz's memoirs. The division of labor has only widened in the years between the Romantic era and the present day. Sociologist Howard Becker observes that, within the Western classical music tradition, "in the mid-twentieth century, [composition and performance] occur separately and are seen as two different, highly specialized jobs. That was not always true. Beethoven, like most composers of his time, also performed, both his own music and that of others, as well as conducting and improvising on the piano."[23]

This process has also paralleled, and helped to engender, the gradual removal of musical performance from the public sphere and its sequestering behind the proscenium (or down into the orchestra pit). As Attali writes, by the eighteenth and nineteenth centuries, "the concert hall performance replaced the popular music festival and the private concert at court."[24]

Origins of the Modern Framework: Figure vs. Ground

The concepts of "figure" and "ground," which are essential to our present-day understanding of musical organization, originate in late-nineteenth and early-twentieth-century gestalt psychological theory. According to this theory, human beings are naturally inclined to divide their visual fields (and, to a lesser extent, their other sensory experi-

Figure 6:
A Rubin vase,
demonstrating
figure/ground
ambiguity.

ences) into a dominant element (the figure) standing out from a less differentiated field (the ground).

Such perceptual organization can be subjective, contingent, and changeable: "What is figural at any one moment depends on patterns of sensory stimulation and on the momentary interests of the perceiver."[25] In one classic illustration of this point, called a "Rubin vase," a drawing of an hourglass, vase, or candlestick can resolve itself into a drawing of two profiled faces and then switch back again for any given viewer within the span of a few seconds (fig. 6). While the figure/ground distinction is typically discussed in regard to visual stimuli such as this, it has been conclusively demonstrated in the case of auditory perception as well. This is commonly referred to as the "cocktail-party phenomenon," describing our ability to follow a single conversation in a room full of talking people (and clinking glasses).

The concepts of figure and ground have been applied to music by numerous scholars over the years. Leonard B. Meyer, one of the foremost Western music theorists operating within the modern framework, relies on it heavily. He concedes that figure/ground distinction may not be as universally recognizable in music as it is in visual art: "In 'aural space,' in music, there is no given ground; there is no necessary, continuous stimulation, against which all figures must be perceived."[26] Yet, for Meyer, this is only further demonstration of his fundamental premise that musical meaning relies entirely on culturally specific stylistic conventions and cues.

This helps to explain why, elsewhere throughout his book, Meyer confidently discusses exactly which sonic features correspond to figure and ground in music. He is specifically describing the Western musical tradition, and thus giving us an excellent description of the prevailing norms within the modern discursive framework. For Meyer, the "ground" in a musical work can be identified through two criteria. First, it "must be more homogeneous" and "have a less palpable, well-figured shape than the other figures of the work so that it is clear that it is not the chief pattern." Second, it must "surround the other figures temporally,"[27] beginning earlier and ending later than the musical figure or figures do. For Meyer, a "well-figured shape" can apply to melodic, harmonic, or rhythmic articulation, depending on the form of the composition. In other words, a polyrhythmic pattern can act as a figure against a uniformly rhythmic ground, a melodic figure can stand out against a harmonic ground, or a dissonant chord can emerge from an assonant background. Like all aesthetic meaning in his model of music, the figure/ground distinction is a factor of our expectations, and of the compositional divergences therefrom.

Cognitive linguist Reuven Tsur builds on Meyers's model, focusing on the ambiguities of figure and ground in both musical composition and performance. Tsur specifically analyzes Beethoven's "Moonlight" Sonata, which he argues is "quite unlike anything previously composed for the keyboard" due to the unique ways in which the composer undermines earlier figure/ground conventions and builds his work around the subjectivity and contingency of aural perception.

Tsur demonstrates that the rising pattern of three-note figures which give the "Moonlight" Sonata its distinctive quality are actually quite similar to a passage in Mozart's *Don Giovanni*. However, while Mozart has "deeply buried" the passage in the background of his opera, Beethoven has chosen to highlight it in his own composition. Tsur emphasizes that he is not accusing Beethoven of theft or imitation; he is merely observing that a similar musical device has been employed in radically different ways by the two composers. In his words, "Beethoven took a piece of ground music, that has a typically ground texture, and placed it in the focus of the sonata movement dominating for no less than six minutes the musical space."

By dislodging a musical device from the deep recesses of the ground and placing it in the figural spotlight, Tsur argues, Beethoven engineered an ambiguous composition, in which "'the momentary interests of the perceiver' can be manipulated to a considerable extent by the performer." To demonstrate this, he cites two recordings: one in which the performer emphasizes the ground-ness of the passage, and another in which the performer emphasizes its figure-ness.[28]

Given that Beethoven is widely considered to be the definitive composer of the modern framework, we may take his radical technique as an indication of the framework's broader treatment of figure and ground. This treatment can be summarized in terms of two key elements. First, figure and ground are signified by stylistically specific musical attributes. Melodic, rhythmic, or harmonic articulation represents musical figuration, while homogeneity represents musical ground. Second, the dialectical tension between figure and ground has become an important tool in the arsenal of modern composers. In order to exploit this tension, composers may transpose musical elements from the ground of one work to the figure of another, creating the potential for ambiguous interpretation. This process has important consequences in the age of digital sampling, as I discuss at greater length later on.

Origins of the Modern Framework: Materials vs. Tools

The distinction between materials and tools is so deeply implicit in our understanding of art that few, if any, scholars have ever bothered to describe it. In practice, the distinction can be distilled down to something paralleling the "natural vs. artificial" Levi-Straussian binary: materials are *unstructured*, while tools are *structured*. H. W. Janson and A. F. Janson, in the introduction to their definitive reference work, *History of Art: The Western Tradition*, argue that "artists work with materials that have little or no shape of their own. The creative process then consists of . . . the artist's attempts to give them form by shaping the material."[29] Put another way, tools are templates, allowing humans to impose organized form (e.g., art) on a chaotic material universe.

Clearly, this distinction raises some problems; paints are no more or less a product of human industry than are brushes, and a Jackson Pollock painting is arguably less structured than the sum of its constituent materials. For the bulk of aesthetic discourse within the modern framework, though, the distinction holds. Another way to understand the materials/tools distinction in relation to the Levi-Straussian binary is to consider the following: regardless of their degree of structure or chaos per se, materials can be considered a metaphorical subset or extension of the natural world, while tools can be considered a metaphorical subset or extension of human endeavor.

Just as tools are defined as "instruments" within the modern framework's broader discourse of art, musical instruments represent the primary toolset within the field of music. Their structure determines the locus of aesthetic possibilities available in the musical work they produce (for instance, the eighty-eight keys on a tempered piano do not readily allow for microtonal melodic variation). Music's intangibility and invisibility make it more difficult definitively to identify the materials involved in musical production. Traditionally, everything from sound waves and the air they travel through to abstract musical notes and rhythms to musical styles and codes to actual compositions have been treated as the material acted on when music is produced.

Within the modern framework, discussions of the Western classical tradition (which tends to emphasize composition over performance) treat the more abstract elements (e.g., notes and styles) as materials for the *composer* to work with. Discussions of popular and folk music traditions (which place more of an emphasis on performative interpretation) often refer to the songs themselves as "material" for the *performer* to work with. Meyer unconsciously reflects this in his differing use of the term. Discussing the general principle that musical styles vary from culture to culture, Meyer argues that they "are not based on universal natural relationships inherent in the *tonal material* itself."[30] On research on Jamaican folk music traditions, Meyer writes, "the folk singers themselves recognize the difference between the fundamental substratum of the *oral material* handed down to them and their own creative actualization of that material."[31] There can be little doubt from the context of these two quotes that Meyer is referring to tonal elements as material in the first case and to actual compositions as material in the second.

Institutional Foundations of the Modern Framework

The modern discursive framework, characterized by the six binary distinctions described above, has held sway in Western culture for two centuries, surviving numerous technological, social, and aesthetic changes over the course of its ascendancy. This durability can be attributed in large part to its emplacement within a dense thicket of what Becker refers to as "art world" institutions. He makes the argument somewhat succinctly:

> For a symphony orchestra to give a concert . . . instruments must have been invented, manufactured, and maintained, a notation must have been devised and music composed using that notation, people must have learned to play the notated notes on the instruments, times and places for rehearsals must have been provided, ads for the concert must have been placed, publicity must have been arranged and tickets sold, and an audience capable of listening to and in some way understanding and responding to the performance must have been recruited.[32]

As Becker's description suggests, the institutions comprising the art world(s) for music may be educational, professional, or commercial in nature. I would add legal institutions to this list, reflecting the increasingly central role of intellectual property as an element of commercial music practices within the modern framework. As you may observe, these institutions serve many of the same functions as the regulatory institutions described in my first chapter. In point of fact, we can assume in most cases that musical regulatory institutions and "art world" institutions are one and the same.

In other words, the institutions surrounding musical production and consumption serve both constraining and enabling roles, reinforcing the discursive framework and serving as a boundary for the processes of regulation and resistance described in chapter 1 (fig. 7). Although a thorough accounting of all the ways in which the modern framework is institutionally entrenched would require a book-length treatment of its own, I briefly outline some key examples below.

One of the early developments within the educational institutional context was the shift from community-based learning and a guild-based system of apprenticeship to a modern academic pedagogical model rooted in universities, academies, and conservatories. Kristeller[33] argues that such a shift among visual artists in sixteenth century Florence played a vital role in the elevation of painting and sculpture to fine arts—and thus, we may conclude, in the shaping of the modern framework. Attali supports this conclusion, arguing that "the conservatories were charged with producing high-quality musicians through very selective training,"[34] thus institutionalizing the separation of artist from audience and amateur. By the end of the eighteenth century, this institutional shift had become widespread across Europe. The Paris Conservatory, for instance, home to Fétis and, later, to Berlioz, was founded in 1795—five years after the publication of Kant's *Critique of Judgment*.

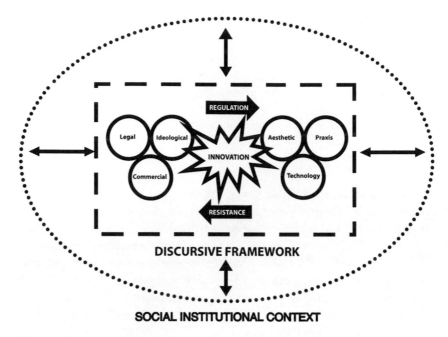

Figure 7: Reciprocal relationship between framework and institutions.

In addition to signifying the elevation of music to a fine art and serving as "special mechanisms [to] sort out artists from nonartists,"[35] pedagogical institutions supported (and continue to support) the other foundational assumptions of the modern framework as well. They reinforce through repetition and convention the other binary distinctions I described above, distinguishing innovation from imitation, performance from composition, figure from ground, and materials from tools in the very language of musical scholarship. Today, the logic of the modern framework underpins virtually all Western music education, from conservatories to kindergartens, constraining resistance and impeding institutional change. As music education researcher E. R. Jorgensen argues (and advocates), to dislodge it would require nothing less than "a revolution in the institution of music education; a pervasive, systemic, ongoing and radical intervention in the status quo."[36]

The professional institutions surrounding music are equally supportive and constituent of the modern framework. As Gross argues, "the ideology of talent and individuality . . . is congruent with the institutional structure of the official, elite art worlds."[37] Gross refers both to educational systems that reserve training in aesthetic competency for a small elite and to professional systems of accreditation (e.g., art galleries, record labels, published criticism) that are institutionally and economically premised on the scarcity of art and artists. He argues that the combined effect of these systems fulfills the post-Kantian definition of art as something irrelevant to and apart from daily life, banishing aesthetic practices and products to a cultural "reservation." This is clearly reflected in Western musical history over the past six centuries, a gradual process whereby musical production has become increasingly professionalized and institutionalized, from the first salaried court musicians of the feudal era to the popular music stars of the present day.

In the professional institutions surrounding the visual arts, the original/copy distinction is enforced both through the practice of signing artworks and through the system of provenance research, which uses "paper trails" and other forensic evidence to link given works back to the artists who created them. In the field of music, a given composer or performer may have a "signature sound," but due to the nature of recording and mass production, uniqueness and originality are established mainly through legal means, which I discuss more fully below. In both music and the visual arts, professional critics serve as the official arbiters of originality, declaring some artists innovative and dismissing others as merely derivative. Even if critics may disagree about which artists deserve which descriptions (although they tend to agree far more often than not, especially as the years expand between artistic production and criticism), they are nearly unanimous in the opinion that innovation and imitation are opposite to and incompatible with one another.

Commercial music institutions help to sustain the modern framework as well. Live music typically occurs in designated performance venues, which architecturally segregate performers from the audience and often make group participation (e.g., dancing, clapping in time, or singing along) difficult or irrelevant at best. The vast bulk of venues increase this already wide gulf by incorporating amplification and transmission technology—such as microphones, sound systems, video cameras, and screens—into the concert experience, technologically enforcing the unidirectionality of musical expression. These interventions both reinforce and render invisible the core assumptions of the modern framework. As concertgoers, we are unlikely to question why the performer holds a microphone and we do not; after all, we've likely *paid* to become a member of the audience, and it's our privilege to hear the artist perform. If we wanted to hear ourselves make music, we could simply stay at home and sing in the shower.

Likewise, the marketing and rhetoric that characterize the recording industry tend to emphasize the exceptionality of artists. Countless instances of news, reviews, and advertisements invoke the Romantic notion of genius, suggesting that the recording industry is structured as a meritocracy, and that its primary function is to discover, facilitate, and share the work of those rare individuals whose native musical capacity vastly outstrips that of the common individual. I personally remember my own naive surprise when, as an intern at a major record label during my final year in college, I realized that, to the A&R executives I worked for, the functional definition of "genius" was simply the capacity to sell a hundred thousand records. This reverse logic, so tacit within the industry that it need never be expressed outright, flies in the face of the mock-meritocratic rhetoric of television shows like *American Idol* and the unwaveringly fawning interviews and reviews featured in popular music magazines and on MTV.

Of course, the Romantic notion of enduring, uncontestable genius is fundamentally at odds with the increasingly abbreviated fashion cycles of the modern recording industry.[38] No amount of rhetoric can hide from the astute observer that last year's genius is today's tabloid tragedy, or that this year's genius likely shares the same fate in due time. The industry has responded to this apparent disjuncture with a brilliant rhetorical innovation: the now-standard narrative of success, failure, and redemption that characterizes quasi-documentaries such as VH1's popular television show *Behind the Music* and E!'s popular show *True Hollywood Story*.

These narratives teach us that a given recording artist's fall from grace is neither the result of a fickle audience changing its tastes nor of a fickle industry shedding its waste. Rather, it is presented as a natural, if regrettable, consequence of the artist's coping with his or her personal demons (a definitively Romantic notion), exacerbated by the rigors of the road and/or the demands of fame. The inevitable "comeback" of an artist (he or she is unlikely to reattain the heights of their initial renown, but it may still be possible to win a Grammy or two) at the conclusion of a narrative cements the Romantic mythos, reestablishing the artist's exceptionality by trumpeting the power of genius over whatever personal failings he or she may possess. This fifteen-to-twenty-year cycle also conveniently reintroduces the recording artist as a commercially viable property just in time to capture a whole new generation of consumers.

If the educational, professional, and commercial institutions comprising the art world for music primarily reinforce the modern framework by emphasizing the exceptionality of art and artists, many of the framework's remaining binaries are supported through legal institutions. Originality and uniqueness, for instance, are both defined and policed through the application of copyright law. In France, copyright was first extended to musical scores in 1527 (less than a century after Gutenberg introduced his printing press), offering publishers the same exclusive rights over reproduction and sale that were then applied to literary publishing. Copyright control was not accorded to composers themselves until 1786. Attali argues that the timing of this shift is evidence that "in the beginning, the purpose of copyright was not to defend artists' rights, but rather to serve as a tool of capitalism."[39] Without disputing him, I would add that the shift also coincides with the birth of the modern framework.

The role of musical copyright in enforcing the unique/copy distinction is fairly narrow in scope, but nonetheless vital to our understanding of music within the modern framework. For any given musical *event*, it makes little sense to apply the binary at all. Performances are both intangible and fixed within a certain place and time; therefore their uniqueness can never be questioned. Compositions, which are defined by their existence prior to expression, are not only intangible, but invisible and inaudible as well; in their case, there is no unique artifact to be copied. Thus, the unique/copy binary may only be applied to recorded musical *expression*, in the form of either a score or a recording. Demonstrably unique artifacts of musical expression may exist, such as handwritten scores or master tapes, but as I have discussed, the uniqueness of these objects is enforced primarily through provenance research.

The vast bulk of musical expression, however, is mass-produced. Printed scores or manufactured phono recordings may not be unique in the sense that applies to handwritten manuscripts, but their place in the *hierarchy of uniqueness*, which distinguishes them from otherwise identical unauthorized and "pirated" scores and recordings, is enforced entirely through the institution of musical copyright. Given the overlapping history of industrial development and copyright law's various extensions to emerging media and behaviors, it is clear that maintaining the hierarchy of uniqueness for mass-produced musical expression is copyright's raison d'etre and its foremost function.

Music copyright law supports other elements of the modern framework, as well. While it primarily enforces the unique/copy distinction in the context of authorized mass production, it is most often applied to the original/copy distinction in the context of litigation over the authorship of a song. Typically, "experts" in the field of music are called on as witnesses to testify whether a given composition crosses the invisible line separating legitimate influence from illegitimate plagiarism. In other words, there can be no objective method for distinguishing between originality and copying, so the best judgments of those steeped in the modern framework are relied on to decide which shades of gray legally should be rendered "black" and which ones "white."

Despite their necessary imprecision, the judgments of these experts are considered more consequential legally than the perceptions of the composers themselves. For instance, in the well-known suit *Bright Tunes Music Corp. v. Harrisongs Music, LTD,*[40] former Beatle George Harrison was convicted of plagiarizing a song previously recorded by the Chiffons, despite the court's acknowledgment that he did so without conscious knowledge or intent. Thus, the regulatory power of the judicial system has been employed to maintain rigidly a definitive binary distinction underpinning the modern framework, even as it acknowledges the imprecision and subtlety of the creative process involved in musical production.

The performance/composition distinction is also reflected both in the structure of copyright law and in the institutions that surround it. The fact that one variety of copyright applies to musical compositions, while another applies to phonographic recordings of performances, is the most obvious instance of this dichotomy. Yet the binary distinction can be observed at every level of copyright's application to musical practice. Another example is to be found in the institutional structure of music licensing. Even for the variety of copyright that applies solely to compositions, one type of license is applied to the performances of that composition, while other types of licenses are applied to other uses. Within the United States, these separate licenses are policed by separate organizations—with collection agencies such as ASCAP, BMI, and SESAC focused on performances of licensed compositions; the Harry Fox Agency focused on mechanical reproduction of licensed compositions; and music publishers themselves licensing such uses as "synchronization" of a composition with a movie or video game.

Finally, we may observe support for the figure/ground distinction in the application of copyright to musicological structure. Melody, which is considered the definitive figural element within the modern framework, is the *only* component of a musical composition that is unambiguously accorded copyright protection (lyrics are protected as well, but for now let us ascribe to them the status of "nonmusical" compositional components).

Other musical elements, such as harmonies, chord structures, and rhythmic patterns, which are more likely to be treated as ground than as figural within the modern framework, are generally grouped by law under the category of "arrangements." According to the 1976 Copyright Act, arrangements may only qualify for copyright protection under one of two conditions: they must be created by the copyright owner of the "original work" (e.g., the melody), or created and copyrighted with the owner's consent. As music industry attorneys M. William Krasilovsky and Sidney Shemel observe, most newly composed and recorded music fails to meet such criteria: "arrangements used on popular records rarely qualify for copyrighting under either of these conditions."[41] Thus, in one fell swoop, modern copyright law legally mandates a distinction between musical figure and ground, and reinforces the creative primacy of the composer and the inviolability of his work. The radical ideas of Berlioz's youth have now become official dogma.

In short, the educational, professional, commercial, and legal art world institutions surrounding musical practice and production provide considerable support for the modern discursive framework, reinforcing the binary dichotomies that characterize this paradigm in theory, structure, and practice. But why should this be? What incentive is there for such institutions to play a role in enforcing the boundaries of musical practice and innovation? There are two possible answers to this question, which are not necessarily mutually exclusive. The first answer is inertia, or simple force of habit. According to this hypothesis, art world institutions emerge to serve narrowly defined purposes in particular places and times, but become more complex, broad-reaching, and resistant to change over time, like a pearl slowly accreting around a grain of sand.

The second possible answer is that art world institutions support discursive frameworks, consciously or reflexively, as a form of self-preservation. According to this hypothesis, the musical codes, practices, and technologies allowable within a given framework are limited to those which will not threaten to undermine the institutional structures comprising those art worlds, and, more broadly, a society's cultural infrastructure.

I argue that both of these hypotheses are true. Institutional inertia can certainly be observed in structures ranging from our labyrinthine and conflicting legal system to our outmoded, underfunded, and overtaxed educational system, but there is also ample evidence that the modern framework helps to sustain the larger social, political, and economic systems in which the art world institutions are located.

Social Functions of the Modern Framework

It is neither a surprise nor a coincidence that the ascendancy of the modern discursive framework has paralleled the rise of modern social, political, and economic structures. As I have argued throughout this book, our musical codes and practices are intimately tied to our social imagination, and they play an active role in the cognitive, psychological, and social processes by which we orient ourselves in relation to others. Thus, we may observe, in the architecture of the modern framework, conceptual patterns that both reflect and help to constitute the organizational patterns on which modern macrolevel institutions are founded.

The philosophical distinctions between art and craft and between artist and audience have helped to remove aesthetic activities from their historical place at the center of social practice and to sequester them within a cultural "reservation." As a result, art's traditional function as the repository of a shared cultural lexicon has been eroded to a significant degree, leading to a fracturing of meaning and erecting higher barriers to cultural participation.[42] This shift contributes functionally and ideologically to macrolevel processes ranging from class differentiation to capitalism to industrialization.

As Pierre Bourdieu argues, aesthetic taste often functions as a marker of social class.[43] For instance, few in our society would argue with the premise that opera (whatever its pedestrian origins) is largely the province of the wealthy and powerful. This is evident in a variety of ways: understanding and enjoying the music requires specialized cultural competence, concert tickets tend to be quite expensive, and the concerts themselves tend to be steeped in other markers of class, such as tuxedoed ushers, well-dressed patrons, lavishly appointed performance venues, and so on.

Social classification is not the only social function associated with the artist/audience binary. Another obvious parallel is with the producer/consumer binary that underpins the modern capitalist economic system. As Attali writes, "the artist was born, at the same time as his work went on sale."[44] Conversely, I would argue, the audience was born at the same time as music became a commodity. In preindustrial societies, music served as a marker of identity, and participation in musical events would help to solidify an individual's sense of belonging to a larger group (national anthems are a vestige of that tradition). In a consumer society, cultural participation is defined not in terms of what we produce, but in terms of what we acquire. Music still functions as a marker of identity, but now it is the music we play on our car stereos and iPods, the music we list and link to in our Facebook profiles, the music we choose on a jukebox in a crowded bar, that communicates our group affiliations and cultural attitudes.

Similarly, the organization of art worlds within the modern framework may be understood as models for political relations in the modern state. The hierarchy of aesthetic engagement (with a handful of artists at the pinnacle, followed by a class of professional critics, followed a class of connoisseurs, followed by the ranks of the uninitiated at the bottom) closely parallels the hierarchy of political engagement (with a handful of politicians at the pinnacle, followed by a class of professional pundits, followed by a class of civically engaged citizens, followed by the ranks of the disenfranchised at the bottom). Whether we are discussing cultural production, class structure, economic structure, or political structure, then, the net effects of the modern framework's art/craft and artist/audience binaries are consistent and clear: stratification, hierarchy, and disenfranchisement. Or as Levi-Strauss puts it, the loss of a society in which "the whole of the population participates."[45]

It would be absurd to suggest, of course, that social stratification is the *only* function of musical engagement. Despite the impossibility of separating these two strands, it is clear that other motivations must exist as well. Music wouldn't work as a vector of dominance and resistance unless it retained some relationship to the cognitive, psychological, and communal functions that fuel its sociopolitical capacity. A performance of Mozart's *Le Nozze di Figaro* can be understood as an intrinsically polysemous event. While the division of creative labor certainly reinforces social hierarchy, the opera also offers both rich opportunities for aesthetic pleasure and a thinly veiled political subtext in the libretto that challenges, rather than reinforces, the primacy of the elite classes. People may also attend to enjoy the camaraderie of fellow enthusiasts, to sneer at the snobbishness of other patrons, or simply for the excitement of dressing up. None of these functions is, or can be, separate from another; I myself have experienced each of these dimensions of the event at one time or another, and often feel many at once.

Other elements of the modern framework help to sustain the logic of modern social, economic, and political structures as well. What is the "hierarchy of uniqueness," after all, but a model for the hierarchy of production and consumption in a commercial culture? Whether we are discussing cars or clothing, the same system of categorization pertains. At the top are the most unique and expensive goods, tailored to fit the needs of elite customers by the product designers themselves—the Queen of England drives a custom-made Bentley, and Julia Roberts wears dresses made exclusively for her by Giorgio Armani. Beneath this tier are the luxury goods, the quality of which are guaranteed by the imprimatur of a top-tier brand and the well-publicized patronage of the elites—standard issue Bentley automobiles and Armani clothes. Beneath this tier are the mass-produced goods—Hondas and Fords, Gap jeans and Armani Exchange t-shirts. Finally, at the bottom, are the untouchables of the commercial sphere—chopped-up "beater" cars, cheap "knock-offs," and bargain-branded sweatpants—goods too cheap and flimsy to warrant an imprimatur of any kind.

Further examples abound. The performance/composition dichotomy may be understood as a model for the division of labor in a Fordist industrial organization, in which the production of a complex product is broken into simpler component parts, each of which is accomplished by a laborer with "specialized" skills. The elevation of melody to figural status and the relegation of harmony, rhythm, and other "arrangements" to mere background may be understood as a model for the separation of the individual from the collective in post-Enlightenment social organization. The materials/tools distinction supports the propertization of culture: if musical production may be described in terms just as easily applied to the timber or fishing industries (entrepreneurs exploit resources, using tools to turn materials into products), then it is only natural they should be accorded the same legal privileges and protections to profit exclusively from their work.

In short, the modern discursive framework, which bounds the discourse of music and thus constrains the processes of musical regulation and resistance, both owes its continuance to and helps to sustain the larger macrolevel institutions that govern and constitute modern society—economically, politically, and organizationally. Overwhelming evidence suggests that this arrangement is one of necessity, rather than simply circumstance; the musical codes, practices, and technologies that are allowed within the modern framework collectively help to support macrolevel social structure, while potentially destabilizing influences are prohibited.

3

The Crisis of
Configurability

I think that the laptop is a folkloric instrument of our time.
Osvaldo Golijov

As I write in chapter 2, our concept of music and its relationship to society—the modern discursive framework—has endured many social, political, and technological upheavals in the last two centuries. This durability can be attributed in large part to the strong reciprocal relationship between the modern framework and modern social institutions; neither would have survived as long without the other.

Discursive frameworks do eventually break down and change under the pressure of overwhelming social or technological reorganization; the modern framework itself was new in Berlioz's youth. While a robust framework may be flexible and strong enough to encompass all manner of unforeseen changes, some shifts in terrain are simply too great not to rock even the firmest edifice. We may be witnessing just such a change today.

Despite two hundred years of institutional entrenchment and cultural inertia, rapid changes in the technology governing the production, distribution, and consumption of mediated communication currently threaten to undermine the very foundations of the modern framework. In the hothouse atmosphere of the networked age, a myriad of new cultural practices have blossomed and bloomed—practices that have no place in the taxonomy of modernity's prim gardens. Whether the modern framework will somehow adapt to these changes, or break under the strain and give way to a new framework, remains to be seen; it is, in fact, the question that drives this book. Before I address that question, I must more fully describe the technological and cultural changes underway today.

Recent advances in communication technology, such as the personal computer, Internet connectivity, accessible media editing software (e.g., GarageBand), peer-to-peer file-sharing software, time-shifting devices (e.g., TiVo), portable media devices (e.g., iPods), portable communication devices, and writable high-capacity media (e.g., DVD-RWs), have enabled a paradigmatic shift in the way people and organizations communicate. The social dimension of this paradigmatic change is commonly referred to as *remix culture*, a term generally attributed to Lawrence Lessig,[1] after the practice of "remixing," or reediting media files such as songs. For reasons I will discuss shortly, I feel the terms *configurability* and *configurable culture* are more accurate and appropriate ways to describe the technological and social aspects of this new paradigm.

What, if anything, is new about configurable culture? As theorists from Raymond Williams[2] to Stuart Hall[3] have argued, culture by definition is plastic and permutable. No two people express themselves or understand the world identically, and everyone changes his or her perspective over time, largely in response to the people and the expressive materials he or she comes in contact with. It logically follows that each of us, in our own way, contributes to the ongoing reconfiguration of culture, whether through a calibrated cultural intervention (e.g., art, rhetoric, resource investment) or simply through the quotidian, and largely unconscious, rituals and interactions of daily life.

What differentiates the newly ascendant paradigm from previous epochs is the reciprocal interdependence between communication technology and culture, to the point of symbiosis; in other words, they may no longer be understood in the absence of one another. To put it another way, the power and scope of communication technology has expanded to the point where mediated expression and interaction have come to approach, and in some cases, to rival, the fluidity, subtlety, and power of face-to-face communication and oral cultural traditions. Although research aimed at directly measuring "presence" and other experiential attributes of emerging media can only hint at the enormity of this change, we may find additional evidence for it by cataloging the unique qualities of these new, transformative technologies and by examining the new social behaviors that both exploit them and help to influence their development.

Like most paradigmatic shifts, the changes in the quality of media technology and the nature of mediated behavior are more gradual and emergent than sudden and immediate. Clearly, society has coevolved with communication technology from prehistory to the present day, and never in a linear or predictable way. Other scholars have chronicled the social changes marked by the birth of language,[4] the emergence of writing and literacy,[5] the development of the printing press,[6] and the mechanical and electronic storage and transmission of information,[7] to name but a few milestones.

Similarly, many elements of configurable culture have existed for generations, from the photographic collage and *musique concrete* experiments in the art world of the early- to mid-twentieth century, to the *samizdat* cassette tapes of pre-Perestroika Soviet culture, to the dub plates, sound systems, and "versions" of 1960s Jamaican music, to the Choose-Your-Own-Adventure genre of children's literature in the 1980s. I myself participated in a proto-remix ritual for many years; along with other fans of the cult film *The Rocky Horror Picture Show* in the mid-1980s, I would engage in an ongoing verbal dialogue with the movie screen each weekend—participating in and contributing to an ever-changing catechism between the audience and the film's script.

I could continue to list such historical antecedents to configurability for some time. My point is that the configurable media experiences of the present day clearly outnumber, overpower, and outpace any of these examples by orders of magnitude. And, most important, the ease-of-use of today's creative technologies and networked organization of today's communications infrastructure ensure that the tools of media configurability are accessible to hundreds of millions of interconnected individuals. As a result, we have a media and communications system that is historically unique, possessing all of the following attributes:

Instantaneous. Electronic and digital media transmit information at light speed.

Global. Although there are still countless individuals, communities, and even regions of the globe with limited or no access to telephones, let alone the Internet, the number and geographic span of those that are connected is greater than at any point in history.

Multisensory. Standard media technology delivers video, spatialized audio, and text. Experimental technology also provides olfactory and kinesthetic/haptic information.

Archival. Older media elements may be stored and retrieved at virtually zero incremental cost or effort.

Transmissible. Media elements may easily be transmitted between two individuals, or multicast from one individual to many. Greater distances no longer introduce significant noise into signals, nor do they represent significant cost increases. Along with archivability, this feature helps produce the "time-space distanciation" Anthony Giddens[8] discusses.

Permutable. Media elements (songs, articles, photos, etc.) may be accessed in any order, or used in conjunction with any other media elements.

Editable. Media elements may be easily broken down into smaller components (such as samples or quotes), which in turn may be reassembled, permuted, or broken down further. The Planck-length equivalent for media elements (e.g., the smallest possible irreducible kernel) is often below the range of human perception, and becomes ever smaller as higher-definition encoding, storage, and rendering technologies continue to emerge.

Networked. The new communications infrastructure is networked, rather than hierarchical, permitting one-to-one, one-to-few, or one-to-many contact between any connected individuals. This infrastructure is crucial to what Manuel Castells[9] calls "network society" and "the space of flows."

Interoperable. Unlike earlier technological eras, in which separate communicative functions were served by distinct technologies (e.g., electromagnetic broadcasts for TV/radio, film for video editing, copper wires for phone calls), all functions are now converging on the same digital platform. This means that, for the first time, all cultural participants can create, retrieve, edit, and share audio, video, images, and text using a single tool (e.g., an Internet-connected computer).

Customizable. Database software, menu-based interface design, and other technologies offer users of communication technology an unprecedented degree of customizability and control over the nature and presentation of the information they send and receive. These same technologies also allow third parties, such as marketing companies, an unprecedented ability to "target" messages to individual recipients.

Hackable. Every technology is hackable (e.g., it can be reverse engineered, or used for purposes other than those it was created for), but new media technologies, by virtue of being built on a common digital platform, require fewer skills and tools to be hacked. This fact is further compounded by the networked communications infrastructure, allowing hacks (many of them malicious, such as trojans, worms, and viruses) to travel autonomously throughout the network.

The net effect of these developments in communication technology is a system within which expression itself, recorded and stored within the distributed nodes of an ever-growing and ever-changing network, joins language and other forms of symbolic and metaphorical representation as a vital element of the expressive palette. There can be little question that this shift enables an unprecedented plasticity (every cultural artifact can be used by anyone, in any way, to create new cultural artifacts of any kind) and recursion (expression becomes expression becomes expression), drastically expanding the locus of expressive possibilities. I am tempted to invoke a metaphor commonly used in software circles to describe a drastic enhancement in the toolset or interface for a given program: upgrading from a box of eight crayons to a box of 128. In this case a more appropriate metaphor would be something along the lines of upgrading from the abstract concept of "color" to a box with an infinite number of crayons in it.

Beyond "Web 2.0" and "Remix Culture"

The social consequences of this shift to a configurable communications infrastructure, and the uses to which we will eventually put these new tools for creative expression, are far from certain. As communication scholars have long argued,[10] new technologies do not necessarily require specific uses. Even technologies designed and distributed explicitly for a given purpose are routinely applied to tasks far afield from the intentions of their makers (as when we use a cigarette lighter to open a bottle of beer, or an electric power line as a conduit for Internet connectivity). Generally, society finds its own uses for new technologies, and helps to shape the future direction of technological innovation by doing so. In the case of configurability, as I have discussed, the holistic infrastructural change has been an emergent consequence of a myriad of smaller, more purposeful changes; the net result would have been difficult or impossible to predict based solely on one subcomponent of the larger process.

It is already clear, however, that configurable technologies have given rise to a multiplicity of new cultural practices running the gamut from art to communications to business and marketing. Several theorists in addition to myself have attempted to grapple with the scope and consequences of these changes in recent years, by integrating these new cultural practices into some larger frame of reference. "Web 2.0"—the popular, albeit vague term[11]—is an often-deployed catchphrase describing the dramatic rise of user generated content distributed via online social network technologies. Henry Jenkins's "convergence culture"[12] improves on this concept by incorporating the participatory and collective dimensions of user behavior across multiple media platforms. Yet both avenues of analysis have found their critics,[13] many of whom find the promises of democratization inherent in these models unjustified and overly optimistic.

Lessig's concept of "remix culture" offers a more robust model. He uses the term to describe a creative environment in which the ability to edit and redistribute mediated expression—such as audio and video—is democratized as a result of lower costs and lower barriers to expertise. Yet despite the techno-pizzazz of his terminology, Lessig downplays the culturally disruptive potential of new media technologies, evidently for rhetorical purposes. His legal advocacy for "thinner" copyright protection and a more expansive creative commons is premised on the notion that remix art simply uses new tools to do what's always been done—namely, to put one's own "spin" on previously existing cultural ideas and creative expressions. In his words, "remix in art is, of course, nothing new. What is new is the law's take on this remix."[14] Lev Manovich makes a similar claim, arguing that "the two kinds of remixability [symbolic and technological] are part of the same continuum."[15]

Although I agree wholeheartedly with the call for a reexamination of intellectual property law and a legal recognition of the right to remix, I must disagree with any claims of continuity between past and present cultural practices. Riffing on a melody written by someone else using a saxophone or piano is a fundamentally different process than chopping up a recording of someone else's rendition of a melody and then resequencing it to produce your own melody using computer software. To be sure, the sense of cultural give-and-take, of participation in a larger dialogue, remains. But a vital degree of abstraction—a buffer, if you will, between the participants in the dialogue—has been removed. The locus of action is no longer limited to the *idea* of the music, located within conceptual mechanisms such as melody, chord changes, or composition. What is acted on in these new practices is the *musical expression itself*, the indexical codification of sound waves in a fixed medium. Yet, in a configurable technological environment, thanks to the universal language of 1s and 0s that constitute digital signal processing and global communications, these sound waves are as malleable and distributable, and nearly as universally accessible, as music's conceptual aspects were in the days of analog media.

To put it a slightly different way, the processes of cultural digestion, assimilation, and reformulation, which were historically limited to the confines of our own minds, have been externalized. They now take place in plain sight (or sound), where we can experiment with cultural permutation phenomenologically and collectively via technological interface, rather than simply letting them reverberate within our mind's eye (or ear).

Another way in which configurable technologies depart from past media is in the scope of their effects. Typically, new media are assessed in terms of their effects on either producers or consumers. Software programs like GarageBand and ProTools LE, which provide millions of aspiring musicians with free or cheap recording studios on their computers, are often understood as agents of *democratized production*. In other words, they lower the barrier for people to become producers. Similarly, products like iPods and P2P file sharing software are understood as agents of *empowered consumption*. These new technologies offer a broader range of "content" to consumers, and provide them with a greater range of control over their "music experience."

While there is certainly some truth to both of these assessments, neither adequately encapsulates the larger picture: namely, that these new technologies do not simply enhance preexisting practices of cultural production and consumption; they help to *undermine the producer/consumer dichotomy itself*.[16] The question of whether cultural production and consumption constitute a binary opposition, or simply exist at opposite ends of a long and fluid spectrum, was effectively moot during much of the nineteenth and twentieth centuries. If any vast region of "gray area" lay between the two poles, it was inaccessible to most members of society because of the limits of commonly available media technologies. With the emergence of configurability, however, we have seen a rapid colonization of the gray area between consumption and production, and an explosion of new cultural practices that range from what a real estate broker might refer to as "consumption-adjacent" (e.g., user-created music playlists, DVD bonus features, video game character setup and design) to those which might be termed "production-adjacent" (e.g., mash-ups, remixes, machinima, game mods). Such behaviors would not only have been impossible before configurability—many of them would have been unthinkable.

Configurability and the Mainstream

At what point does an "underground" cultural practice or community become so prevalent that it deserves to be called mainstream? And what are the social consequences of this phase shift? For the past few years, configurability has been simmering just below the threshold of cultural ubiquity. A decade ago, many still marveled at the rapidity with which a new movie trailer, political gaffe, popular song, or embarrassing celebrity photograph would appear online, circulating "virally" through social networks via e-mail, instant messages, or Web links. Today, no such meme can enter the public sphere without instantly becoming the subject of countless remixes, mash-ups, and creative appropriations, which then become circulated with a rapidity and scope that is often equal to or greater than that of the artifacts they are derived from. The infamous photo of Elián González at gunpoint, Bill O'Reilly's expletive-ridden on-camera rant, Paris Hilton's home sex video, and the clumsy, videotaped broomstick-wielding of a teenage Canadian would-be Jedi named Ghyslain Raza are just a few of the myriad cultural artifacts that recently entered popular consciousness in one form, but became enshrined in our cultural memory only after being refracted through the lens of a thousand subjective reinterpretations.

Some recent theorists[17] have invoked Habermasian concerns about the effects of configurability, arguing that, far from becoming an element of the mainstream, these new practices are undermining the very notion of common culture and fracturing the public sphere. If each of us has the ability to select and reject the nature of the information we encounter based on our individual tastes and preferences, the argument holds, then each of us will have a completely different sense of what is going on in the world around us. Furthermore, if each of us has the ability to alter and recirculate information as we see fit, there can be no confidence in the quality, veracity, or objectivity of the information we encounter. And if we cannot agree on a consistent worldview, based on authoritative information, then we cannot make intelligent collective decisions; in effect, democratic society is doomed in the era of the blog and the remix.

Others are concerned about the growing prevalence and visibility of configurable cultural practices for an entirely different reason: they feel that the commercial embrace of the remix amounts to a form of neutralization. According to this argument, the ethic of participatory culture that informs configurable practices is lost, once the institutions comprising the culture industry become involved in the production and distribution of configurable content. In this scenario, the remix becomes simply another generic category, a new and exciting flavor of prepackaged culture available to paying customers. Hacker culture researcher Doug Thomas, for instance, argues that far from being a tool for the empowerment of computer owners, an accessible and configurable interface only "serves to separate the user from the machine, effectively rendering the computer as an opaque object."[18] Similarly, technology theorist Alex Galloway[19] echoes this argument in his discussion of Internet protocols as a mechanism of social control, and many others[20] make analogous arguments about historical musical forms, describing how community-driven musical practices were appropriated by corporate interests and stripped of their sociopolitical underpinnings before being marketed to consumers as hip-hop, reggae, and soul music.

In short, the increasing prevalence of configurable cultural practices has evoked concerns among some that individuals will use new technologies to undermine institutional authority, and concerns among others that institutions will use new technologies to undermine individual liberty. Both sets of concerns share a similar premise: if the delicate détente balancing individual freedom against institutional authority is tipped too far in either direction, the foundation for our social and political system will erode, conjuring the twin specters of anarchy and fascism.

Although both arguments have their merits, each has its weak point, as well. Three decades of postmodern theory have provided us with ample reasons to question the notion of a master narrative, and to mistrust the authority of institutionalized information brokers. The idea that society can—and must—agree on a consistent worldview, supported by a canonical subset of information sources, has been revealed as a convenient mask for the exercise of power. Donna Haraway famously dismisses the single-worldview concept as the "god-trick," equally shunning uncritical relativism for what she calls "situated knowledge": the notion that any honest, accurate, and therefore socially egalitarian worldview must account for a "multiplicity of local knowledges," due to the unique and limited frame of reference embodied by each member of society.[21] Arguably, this is exactly the function of remixes, mash-ups, and many other elements of configurable culture: they are the instantiation of situated knowledges, manifested and distributed via the very media that were once reserved exclusively for elements of the master narrative. By this argument, then, it is not democracy per se that is under threat in the age of the remix, but vested power, enforced by authoritative (or authoritarian) information.

Similarly, concerns that configurable technology (at least when employed at the "consumption-adjacent" end of the spectrum) will undermine, rather than enhance, the agency of individual users, echo Marxian fears of "false consciousness." People might *think* they're being given more control over their lives, this argument holds, but *in reality*, they're being ensnared within an invisible prison, deprived (like the hapless extras in *The Matrix*) of even seeing the walls that hold them.

This argument both underestimates the agency of individuals and overestimates the powers of institutions. The relationship between individuals and institutions in the production of culture has always been more of an ongoing negotiation than a matter of outright revolution, wholesale appropriation, or pitched battle between polar opposites. As media historian Thomas Frank[22] argues, 1960s counterculture was neither the revolutionary uprising many feared, nor a cleverly packaged marketing ploy aimed at capturing teenage spending allowances. Rather, it represented a new organizational, aesthetic, and ethical paradigm that many corporations embraced wholeheartedly (perhaps to a greater degree than their own customers) for their own good. Without such a corporate embrace, which both mainstreamed and amplified its message, he argues, the counterculture as a social phenomenon may never have existed.

This symbiotic dynamic, characterized by negotiation rather than all-out warfare, is even more vital in the age of configurability than it was during the 1960s. The blurring of the lines and colonization of the gray area separating cultural production from consumption has just as many implications for culture industry institutions as it does for the individuals who constitute culture. As configurability emerges into the mainstream, it is changing the very notion of what a "mainstream" is, altering the traditional media interaction habits of individuals as well as the business practices of media organizations, and thereby requiring a considerable renegotiation of the relationships between the two. This process can be witnessed in nearly every sector of the cultural landscape today, and in the practices and products that traditionally comprise the mainstream.

One recent example is the hit song "Crazy" by Gnarls Barkley, a 2006 collaboration between rapper/singer Cee-Lo and DJ Danger Mouse, who rose to prominence two years earlier through his extraordinarily popular yet unauthorized and noncommercial mash-up of Jay-Z and the Beatles, dubbed *The Grey Album*. The song was a critical and market success, the first ever to reach the top of the UK singles chart based entirely on download sales (a CD version was released a week later). These facts alone, though, do not capture the true scope of the song's success. Its cultural impact can also be seen in the details of its life before and after its market penetration.

The song itself was the product of configurable cultural practices; its instrumental track samples Gianfranco and Gianpiero Reverberi's "Nel Cimitero Di Tuscon," from the soundtrack to the 1968 film *Django, Prepare a Coffin*. Thus, the very same techniques that had made Danger Mouse persona non grata in the music industry in 2004 also made him its darling in 2006. Even more interestingly, the song instantly became a configurable touchstone, as an extremely popular subject for mash-ups, remixes, covers, and other creative reinterpretations, thousands of which are widely available through both commercial and "underground" music distribution channels. In other words, the song's moment in the sun atop international sales and airplay charts was only a snapshot of its creative evolution, constituted and reconstituted through sampling and other configurable practices; as the King James Bible might put it, "ashes to ashes, remix to remix."

Although music is arguably the best-known venue for cultural experimentation with configurability, it is hardly the only area in which this new paradigm appears to be exerting a growing influence. Another recent example is the 2006 New Line Cinema film *Snakes on a Plane*, which owed both its significant prerelease popularity and elements of its plot to innumerable blog posts, video mash-ups and remixes, doctored photographs, and other configurable cultural artifacts produced by members of the general public in anticipation of the film's release. Although the film didn't perform as well as "Crazy" in the marketplace, its cultural impact before and after its market debut was nearly as great, and its story is equally instructive.

After advance word of the film was leaked via a screenwriter's blog in the summer of 2005, the one-two punch of its absurd title and a star turn by Samuel L. Jackson (perhaps the most remixed and mashed-up actor in cyberspace) attracted legions of film buffs, satirists, and fans to produce everything from songs to clothing to mock trailers about the film. The unexpected buzz influenced New Line's production and marketing strategy considerably. The studio undertook additional shooting to add new, racier scenes to the film—including dialogue that originated in online parodies, such as Jackson's expostulation: "I've had it with these motherfucking snakes on this motherfucking plane!"[23] Additionally, the studio leveraged the advance Internet hype in its own marketing strategy, offering visitors to the movie's official site a chance to win prizes and recognition simply by accumulating votes from other online users in a contest to be named "the #1 fan" of the film.

Configurable practices appear to be increasingly influential in the business and culture of video games, as well. The game *Counter-Strike* is probably the most popular "first-person shooter" online game in history. According to the game's publisher, Valve Corporation, which also runs Steam, the primary online gaming network that supports such games, *Counter-Strike* and two of its sequels are, at the time of writing, the first, second, and fourth most popular games out of the hundreds on the network. At any given moment, they account for about 150,000 simultaneous players on the site, or roughly 73 percent of its total gaming traffic.[24]

In the fast-paced business of video games, in which four or five years constitutes a new generation of gaming technology (and a new generation of gamers), it is unusual for a single title to maintain its dominance for even a few years (although multititle franchises, such as *Grand Theft Auto* and *Call of Duty* can remain powerful brands for far longer). Thus, it is impressive that *Counter-Strike* has maintained its high degree of popularity virtually from its initial beta launch in 1999 until the present day.

What is extraordinary, however, is that *Counter-Strike* wasn't created by a commercial game developer, or distributed initially by a commercial publisher. It began as a "total conversion mod" of another game called *Half-Life*. Two fans of the game, Minh Le and Jess Cliffe, decided to replace its futuristic alien-battling plot and artwork and single-player game play with a more contemporary counterterrorism-themed plot and artwork, and multiplayer game play. Although they retained *Half-Life*'s "game engine"—the fundamental software responsible for rendering graphics and organizing the data structure—they replaced all of the visual and auditory elements driven by that engine with their own artwork, and reorganized the structure of the game to match their needs.

In 2000, Valve hired Le and Cliffe to create a commercial version of *Counter-Strike*, which was released to retailers in time for that year's holiday season. The stand-alone retail version of *Counter-Strike*, unlike the earlier, unofficial versions, does not require that *Half-Life* be installed in order to play it. However, existing *Half-Life* owners can still freely download the *Counter-Strike* mod, and the mod has been bundled with retail versions of *Half-Life* as a value-added feature.

The ethic of configurability is on the ascent even within the rarefied world of "high art." In a way, this cultural sector has come full circle. In the years following World War II, avant-garde composers like Pierre Henry, Pierre Schaeffer, and John Cage—recognizing the aesthetic cul-de-sac presented by Schoenberg's twelve-tone compositional technique and the serialist experiments that followed—began to experiment with sampling, tape manipulation, and sound synthesis to expand the musical palette beyond the harmonic, rhythmic, and timbral limitations of the traditional Western orchestra. Although these techniques have remained vital among avant-garde composers in the intervening decades (and have broadened with the introduction of digital sampling and sound editing), they never achieved the kind of widespread adoption and mainstream appreciation within the classical world that sample-based musics like hip-hop and techno have achieved among popular audiences and performers.

This finally appears to be changing. In the summer of 2006, the Canadian Broadcasting Corporation's Radio Two channel—which primarily broadcasts opera, classical music, and jazz—initiated a new programming feature: a series of contests called "Compose Yourself," inviting listeners to submit their own music to be featured as on-air programming. The first contest in this series was called "Remix the Ring": "You are invited to Remix The Ring! Well, actually just part of it—the famous Ride of the Valkyries. Download the file of Richard Wagner's Ride of the Valkyries and remix it in any way you see fit. Mash it, chop it, layer it, turn it upside down. Your remix can have a dance feel, or be completely avant-garde. Let your imagination be your guide."[25]

The CBC reserved $3,250 in prize money, as well as airtime, to reward the contest winners. Needless to say, a paid contest, hosted and promoted on the website of a Western nation's premier classical music broadcaster, inviting people to inject a "dance feel" into Wagner's operatic work, is a far cry from the relative marginality accorded to Henry, Schaeffer, and Cage. "Avant-garde" is still a stylistic option according to the contest description—in this case, the term appears to mean "lack of a danceable beat"—but there is no question that the configurable techniques themselves are becoming mainstream fare, even within the classical music community.

The CBC is not only reflecting the growing popularity of the remix *aesthetic* in its programming decisions; by soliciting remixes from all of its listeners, rather than established composers, it is also acknowledging the inherent participatory cultural *ethic* associated with the remix movement today. In the days of Henry, Schaeffer, and Cage, the notion of a classical music broadcaster opening its gates to compositions submitted by its listeners would probably have seemed absurd.

In short, the growing incidence and influence of configurability in the entertainment industry and other art worlds has thus far neither extinguished art world institutions, nor lulled individuals into a false sense of control over their cultural environment. Rather, configurable technologies have intensified and augmented the ongoing negotiation between individuals and institutions in the production, distribution, and consumption of cultural information. Many people who may have listened to music or watched a film passively (or even critically) a decade ago are now making their criticism manifest, expressing their situated knowledges through the medium of the mash-up or the remix. Cultural institutions that may have relied solely on market research and rote formula as the keys to profitability a decade ago are now learning to harness the collective intelligence of their customers— not only as a way to learn more about their market, but as an engine of innovation and a means of reanimating moribund styles and material.

The process is far from flawless, and the outlook is not necessarily rosy. For every successful negotiation, there are countless cease-and-desist orders, hacks, counter-hacks, and other missed opportunities. The problem isn't necessarily ignorance or malice on the part of either institutions or individuals, but rather one of language and precedence. The modern discursive framework, which sets the boundaries within which these negotiations take place, is simply being stretched beyond its capacity by configurable technologies and practices, rendering meaningful discussion—and therefore effective negotiation—difficult at best. This becomes apparent when we recall the set of definitive binaries that constitute the modern framework, and consider their application within the context of configurable culture.

Crisis: Configurability and the Modern Framework

I have just discussed the ways in which configurability pries apart the production/consumption dichotomy, revealing an expanse of newly accessible gray area between the two polar extremes. Earlier, I discussed the role of the modern framework in sustaining the production/ consumption dichotomy, and the ways in which modern social, economic, and political institutions predicated on that dichotomy help to maintain the framework's dominance. It should come as no surprise, then, that configurability's destabilizing influence extends far beyond production and consumption, to the foundations of the modern framework itself.

The art/craft dichotomy, which is the most pivotal element of the modern framework, faces an immediate challenge in the age of configurability. For just as configurable cultural practices defy the logic of pure production and consumption, they also defy the logic of pure aesthetics. Photography, cinema, and recorded music are all widely held to be located comfortably within the pantheon of legitimate Arts-with-a-capital-A (although each has its stalwart detractors), taught at conservatories, and picked apart with the same critical ferocity as is commonly applied to painting or literature. Yet leading practitioners of each of these fields today routinely use the techniques of configurability (and thus the language of configurability) to produce their works.

From the composite digital photographs gracing the covers of today's glossy magazines (a nose from photo 12 matched with a mouth from photo 27) to the post-production-centric direction techniques of filmmakers like George Lucas and Robert Rodriguez (a performance by one actor from take 3 sharing the frame with a performance by another actor from take 7) to the studio wizardry of music "superproducers" like the Neptunes and Dan "the Automator" Nakamura (layers on layers of diverse samples seamlessly harnessed to a single groove), commercial and fine artists across a broad spectrum of aesthetic discourses are taking advantage of the unprecedented opportunities for plasticity and pastiche offered by configurable technologies.

Yet if these practices are unequivocally deemed "art," then what of production-adjacent practices, such as mash-ups, remixes, and Photoshopping? And if the rubric somehow stretches to include them, what of configurable practices located even deeper within the gray area, such as karaoke or anime music videos? And what of consumption-adjacent practices? In the final analysis, if every customized MP3 playlist and digital photo slideshow is to be considered a work of art, then the category has lost any vestige of meaning it had within the modern framework; the line must be drawn somewhere for the category to hold. Yet, as the gray area between production and consumption becomes increasingly populated with new cultural practices, the boundary separating art from craft is becoming increasingly difficult to locate.

A similar ambiguity confronts the artist/audience distinction as configurability becomes ascendant. From a theoretical standpoint, configurable practices challenge Kant's dictum of "disinterested" aesthetic pleasure, which introduces a distance between artwork and audience that precludes critical inquiry, let alone tinkering. Instead of enjoying art in reverent awe, an increasing number of people are confronting it head on, treating artworks as the starting point for cultural engagement, rather than the endpoint of a one-way conversation. Perhaps this was always the case on some level; Kant notwithstanding, there is ample reason to believe that audiences have always had an "interest" in the art they encountered. Configurability, however, presents people with the tools to turn that interest into expression, allowing us to share our responses with other interested parties, and to invite responses of our own.

From a practical standpoint, the sheer number of people engaging in configurable cultural practices undermines the premise of artist exceptionality. If it is becoming increasingly difficult to say which practices and products qualify as art and which do not, it is becoming equally difficult to say who is an artist and who is not. Mid-twentieth-century fine arts movements such as pop and conceptualism pioneered the concept of curatorial art, suggesting that simply organizing the work of others is a legitimate aesthetic enterprise in its own right. The rising profile and power of the DJ in popular musical culture from the 1970s to the present echoed this elevation of the curatorial role to artist status. Today, configurability allows everyone with an iPod, TiVo, or personal computer to become what cultural policy researchers Bill Ivey and Stephen Tepper[26] call the "curatorial me," wading through the volumes of cultural information now available via digital communication networks and selecting and organizing subsets of that information for personal or public consumption.

Paired with the power to remix, mash up, and otherwise reconfigure such cultural information, the rise of the "curatorial me" makes it virtually impossible to arrive at a functional distinction between artists and audiences in the age of configurability. Of course, the traditional rationales of "genius" and "talent" are still very popular currency, but today these concepts are more amorphous than ever. What does skill mean in a curatorial context? How can we separate the quality of a DJ's work from the quality of the work he or she is showcasing? If the concept of genius is predicated on an artist standing apart from or rising above his contemporaries, how can we apply it to an artist whose palette *consists of* his contemporaries' work? Of course, there are many potential answers to these questions; remixes and mash-ups may be understood as the next step in the evolution of subjective distortion, and therefore proof positive of an artist's quality, or they may be understood as simply another form of derivative work, proof positive of an artist's mediocrity.

These open questions suggest that the dichotomy distinguishing an original from a copy is as deeply undermined by configurability as are the distinctions between art and craft or artist and audience. Obviously, the techniques of digital pastiche, whether applied to images, sounds, video, or other forms of expression, are premised on the act of reproduction. If the "aura" of the original was threatened by mechanical reproduction in Benjamin's day, then the "authenticity" that replaced it is threatened by digital reproduction today. Technology is no longer being used primarily to produce straightforward facsimiles, flawed only in their "perfection" relative to an original work; in its own way, such an act reifies the primacy of the work being reproduced. Today, configurable technology is often used to consciously distort even as it reproduces, according little or no primacy to the "original" work.

This subversion of the mechanism of authenticity has its correlative in an inversion of the hierarchy of uniqueness. The ostensibly unique and irreplaceable artifacts at the top of the pyramid become immediately suspect; if reproduction has become the dominant mode of creation, what are we to make of something that makes grand claims to have been born ex nihilo? It requires the same degree of faith and suspension of logic as the story of Adam and Eve. In the meantime, the untouchables from the bottom of the pyramid—the unauthorized and rough-hewn reproductions of the economic or cultural underground— have become increasingly glorified as truly authentic. An excellent example is the burgeoning popularity of hip-hop mixtapes, music collections by aspiring rappers and DJs that eschew traditional record label distribution (and sample licensing), but often sell thousands of copies or more. Mixtapes are widely held to be a more genuine reflection of urban American culture than commercially distributed hip-hop, and ironically (but not surprisingly) are being used by record labels themselves to identify—and unofficially promote—promising new acts.[27]

Configurability challenges the performance/composition dichotomy as well. One immediate problem is the question of process. According to the modern framework, composition precedes expression, and is therefore more fundamental and worthy of our respect and admiration. This linear model breaks down when it is applied to a creative process in which composition requires expression as a precondition. In its place, we have a cyclical model in which expression and composition alternate, with no clear origin or terminus: X samples music by Y, who in turn samples music by Z, ad infinitum.

Further compounding this is the fact that the line separating performance from composition (like those separating art from craft, artist from audience, and original from copy) is becoming increasingly difficult to discern. Although some configurable musical practices involve performative aspects, such as DJs spinning vinyl in front of a live audience, such practices are neither necessary to the form nor clearly demarcated from composition itself. In a way, configurability combines two preexisting challenges to the performance/composition dichotomy—improvisation and mediation—into a single, formidable challenge.

Improvisation has been the hallmark of African American (and, more broadly, Afro-diasporic) musics for centuries, from the jubas and field hollers of slavery-era rurality to the jazz and hip-hop of twentieth- and twenty-first-century urban life. Each of these forms involves a structure or template within which collective improvisation can take place, providing a distinctive balance between individual liberty and communal responsibility. Thus, performance becomes integral to composition; songs may exist in inchoate form prior to performance, but their expression cannot be predicted or determined until the moment the music unfolds.

Mediation—the production of music for recorded rather than "live" expression—is a newer threat to the performance/composition dichotomy than improvisation, but it predates configurability by decades. As art philosopher Theodore Gracyk[28] argues, rock music was the first musical form in which the recording—rather than the score, the live performance, or any other manifestation of the music—was the definitive artifact. Works like the Beatles' *Sgt. Pepper's Lonely Hearts Club Band* and the Beach Boys' *Pet Sounds* can no more adequately be represented by a live concert than they can by a series of black marks on a white page. Thus, composition and performance collapse into a single, indivisible entity. Configurability pairs this singularity with the collectivity and unpredictability of improvisation—not only are configurable musical forms like hip-hop and mash-ups replete unto themselves ("autographic," to use the terminology of Gracyk and Nelson Goodman),[29] they are also unfixed, living works that may be tailored to the time, place, and company in which they take form.

Configurability (as the word's second and third syllables may suggest) calls the figure/ground distinction into question, as well. As I have discussed, the modern framework defines figuration in terms of specific music elements (e.g., temporal emplacement within a given sonic ground, melodic articulation against rhythmic and/or harmonic patterns), and affords composers the ability to produce "ambiguous" works, in which given compositional elements can be performed as either figure or ground. With configurability, the distinction is even further eroded. Figure or ground from one work, when sampled or sequenced, quite literally becomes ground or figure in another work, as when the "break" from a given song—the disruptive rhythmic articulation emerging from an otherwise consistent drum beat—is looped to produce the consistent "breakbeat" serving as the background of a new song.

New technology also allows us to expand our understanding of the sonic landscape beyond music. Leonard Meyer's argument that "in 'aural space,' in music, there is no given ground"[30] rings hollow once we have learned to listen through the metaphor of sampling. Industrial noise, public conversations, and even environmental music are all part of our daily soundscape. When music was made exclusively with acoustic instruments, these noises generally seemed far enough beyond the locus of compositional applicability as to be rendered irrelevant, or at best a diverting nuisance.[31] Today, such noises are a prime subject of sampling, and thus they become relevant to our musical codes. This relevance turns ambient noise into an ongoing ground against which all music (and silence) is interpreted figurally. It is no surprise, then, that the mash-up should emerge in the age of the iPod. We are now accustomed to hearing two or more sonic events at once, on different levels of perception, as we navigate public spaces while listening to our own private soundtracks; it was only a matter of time before this schizophonia was addressed dialectically and aesthetically.

Another effect of sampling technology is that melody has ceased to be the necessary figural component in compositions; in many hip-hop songs, for instance, a sampled melodic riff will play in the background while a rapper dominates the foreground. Given that copyright law and other music institutions are built around the premise of melodic figuration, this has become a practical problem in addition to a philosophical one.

Finally, configurability undermines the materials/tools distinction just as it undermines the other fundamental dichotomies of the modern framework. In 1967, the philosopher James Feibleman wrote that, because of recent developments in material science, "the distinction between materials and tools has at last been broken down. Man constructs the matter he wants in the way he wants it."[32] One could make an analogous argument about cultural production today. If the atomization of chemical processes drastically expanded the creative horizons for industrial manufacturing by liberating us from the constraints of preexisting chemical formations, then the atomization of cultural processes is drastically expanding the horizons for creative expression by liberating us from the constraints of preexisting cultural formations. As Feibleman might say: Man constructs the culture he wants in the way he wants it.

This atomization of culture undermines the categorical distinctions between materials, tools, and products (e.g., art), because those distinctions are premised on structure. By the definitions I cited above, materials are chaotic, while tools are organized. In an age when culture is infinitely permutable, when it can be decomposed and recomposed as often and as easily as the imagination permits, such definitions have no basis. Is an MP3 of a song a piece of material, a tool, or a finished product? The answer, of course, is all three; the categories still exist, but their definitions have changed from inherent to relational. One man's product is another woman's tool is another man's material, and so on. As for the Levi-Straussian binary undergirding the materials/tools distinction, both material and cultural atomization present a significant challenge. Today, one could argue, either everything is natural, or nothing is.

In short, configurability presents a significant challenge to each of the binary distinctions that comprise the core of the modern discursive framework, forcing us to confront the fundamental ambiguities that have always existed at the heart of those distinctions. As a result, the framework itself faces a fundamental crisis: either it will be significantly reworked to accommodate the myriad new configurable cultural practices, or it will give way to a new framework altogether; either way, the crisis demands resolution.

This is not solely an academic concern; the resolution of this crisis has significant social and political repercussions. Because the framework sets the boundaries of discourse about music, because music can be considered a form of cognitive–affective capital influencing macrolevel social structures, and because this capital has been the site of fiercely contested regulation and resistance in so many times and places, we must acknowledge that the resolution of this crisis will help to determine the organizing principles of postindustrial society for years or perhaps for centuries to come.

Of course, no one—not musicians, record executives, federal commissioners, or even academic theorists—can possibly predict macrolevel change, especially on the basis of purely microlevel events. Yet every lawsuit, every municipal statute, every aesthetic innovation contributes in some small way to the ongoing negotiation between institutions and individuals, to the shifting balance of power between regulation and resistance, and to the eventual resolution of the crisis of configurability.

In the chapters that follow, I will attempt to weave these slim and disparate strands together into a tapestry that tells a story—in other words, to examine musical discourse for clues about social change. How are musicians, commercial organizations, legal institutions, and other members of society reacting to the crisis of configurability? How are they changing their conceptions of "art," "artistry," and "originality" in the context of new technologies and musical practices? Which ideas are being abandoned, which are altered, and which will be maintained intact? And what are the potential social ramifications of these changes? In order to address these questions, I will draw on extensive interviews with dozens of artists, executives, and legal practitioners, survey data reflecting the behaviors and beliefs of thousands of individuals, and a healthy dose of cultural exegesis.

II

DRAWING LINES IN THE SAND

The first section of this book is about theory. In it, I discuss the discursive framework that bounds musical regulation and resistance, and argue that new communication technologies may help to undermine that framework, requiring us to reevaluate some of our oldest and deepest assumptions about culture and society.

The next part of the book is about practice. Specifically, it's about the ways in which actual musical practitioners, music industry executives, and the rest of our society appear to be making sense of these radical changes, and about the larger social implications of these new sensibilities.

To address these questions, I rely on two sources of data. The first is a survey, fielded in the summer of 2006. Written and analyzed by myself and Marissa Gluck under the aegis of our consulting firm, Radar Research, and fielded by another commercial research firm called Intellisurvey, the survey aimed to gauge awareness, attitudes, and behaviors surrounding configurable cultural practices in the United States. In all, we surveyed 1,779 U.S. adults from a diverse age range (39% age 18 to 34, 46% age 35 to 54, and 14% age 55 and up), significant representation by both genders (27% male, 73% female), a diverse range of annual income levels (39% below $40,000, 37% between $40,000 and $80,000, and 19% above $80,000), as well as representation from all fifty states.

Although the survey yielded fascinating statistical data, both the quantitative methodology and the broad, sample-based findings are somewhat off topic for this book. Instead, I have chosen to use the survey's qualitative data, taken from an optional, open-ended survey question, which was worded as follows: "We welcome your general thoughts about remixes and mash-ups, as well as any feedback about this survey." The 611 responses to this question were diverse and illuminating, and directly relevant to my discursive analysis, and I cite them liberally in the pages that follow.[1]

The second data source I rely on is extensive interviews, conducted primarily in person and over the phone, with configurable music practitioners, music industry executives, and music attorneys. If the Radar Research survey was intended to discover the attitudes and behaviors of people more likely to engage in what I have termed consumption-adjacent practices, these interviews focused more on the production-adjacent side of the spectrum. In all, I conducted about sixty hours of interviews with roughly three-dozen sources. Most of these interviews were conducted in the fall of 2006; however, some were conducted as early as 2003, and some as recently as the summer of 2008.

Because the use of language as discourse is so central to my research premise, I cite my interviews verbatim whenever possible; however, on some occasions, I have stripped the quotes of extraneous "ums," "y'knows," and half-finished words or phrases, for the sake of clarity on the written page. In no way have any of these emendations changed or altered the meanings of the quotes themselves. I also refer to my interviewees by the names for which they indicated a preference—in many cases, it is a musical alias, rather than a given name.

The following six chapters each focus on one of the core binaries I outline in chapter 2, discussing the ways in which the lines separating traditional dichotomies such as art vs. craft and materials vs. tools are being blurred, erased, and redrawn in response to the crisis of configurability. On its own, each short chapter tells an interesting story. Collectively, I believe they point to a profound change in the discursive and organizational foundations of our society.

4

Yes, But Is It Art?

The Art/Craft Binary

> How thoroughly blurred the lines dividing art, craft and design
> have become over the past few decades. Unfortunately, [it] is a
> strategy that has reached epidemic proportions in the larger art
> world: the use of many small recognizable things to make one
> big recognizable thing.
> Roberta Smith

It's not always easy to spot art when you see it. Even during the peak of
modernism, the concept was continually being challenged, tested, and
sometimes found wanting. Marcel Duchamp famously converted the
most functional of objects—a urinal—into an artwork simply by nam-
ing it, signing it, and entering it into an art show (after much debate,
the piece was not exhibited). Pieces like Duchamp's *Fountain,* though,
tended to be the exceptions that proved the rules; they existed to prod
and provoke, and to call attention to the limits of the modern framework. If most people had trouble accepting the latest avant-garde artwork as legitimate, it only served to reinforce the legitimacy of mainstream aesthetic conventions.

Configurability has complicated this process. Today, the surest sign
that something is an artwork is its sponsorship by a SoHo gallery or its
ability to provoke discussion among the readers of *Art in America;* yet,
mainstream cultural behaviors and artifacts are increasingly difficult
to categorize. In 2008, for instance, the artist Cory Arcangel exhibited

new work at the Team Gallery in New York. The exhibition included *Self Playing Sony Playstation 1 Bowling*, a piece in which Arcangel rigged a video game console to play endless rounds of virtual bowling, throwing only gutter balls. Visitors to the gallery could sit on a small couch and watch the action unfold on a large projection screen. The show was positively reviewed in the *New York Times* and elsewhere, and although many observed Arcangel's playful intertextuality and references to the elusive promise of technotopian democracy, few appeared to question whether his work was, in fact, art.

The *Times* review praised Arcangel for having the "blithe attitude of a YouTube satirist."[1] Yet, as I write these words in 2009, a quick search for the term "machinima" (which means cinema made from video game technology, mostly by nonprofessionals) yields over 95,000 results at YouTube.com, and a search for "video game walkthrough" (a tradition in which gamers post the entire process of playing a given game from beginning to end as a video for instructional or reputational purposes) yields 759,000. I doubt whether many of these works have been reviewed by the *Times* or any other major organs of the art world, or whether most of them would even be recognized broadly as "art." To be sure, not all of them capture Arcangel's canny combination of humor and critique, and many of them likely relied on less innovative technological means than Arcangel's "self playing" console hack. Yet the fact remains that taking video game elements and using them as a tool for public self-expression is far from an arcane practice—it's a mainstream aspect of digital youth culture, with millions of active participants.

Do the hundreds of thousands of videos I mentioned above count as "art"? If not, what distinguishes them from Arcangel's work? Is the difference simply contextual and institutional, or are there formalistic distinctions we can make in the use of interactive media for public self-expression? Clearly, there's no simple answer to these questions; I raise them simply as a way to highlight the ambiguities presented by configurable technologies and culture. And, in a way, the conclusions we may reach are less interesting than the means by which we reach them; it is the process of grappling with basic cultural categories that defines the present era.

In my interviews with DJs, music industry executives, and copyright attorneys, the terms "art" and "artist" were frequently applied to a broad range of configurable musical practices. There was also widespread acknowledgment, both tacit and explicit, that these terms are a challenge to define precisely in the context of sample-based music production, and that the distinction between art and craft may not be as meaningful as it once was.

Si Begg, a London-based techno DJ and producer, echoed a prevailing sentiment, saying, "I think you can't really draw a line. I think because there's no real moment when it flips over from one to the other . . . it's a very gray area."[2] James Kirby, a Stockport, UK-based sound collagist who produces under the name V/VM, expanded on this notion, specifically associating the blurring of the lines between art and craft with the convergence of expressive media: "I don't think it makes sense to distinguish [between art and craft]. The way I think these days is, that you can just use anything these days and be creative, in all forms, such as video."[3]

Mysterious D, a San Francisco-based DJ and cofounder of the popular mash-up club franchise Bootie, expressed ambivalence on the question, finally focusing on the distinction between teachable skill and innate talent (a subject I will address in greater detail in the following section on the artist/audience binary) as the deciding factor: "Is it a craft or is it an art? It's hard to explain . . . I see art in it besides craft. 'Cause basically as a craft almost anyone can learn. And not anyone can really make a great mash-up."[4]

Survey respondents offered a range of opinions on the subject. Some, such as this California woman in her fifties, offered qualified support for mash-ups and remixes as art: "I have never done any but would consider it an art form, therefore, any use of existing material would be changed into something new, and would not be plagerizing [sic]. I do think getting permission would be the ethical thing to do, though." Others, such as this Utah man in his twenties, expressed a greater degree of ambivalence, reflecting support for the institutional regulation of musical production: "It can be an art, but is a kind of art that may turn into a threat to the creators of the original content if it is not governed in some way." Finally, some respondents, such as this California man in his forties, rejected any claim of configurable music to the category of art: "You might as well let a chimp play the pianno [sic]."

Interestingly, this pejorative comparison of a new expressive form with the work of animals has a long history in the rhetoric of music criticism. As Nicolas Slonimsky relates: "An anonymous cartoon printed by G. Schirmer in New York in 1869 under the title, 'The Music of the Future,' displays eight cats (labeled A, B, C, D, E, F, G, A), several donkeys, and a group of goats, as participants in a Wagnerian orchestra. The score on the conductor's stand reads, 'Liszt's Symphonic Poem.'"[5]

Rupture and Continuity

While many of the interviewees and survey respondents expressed ambivalence about the art/craft binary in light of configurable music practices, they nonetheless drew on a variety of traditional concepts in attempting to maintain a distinction in the face of discursive uncertainty. One of the primary analytical methods, familiar from some of the academic literature on "remix culture," was the attempt to demonstrate continuity between past cultural forms and configurable ones. As Mark Vidler, a Watford, UK-based mash-up producer, DJ, and professional remix producer who works under the name Go Home Productions explained of his work, "you still borrow from things, whether you copy licks on a guitar or on a sampler. To me, it's still art. It's a blank canvas, you're taking pieces and adding them."[6]

This argument is especially interesting in light of the fact that configurable music's *derivativeness* is used as evidence to justify its categorization as art. This line of reasoning seeks to undermine the exceptionality and originality that routinely characterize the category of art (as I have touched on previously, and will discuss in greater depth later in this chapter)—not in order to destroy the categorical distinction itself, but to admit a broader range of practices into the category, thus ultimately reinforcing its legitimacy.

Go Home Productions' characterization of mash-ups as "pieces" added to a "canvas" echoes another common approach people took in attempting to locate configurable music within the art/craft dichotomy: comparison to visual art forms. Like many configurable music practitioners, Go Home Productions explicitly invoked Warhol in his discussion of mash-ups: "Andy Warhol was an artist, yet he would paint a Campbell's soup can. So what's wrong with someone taking something that exists and putting it in a different context with your own added flavors? It's still an art form."[7] Marc Geiger, a senior vice president in the music division at the William Morris Agency, which represents musicians such as Britney Spears, Gnarls Barkley, and Prince, made an almost identical comparison: "I don't think personally it's fair to not call Warhol an artist because he didn't actually design the soup can. So I don't think it's fair to not think of a remix artist or a remix or a rearrangement of existing source code and not call it art."[8] Some survey respondents made this connection as well—for instance, one Illinois woman in her fifties wrote: "I think there are some copyrighted materials that are considered so much a part of our society (an image of a

Campbell's Soup can, for instance, the label of which I would assume has some protection as to its design, etc.) that their use should not be considered theft, particularly because it is clearly owned by Campbell and not by the creator of the art."

Other twentieth-century visual art forms were frequently invoked as well. In speaking of mash-ups, music journalist and critic Bill Werde opined: "I feel it's a legitimate art form that falls into the paradigm of collage."[9] Many musicians made the same comparison, in the same context. Mark Nicholson, a UK-based mash-up and breakbeat producer who records and performs under the name Osymyso, argued that "sampling is collage. It's like cutting out pictures and putting them together. That's the obvious equivalent."[10] DJ Adrian, a San Francisco DJ and guitarist, and cofounder of mash-up club Bootie, argued that a larger ethic of pastiche unifies mash-ups, collage, and other tactile, visual, and digital forms: "Part of the appeal of mash-up music is the juxtapositioning. But you can apply that juxtapositioning to any kind of art form, really, whether it be fashion or visual arts."[11]

I asked DJ Adrian and Mysterious D (who refer to their collective efforts as "A + D"—a linguistic homage to the "A + B" formula for mash-up construction) why artists like Warhol, Duchamp, and the collagists were so often invoked by sample-based musicians. They acknowledged that the comparison is explicitly strategic—in effect, a rhetorical comparison to legitimized art forms of the past as an appeal for artistic legitimacy today:

> *Aram:* You guys are using all these visual art metaphors to describe what you do.
> *DJ Adrian:* True.
> *Mysterious D:* Yeah.
> *Aram:* Why is that?
> *DJ Adrian:* Probably because it's there's a historical precedent of–
> *Mysterious D:* People understand that more. So you use what people have already understood and accepted as art. You know, nobody accepted pop art as art when it began. They didn't believe it was art at all. And now years later they do.
>
> . . .
>
> *DJ Adrian:* If someone, you know, kind of disses what's happening, you know with audio collage, let's call it. We call it mash-up. But, you know you could say audio collage. And, you know, does that make it sound, you know it's like, oh, see this actually is an art form as well. And there's a historical precedent there. And this is it.[12]

The strategic use of visual art metaphors in reference to sample-based music didn't necessarily mean that *every* configurable music practice merited inclusion in the "art" category. Some interviewees were quick to emphasize that the comparison didn't eliminate the need for discriminatory evaluation. As Steve Stein, a legendary New Jersey-based DJ and hip-hop producer who records and performs under the name Steinski, explained when invoking Duchamp: "If you put a urinal on the wall of an art gallery and you sign it, then you're making all kinds of statements, and it is art. I'd have to hear and see the DJ to see if he's putting the urinal on the wall, or if he's just taking a leak."[13]

Thus, many of the people I spoke to sought to legitimize configurable music by placing it within the "art" category—even as they acknowledged that the art/craft distinction was breaking down. In order to account for this seeming contradiction, interviewees relied on many traditional categorical markers of art to draw a "line in the sand"—a signpost in the gray area separating the configurable music they considered art from other configurable practices that didn't make the cut. These signposts included creativity, innovation, authorship, labor, and—significantly—Kantian disinterestedness (although Kant was never explicitly referenced).

Defining "Art" in a Configurable World

Creative transformation and aesthetic innovation were the most-often cited markers of artistry among configurable musicians. As Jordan Roseman, a San Francisco-based mash-up producer who records, performs, and publishes books under the name DJ Earworm argued, "if you're gonna be creating art, you've transformed it. And so the degree to which you've transformed it is the degree of artistry involved." Significantly, DJ Earworm defines transformation more by intellection than by measurable artifacts: "Evidence of thought, you know. Evidence of decision making . . . each decision that you make that alters the sound of it is a creative step. . . . So the number of decisions you make is related to how much of the act of art making you're doing."[14]

Other configurable musicians echo this emphasis on intellectual transformation, reflecting Larry Gross's[15] observation (discussed in chapter 2) that the definition of artistry in the modern and post-modern eras has shifted from execution to intellection, consigning mere technique to the craft category. Osymyso, for instance, said that he divides configurable music into "two areas." The first consists of "things where you're just cutting things up and editing. I suppose there's an art to it, but it's not as creative as coming up with something yourself." But he emphasizes that "there's a sliding scale. Just chucking two songs together is not as creative as chucking 101. [Osymyso is perhaps best known for his 2002 mash-up "Intro Inspection," which uses samples from 101 songs.] One is a little more cerebral, it gets you excited. The other is just DJing. It's not uncreative, it's just not pushing the boundaries or anything."[16]

This notion of "pushing the boundaries"—of innovation, a classic badge of artistry within the modern framework—was echoed in Si Begg's evaluative criteria, as well. On the "art" side of the fence, Begg told me, is Freelance Hellraiser's classic 2001 mash-up, "A Stroke of Genius" [often referred to as "A Stroke of Genie-us"], which combines instrumental music by retrorockers the Strokes with pop vocals by Christina Aguilera: "He didn't even change the vocal structure, but to me that was an incredibly creative and inspired move to do that. Even though he didn't write one note of music and he only used two sources, it was a very creative move." Begg adds, "the craft end of things" is characterized by "a working DJ who just has created his own edited [version of a song, for use at a club] . . . because it's probably not that much different from the original." In the murky gray area between these two extremes, he told me, is Madonna's 2005 single "Hung Up," which prominently uses an ABBA sample, "because she didn't change the context. It was still a disco record. ABBA intended it to be a disco record."[17]

Survey respondents echoed musicians' concerns about the "creativity" involved in sample-based music, although many were unwilling to draw a line between legitimate and illegitimate work,[18] electing instead to simply categorize *all* configurable music as uncreative. As one Pennsylvania man in his sixties wrote of configurable cultural forms: "it's a way for someone that is 'uncreative' to use someone elses work as a base so they can 'create' something of their own. I think lazy is a word that covers their work. Like adding one letter in a scrabble game to profit from someone elses ideas. [*sic*]"

The ambiguity regarding creativity in the context of configurable music contributes to ambiguity surrounding a related concept, as well: authorship. As I discuss in the context of the artist/audience binary, authorship typically functions as a badge of artistry and exceptionality, creating value for a work through its association with an individual (and vice versa). In discussing art and craft in the context of configurable music, many interviewees invoked authorship as a gauge of creativity, and therefore as a conceptual boundary of artistry. Osymyso, for instance, argued that, for the majority of mash-ups, "It's not making an individual piece of music as such, it's a DJ tool. It's something to facilitate the DJ set, and I don't think many people would honestly say 'this is my creation.'"[19]

Similarly, Si Begg acknowledged that configurable technologies are eroding the boundaries between art and craft, and invoked authorship as a dividing line between them: "Everything's getting so digital that people are just re-editing tracks themselves just for the way they like and they're not trying to pass them off as their own. They're just saying, 'Well, I prefer it like this. I didn't like that bit so I just took it out,' kind of thing. So they're not professing to be particularly artistic. They're just— it's . . . more of a craft or something." Begg acknowledged, however, that between these two extremes, "there's a big gray area."[20]

Not every configurable music practitioner accepted authorship as a marker of the art/craft distinction. Kevin Foakes, a British DJ and mash-up producer who records for the Ninja Tune label under the names Strictly Kev and DJ Food, told me he hadn't released a commercial record in five years, but had released three or four albums worth of material in that time over the Internet. "They're still works that I've put my name to," he said. "Whether they're works of art is debatable."[21]

The emphasis on creativity, innovation, and authorship as the badges of artistry espoused by many interviewees and survey respondents is not only a staple of modern aesthetic theory and a common belief among Americans in general, it's also an institutionalized distinction, enshrined in the very language of copyright case law, and in the constitutional articles that are the sources of the law. A 1991 Supreme Court decision written by Justice Sandra Day O'Connor in *Feist Publications, Inc., v. Rural Telephone Service Co.* argues that telephone book listings do not constitute authorship, because "the sine qua non of copyright is originality." Originality, the decision continues, necessitates "a modicum of creativity."[22] As intellectual property attorney Bob Clarida explained to me, *Feist* essentially draws a line between art and craft, using creativity and originality as standards, because "a copyright only protects authorship. It doesn't protect, in that case, what it called 'industrious collection.'"[23] Whether and when configurable music practices live up to *Feist*'s "modicum of creativity" standard, Clarida told me, has yet to be tested or established in a court decision— although he said that it's "hard to imagine that someone doing a remix or sample collage" would not live up to this threshold.[24]

I treat shifting definitions of "creativity" and "innovation" within a configurable context at greater length in chapter 6, when I discuss interviewees' treatment of the original/copy binary. In the matter of the art/craft dichotomy, it is simply enough to say that an evaluation of the former binary is essential in the evaluation of the latter. However, interviewees brought other evaluative criteria to bear on the art/craft distinction, as well.

One concept that emerged from my interviews is the notion that the degree of effort involved in production has some bearing on whether configurable music counts as a legitimate art form—and that *conspicuous* labor is an essential factor of the aesthetic. As Osymyso put it: "I want to see that there's a labor of love involved, that there's some sweat involved, because the software makes it just so easy. I like to make it clear that what I've done was not done in just two seconds. That's where *Intro Inspection* came from—you can't deny that it just took many hours. Of course, I could do it quicker now and probably better on the newer software, but it wouldn't matter as much."[25]

Similarly, DJ Paul V, a radio DJ who hosts a mash-up show on KDLD 103.1 FM in Los Angeles (as well as producing his own mash-ups and hosting mash-up clubs at local venues) told me that he's not impressed by mash-ups that use preexisting, commercially released a capella rap vocals as a starting point, because it's just too easy: "I'm more blown away when someone has to take a track as it is and somehow strip out the vocals themselves, and really put that effort into putting it with something else."[26]

Survey respondents echoed this sentiment in their responses. The Pennsylvania man I cite above alluded to it in his characterization of configurable cultural forms as "lazy." This New York woman in her forties made the point more explicitly: "Derivative works only become original creative content in their own right when a decent amount of work goes into producing something new." Music attorney Ronald Bienstock shared this assessment as well, telling me that, in his opinion, "sometimes, sampling is just laziness."[27]

The labor standard for artistry in the context of sample-based music was accompanied by caveats from all quarters. The survey respondent from New York added that "there are some situations where it's theft and unethical, no matter how much work is put into it." Osymyso, on reflection, decided that given his own creative experience, the standard was insufficient: "I sometimes have an idea that will take five seconds, and it's sometimes better than one that would take five days, so artistry's not all about time. It's in the end product."[28] And University of Southern California law professor Jennifer Urban, who also serves as director of the university's Intellectual Property Clinic, reminded me that, from a legal standpoint, "copyright doesn't care how much work you put into it. Copyright only cares about creativity."[29]

Another standard sometimes applied to the art/craft distinction in the context of configurable music was commercialism or market viability. Reflecting the post-Kantian precept that art is defined by its absence of functionality, several interviewees expressed mistrust, disdain, or devaluation of music produced with marketability in mind, and expressed support for the concept of aesthetic purity, or "art for art's sake." As Mark Gunderson, a Bay Area-based instrumentalist and DJ who cofounded the band Evolution Control Committee and goes by the name Trade-Mark G, explained: "On the craft side, I would put things like Coldcut in their more poppy vein. Because their music is reasonably sellable. . . . On the art side, I see things like Negativland. They are totally not interested in rocking the house. They are interested in cutting up tapes and assuaging their sociopathic senses. They're really about trying to exhibit their iniquities in an artistic way, made for music's purpose and not to sell. . . . I'm kind of collapsing craft with marketability."[30]

Survey respondents also expressed a belief that configurable cultural products produced outside of a commercial context are exceptional, and should be accorded a special, protected status. This Illinois man in his forties echoed the sentiments of many others: "I personally don't see anything wrong with that as long as it's not used in a commercial way (i.e., to make money from it's [sic] use)." DJ Adrian made a strikingly similar comment: "I think you should be allowed to do whatever the hell you want to do with these tracks, as long as you're not profiting from it."[31]

Record industry executives drew a distinction as well. Hosh Gureli, former club DJ and vice president of A&R (artists and repertoire) in the dance music division at major label Sony/BMG, put it bluntly: "I'm having trouble with the whole 'art' question because my job is to make records that sell. The record companies don't think in terms of art, they think in terms of business and commerce." While Gureli expressed doubt that music produced by amateurs would be considered "art" by most people, he also emphasized that "having a commercial hit doesn't mean you're making art either, because it could be very bland."[32]

This Kantian logic is also reflected in our legal system, according to law professor Jennifer Urban. As she explained to me, "useful articles are not copyrightable. . . . The creative elements, however, are—so long as they can be separated from the utilitarian function."[33] Therefore, insofar as configurable music products such as mash-ups are denied copyright protection (a point I touch on further later in this book), one can argue that they are consigned to the "craft" side of the fence by existing legal theory and practice.

The Ear of the Beholder

Despite the many evaluative criteria interviewees and survey respondents cited in their efforts to draw a line through the gray area separating art from craft, several people I spoke with acknowledged that categorical judgments represent the opinion of the listener or viewer more than they do any truth about the work under assessment. As Strictly Kev told me, "it's an incredibly subjective thing. I can listen to one mash-up and it's art, and I can listen to another one and it's just crap."[34] Marc Geiger of WMA shared this sentiment: "I have a very egalitarian view on content that's only separable by good and bad. And good and bad is ultimately subjective anyway."[35] Survey respondents echoed this as well. As one Florida man in his forties wrote, "it is a fine line between art and copying, only the true artist knows the difference."

Matt Wand, a sample-based musician from the UK, best known as a founding member of Stock, Hausen & Walkman and as head of independent record label Hot Air, agreed that art/craft distinctions are subjective, but he also linked this subjectivity to increasingly open-ended standards and practices associated with noncommercial production in a configurable technological environment. In his words, "it's definitely an art form, *by today's standards* . . . it is just activity, and it's open to everybody, and the most naive people can make something that's appealing."[36] In other words, he associates the ambiguity and subjectivity surrounding the art/craft binary with the newly democratized capacity for music production and distribution and the emerging social, ethical, and aesthetic codes associated with configurable culture.

Conclusion

In short, although the line separating art from craft appears to be getting blurrier with the advent of configurable musical production, both musicians and the public at large have developed a variety of evaluative mechanisms to make the distinction clearer. Many compare configurable music to historical visual art movements, drawing on collage, pop, and ready-mades as a way to better justify the elevation of mash-ups and remixes to art status. Some look to authorship as a badge of artistry, others attempt to establish formalistic or aesthetic criteria, and still others use economic criteria, making quantitative assessments of the labor or capital involved in production, or using marketability as a negative criterion. Yet nearly all of my interviewees and many survey respondents acknowledged that these criteria are largely insufficient to the task, and that configurable musical practices have made the concept of "art" harder than ever to define.

The ambiguity and subjectivity surrounding art/craft distinctions, and the rhetorical and evaluative strategies that musicians and others bring to bear when trying to make sense of configurable music in this context, have their analog in the treatment of a closely related binary, the artist/audience distinction. If we cannot clearly say what constitutes an art and what does not, then how can we continue to speak confidently of the traditional division of labor separating artist from audience? I explore this and other questions regarding the role of the "artist" in a configurable music context in chapter 5.

5

Some Kid in His Bedroom

The Artist/Audience Binary

> The distinction between author and public is about to lose its basic character. The difference becomes merely functional; it may vary from case to case.
> Walter Benjamin

> The line between artist and audience is pretty much gone. I remember when I got my first digital production rig, I was like, "My god, man, this is like communism—the means of production are in the hands of the people."
> Steinski

As with the distinction between art and craft, the line separating artist from audience has always been somewhat tenuous. The elevation of the artist from the category of mere craftsman during the early Renaissance to its apogee in the nineteenth and twentieth centuries (discussed in chapter 2) required a lot of extra philosophical baggage, including the problematic concept of genius, and the belief that cultural production could spring, ex nihilo, from the labors of one exceptional individual. This baggage was a small burden in comparison to the benefit it brought to its adopters: the Romantic artist served as a model and a justification for our modern economic and social systems, premised on the privatization of hitherto public goods and on the atomistic individual as the central unit of social agency.

The deep and symbiotic interrelationship between the concept of artistic exceptionality and our modern economic and social institutions has always been evident to those who chose to look; there was perhaps no better indication than the fact that, for aesthetic communities excluded or otherwise separated from the commercial matrix, the whole premise often went right out the window. An excellent example is Gee's Bend, a relatively isolated African American community in rural Alabama, known for the glorious abstract quilt patterns produced for decades by the women of the town. As William Arnett and Paul Arnett note, there is a correlation between the communal aspect of Gee's Bend quilt production, in which individual innovation and intellectual property play little or no role, and the absence of commercial or broader social influence: "While some individual southern artists still create visual artworks in this traditional black vernacular idiom, Gee's Bend is one of the few known *communities* of traditional black artists who have worked across several generations and developed a coherent graphic style absent outside patronage or commercial incentive."[1]

Ironically, intellectual property and individual ownership came into play for the quilters of Gee's Bend only when their work was commercialized by a source outside of their community—namely, the authors and art dealers whose book I cite in the above paragraph. A 2007 lawsuit by three Gee's Bend quilters accused the authors and others of appropriating their intellectual and material property in the form of quilt patterns, photos of quilts, and a few actual quilts. The suit was settled out of court in 2008.[2]

Erosion of the Artist/Audience Boundary

While configurable music is hardly produced within an isolated setting analogous to Gee's Bend, the necessarily communal nature of sample-based production (almost by definition, the task requires multiple contributors), combined with the stringency of contemporary intellectual property laws, has disconnected the vast bulk of production from commercial and legal institutions. Some practitioners rebel actively against legal and commercial strictures, while others simply avoid them as a matter of course; in both cases, these factors have contributed to the erosion of the artist/audience binary.

Matt Wand summed up the prevailing opinion among my interviewees the most succinctly: "I can't draw the line, I definitely don't draw the line—he's artist, she's audience—I can't do that at all."[3] Similarly, Pete Axelrad, a Los Angeles-based mash-up producer and DJ who goes by the name DJ Axel by night and works as director of music finance at Warner Bros. Studios by day, told me that "it's just a gray area. . . . I don't know if you can separate it any more, really. . . . I mean, is a DJ an artist?" I asked him whether he could answer his own question, and after struggling for a definitive response, he told me he couldn't, because "it's too gray."[4]

Eric Kleptone, a Brighton, UK-based mash-up producer, expanded on this notion, attributing the ambiguity to a larger shift in the logic of production and consumption, and supporting the shift as a positive development:

> Everything is breaking down in a good way. . . . Once upon a time . . . there was a line. You know, the edge of the stage was *there*. The performers are on one side. The audience is on the other side, and never the twain shall meet. . . . [Now] this really is becoming part and parcel of what people are starting to expect from media that they're purchasing. That they should be able to personalize it or manipulate it in some way. Or at least have the freedom to do so. . . . Now, being an artist is not the same as—you're not necessarily giving people finished product. You're giving people an unfinished product. A platform that they can do stuff on.[5]

The notion that both aesthetic production and consumption are fragmenting, with new roles and behaviors rushing to fill the untracked gray area opening between them and allowing an unprecedented degree of communication, collaboration, and fluidity between makers and users, was echoed by many interviewees. Several said, however, that the existence of a gray area between the traditional polarities doesn't necessarily mean that everyone plays the role of artist or audience to an equal degree. To the contrary, many remarked on the increasing subtlety of the shades and gradations within this gray area. In Kleptone's words, "if you *do* want to draw a straight line between the artist and the consumer, then there are a million points on that graph. And there's another million arriving every day."[6]

Similarly, DJ Earworm echoed Bill Ivey and S. J. Tepper's[7] argument about the "curatorial me," metaphorically comparing the configurable gray area between music producer and consumer to the traditional curation that takes place within the visual arts: "If I put a painting up on the wall no one's gonna say I've made art, right? . . . But what if I had one hundred paintings and I arranged them in some sort of mosaic form? Well that might be art. And I might be an artist. But . . . where's the point where I have made art and I am an artist? And that's a gradual, fuzzy thing . . . you can always find points in between on the continuum where it's gonna stump almost anybody."[8]

DJ Earworm's metaphor of mash-up practitioner as curator reflects a larger thread that ran through many of my conversations. Once they had acknowledged that several distinct points lay on the spectrum from artist to audience member, a great many of my interviewees sought to *define* these points—in effect, to draw multiple lines in the sand. DJ Adrian, echoing Lawrence Lessig,[9] argued that a new category of engaged consumer is emerging: "it's active entertainment. You're not just passively downloading music and consuming it, you're actually altering it to your own tastes."[10] DJ Paul V shared this sentiment, placing the newly engaged consumer within a graded continuum: "I think it goes from passive fan to active fan to the next level. . . . Whether they're all artists, that's debatable. There's levels of technical skill, musical skill, execution. It's kind of like an onion, layered. I don't know if it's so black and white."[11]

While DJ Earworm and DJ Adrian focused on the emergence of an engaged audience developing a consumption-adjacent relationship to media, TradeMark G sought to identify his own role at the midpoint of the scale between artist and audience: "What I think is happening is that there's been a real rise of an intermediary level. The DJ has become a very big class in music. . . . They're not necessarily artists, but they kind of are. They're not necessarily the audience, either. There is definitely some kind of blurring of the lines, but it's happened in a way that we've sort of added a new level."[12]

In some ways, the emergence of the category of the DJ as an intermediary level between artist and audience overlaps with more traditional roles in the art worlds of the modern framework. I have already mentioned curation. Other concepts, such as criticism, connoisseurship, and appreciation bear some resemblance as well. As Mysterious D told me, people often begin making mash-ups "because you like so many diverse styles of music to begin with. The mash-up [producer] is both the consumer and an artist, you know. I mean mash-up artists generally have huge music collections and love music."[13]

Far from viewing the double-consciousness of the DJ as a deficit or evidence of inferiority, many of the configurable musicians I spoke with said they considered the fandom implicit in much sample-based music to be a key asset, and a favorable quality in comparison to traditional definitions of artistry or musicianship. As Matt Wand told me, "that's a really important part of being an artist—is being a good, informed and slightly fanatical audience." In fact, he said, "that might be all there is to it, to being an artist. The rest of it is just time [required for] the skills that you develop."[14]

The existence of a connoisseur or critical class of aesthetic appreciation has often—and reasonably—been viewed as a social marker of elitism or socioeconomic class distinction.[15] Many of the configurable music practitioners I spoke with, however, saw it from the opposite vantage point: rather than raising the bar for entry into practices of consumption, the emergence of the DJ lowers the bar for production, allowing a larger number of people to enter the ranks of the creative. Viewed from this standpoint, DJ culture is inherently communitarian (or, as Steinski remarks, in the epigram to this chapter, "communism"),[16] rather than elitist.

DJ Adrian told me he feels that mash-ups share much in common with earlier aesthetic movements premised on a lower barrier of entry and a grassroots production ethic—specifically, with punk: "I think that bootleg and remix and mash-up culture is basically the new punk rock . . . because twenty years ago, punk rock was the reaction against the bloated, so-called corporate rock. It was a total DIY aesthetic. Do-it-yourself. Anyone could do it. Anyone could pick up a guitar, learn three chords, and play punk rock."[17]

Similarly, Matt Wand associated configurable music with the folk revival movement of the 1960s, and with the (quasi-mythical) folk musical culture the earlier movement valorized, in which authenticity was premised on oral transmission and an absence of property relations to music: "Music has shifted back to feudal times . . . there's no more money in content, is there? Music making has become a folk thing, there isn't much of a career to be made in it. It's just something that people do, making content for each other."[18]

Wand's comment reflects a sentiment echoed by many I spoke with: namely, that configurable technologies are a proximate cause of the communitarian ethic associated with DJ culture. This is because, as Wand observes, technologies such as peer-to-peer file sharing undermine the economic mechanism by which creators are compensated for their work. It is also because the new networked communications infrastructure allows for the emergence of communities of shared interest on a global scale. In fact, some have argued that mash-ups constitute the first new musical movement without a geographic center. As mattcatt, a London-based sound designer and DJ, told me during the early years of the mash-up movement, in 2003, "this is the first true Internet based music culture with two-way appeal, because we can share tracks and play radio to each other and chat about interests."[19]

Definitions of Configurable Artistry

While configurable music practitioners acknowledge a breakdown of the traditional artist/audience dichotomy and celebrate the communitarian values surrounding the emergence of liminal roles such as the DJ/active fan/curator/connoisseur, many are quick to emphasize that gradations of quality, professionalism, and artistry still do exist. And in making these qualitative judgments, many of the people I spoke to—including some of those who championed the DIY ethic of inclusiveness—felt compelled to reinforce the artist/audience dichotomy, and the premise of artistic exceptionality, by setting forth new evaluative criteria. As DJ Adrian told me, "like punk rock, just because you can do it doesn't mean it's going to be good. There's definitely people who rise to the top."[20]

Some people I spoke with were willing to extend the mantle of artistry to all or most configurable music practices. V/VM told me, "I think people who use samples are artists. Why not? It's just what's there, isn't it? If you take something and do something with it, yeah I guess you're an artist." He went on to acknowledge, though, that he does not invest much significance in the concept of artistry: "but how relevant is that term today, anyway?"[21] Similarly, DJ Earworm told me, "I consider a lot of mash-up artists to be artists. I mean, most of them."[22]

On the other side of the spectrum, some—mostly those with predominantly noncreative roles in the music industry—were unwilling to label any sample-based musicians as artists. For instance, Tony Zeoli, a dance music industry veteran and vice president of music at StarStyle. com, told me that, in his opinion, popular DJ and producer Peter Rauhofer "is a remix producer. He's not an artist in his own right."[23] Zeoli emphasized that this assessment was in no way a negative reflection on Rauhofer's work, which he enjoys and respects—it was simply a taxonomic categorization.

Similarly, music attorney Ronald Bienstock, who has been involved in sampling litigation since the 1980s, told me, "I'm a pro-artist guy. I'm always gonna say that the composer of a true piece of composition should be . . . protected from those who would claim that they now have some ownership rights in that by merely [making] a technical change."[24] In other words, in Bienstock's estimation, remixers and mashers never constitute artists in their own rights, and as mere "technicians" (or *craftsmen*) do not deserve to wear the badge of authorship. Some survey respondents reflected this absolutist assessment as well. As one California man in his thirties opined, "people who do this are leaches [*sic*] on the real creative society."

Although it was less common, some configurable music practitioners shared this absolutist negative assessment. Go Home Productions, for instance, told me that "DJs should be playing between bands. I really hate the ethos of the DJ being an artist . . . it's not something I'd want to stand up for an hour and a half to watch."[25]

Most of the people I spoke to espoused a belief that the tipping point between artist and audience lay somewhere in the middle of the configurable music landscape, among the many shades of gray. Many of the evaluative mechanisms they mentioned reflected the ones I've already discussed in the context of the art/craft binary; most frequently, the concepts of originality and creative transformation were invoked. As Trade-Mark G told me: "The way that you use samples can also define whether you're using them as a DJ or as an artist. The longer, the more recognizable the samples, the less your personal artistry or sense of style and technique gets through. I'm more inclined to think of someone who fragments samples as an artist than someone who uses whole phrases."[26]

Another evaluative criterion that emerged from my conversations— almost entirely from interviews with music industry executives—was the notion that artistry is *defined by* the presence of an audience. As Marc Geiger of WMA succinctly put it: "If the audience thinks it's art, then it's art."[27] As Hosh Gureli of Sony/BMG—himself a former club DJ—told me, "All of it's art. Even the DJ just playing one record after another, if he's playing to a crowd, like a comic standing up there or a person in a play, the person's job is to make sure that the dance floor's filled."[28] While it may seem surprising that members of musical regulatory institutions would be willing to extend the mantle of artistry so easily to emerging configurable practices, it also makes sense. To define an artist solely by the existence of an audience—regardless of creative process, output, or qualitative criteria—is the purest possible expression of the modern framework, because it prizes the artist/audience binary above all other considerations.

Skill, Talent, and Genius

Although interviewees were largely ambivalent and divided regarding the concept of artistry within a configurable context, there was a surprising degree of consistency in their approach to related concepts: those of skill, talent, and genius. Configurable music practitioners tended to agree that skill is an essential ingredient of successful sample-based music, and that it's an acquired trait, rather than an innate one. As DJ Adrian told me, "you can throw together a mash-up without that much skill. But to throw together a good one you definitely need skill. And skill is something that's learned, really."[29]

Echoing the modern framework, interviewees defined skill in terms of a capacity with both physical and conceptual tools. V/VM compared facility with music editing software to instrumental expertise: "You still have to invest a hell of a lot of time learning a certain software to get a good result. It's just like learning to play the guitar or something."[30] DJ Earworm identified specific conceptual skills necessary for making mash-ups. In his estimation, skill is "knowing how to make songs, keeping rhythm, knowing how to keep them in time. Knowing how to arrange them. Knowing how to produce them. Knowing how to choose them."[31] Many interviewees told me, however, that, while skill is a necessary component of artistry, it is not sufficient in and of itself; as Osymyso remarked, "you can have someone technically skilled who's got no creative side."[32]

The "creative side" of artistry in a configurable context, according to many of the people I spoke to, is reflected in the notion of talent, which is more conceptual and less procedural than skill. As Osymyso told me, "talent is the ability to know what's going to work with what."[33] For Strictly Kev, talent in mash-ups is a state of mind, or a mode of receptivity to aesthetics: "You put two things together from two different times that would never, ever go together. That, to me, is talent—hearing that, listening melodically." He also associates talent with the concept of creative transformation and innovation, defining it as "originality and flair and the ability to keep going, keep changing and mutating, doing the unexpected, confounding people's expectations."[34]

In keeping with this traditional conceptualization of talent, many interviewees also espoused the belief that the trait is either innate, exceptional, or both. DJ Axel proposed the former: "I think that you could have like raw talent. And the skill is the refinement."[35] Tony Zeoli proposed the latter: "not everyone has talent. . . . [It's a] a special gift of being able to create something that other people enjoy."[36] And Si Begg proposed both: "On the talent front, I think you have to have a certain ear for it. You have to have an ear for what will work. And which some people just have . . . that's a kind of talent which I think you can't—which is comparable to a musical talent in that you can't teach someone that. I don't think you really learn it."[37]

Not all interviewees supported this formulation. Steinski, while accepting the concept of talent in the context of configurable music, questioned the notion that it constitutes a building block of artistry: "I would not say that a DJ set with beat matching is art. It's a talent. It's like, what record are you picking, and how are you playing them? DJing is a talent, I don't know if it's an art."[38]

Eric Kleptone rejected the concept of talent altogether, arguing that it is simply a subjective judgment imposed on creators from without: "Talent is really—it's in the eye of the—that's more in the eye of the audience."[39] Interestingly, this formulation echoes the assertions of Geiger and Gureli that artistry is defined by the presence of an audience; however, while the music industry executives used this argument to reify the concept of artistry, Kleptone used it to the opposite effect.

While most respondents adopted the modern framework's treatment of skill and talent more or less intact, they were generally much more ambivalent about the concept of genius. The most traditional treatment of the concept came from Mysterious D, who emphasized its extreme exceptionality: "Genius I actually only ever use with [DJ] Earworm. Everybody else is talented. Genius is a rare thing."[40] Si Begg espoused a fairly traditional treatment of genius as well, proposing the notion that geniuses are the rare individuals who reformulate aesthetic codes: "I think the geniuses to me were probably the people that go further back, like Afrika Bambaataa and people like that—the early pioneers of hip-hop who were doing it before anyone really knew what they were doing. There was no words for it and they just did it."[41]

Osymyso echoed Begg's assessment about the genius of configurable music innovators, but with an important distinction: "I think a genius is someone that comes up with a concept from nowhere that no one had before. Like scratching. The guy that came up with the idea of the mash-up wasn't necessarily a genius, but he had a genius moment."[42] This midthought shift points to a common thread in my conversations with configurable music practitioners: *individuals aren't geniuses*, but they are capable of having "genius moments."

Several interviewees used almost exactly the same term. DJ Earworm (himself a genius, in Mysterious D's estimation) told me, "I can say there's definitely moments of genius in many producers. Whether I would call them, you know, a consistent—I don't know. There's definitely, you hear these moments of inspiration in certain times."[43] Eric Kleptone was even less equivocal: "I don't think there's been any genius [in configurable music]. There's been some moments of genius. And that goes for everyone from John Cage to Stockhausen, Steinski, Cold Cut, The Art of Noise, Negativland. You know, Public Enemy. People like that. They have intense flashes of genius. DJ Shadow. But none of them are actual geniuses, they're just very good at what they do. . . . I think it's something that you channel. It's not something that you are."[44]

Other interviewees made a slightly different, but analogous argument: individuals aren't geniuses, but their works or ideas can be. As DJ Paul V told me, "An idea can be genius, or someone's passion about it can be genius, but that doesn't make *them* a genius."[45] Similarly, DJ Drama, the Atlanta-based hip-hop and mixtape producer, told me that *The Grey Album* was "an ingenious work,"[46] but that the DJ who made it, Danger Mouse, doesn't necessarily qualify as a genius. V/VM was even more reticent to use the label, combining the concept of "genius moments" with the concept of "genius works," focusing on the exceptionality of individual products created at discrete moments in time: "Maybe some works are works of genius that they've done. But I don't think anybody's body of work is genius."[47]

Finally, some interviewees focused on the inherent subjectivity of the term. Echoing Eric Kleptone's assessment of talent, for instance, Trade-Mark G opined that "genius is in the ear of the listener."[48]

Thus, most configurable music practitioners seemed uncomfortable with traditional formulations of genius, as characterized by the exceptional individual single-handedly reordering aesthetic codes through sheer force of will. Music industry executives and survey respondents were much more willing to use the term—both positively and negatively—in the context of configurable music.

When I asked Hosh Gureli of Sony/BMG about whether there are any geniuses of sample-based music, he responded:

> *Hosh:* I really think you have to give Puffy [hip-hop superstar and impresario Sean "Diddy" Combs] his due, because he really brought sampling to a whole new height with the *I'll Be Missing You* tribute to Biggie [Smalls]. He did that without even getting permission [from Sting, whose composition

he sampled], and he used so much of the record, but he got permission and they even performed it together. That was a groundbreaking record.

Aram: So that was genius?

Hosh: Yes. Biggie did that with a lot of records too.[49]

The fact that Gureli cites Diddy as a genius of configurable music is significant for a number of reasons. Most obviously, Diddy is one of hip-hop's most successful recording artists, and in music industry parlance, "genius" has often been used interchangeably with "consistently profitable." Gureli clearly means more than this in his analysis, however; for him, the genius of Diddy seems to reside in the magnitude and brazenness of the rapper/producer's sampling relationship to his source materials. Ironically, as I discuss in greater detail in chapter 6, these are the very qualities that made Diddy almost universally *reviled* among the configurable music practitioners I interviewed.

Other music industry executives were equally willing to apply the term "genius" to sample-based musicians. Pete Ganbarg, currently the executive vice president of artists and repertoire for Atlantic Records, cited Diddy, as well. He also cited DJ Danger Mouse, the mash-up artist who vaulted to fame and eventually to commercial success with the group Gnarls Barkley after his 2004 release of *The Grey Album,* an unauthorized mash-up of Jay-Z's *The Black Album* and the Beatles' eponymous release, typically referred to as "The White Album." In Ganbarg's words, *The Grey Album* is "a brilliant piece of music, and the artist is basically utilizing two classic canvases to create his art."[50]

Tony Zeoli, despite denying the title of "artist" to remix producers (as quoted above), supported the notion of genius in a configurable context, tacitly reinforcing the artist/audience dichotomy by defining the term through the scope and scale of a work's reception: "Can some people consider a remixer a genius? I think absolutely, if you recognize the fact that there's a human being that can sit down at a board and basically create music from scratch, and have thousands of people all over the world dance to it."[51]

The only categorical rejections of the term "genius" in a configurable musical context came from survey respondents. Though they were not asked about the concept of genius explicitly, some used it in their survey responses anyway. As one Florida woman in her thirties remarked of configurable cultural products in general, "I'm sick of the sameness of these forms. After more than a decade of remixed music, remade movies/tv shows [sic] and mashed-up video footage, I am ready for some originality again. Genius is original, not re-used."

Artistry and Copyright

Currently, the legal treatment of the artist/audience dichotomy within a configurable musical context is as ambiguous and contradictory as the attitudes and beliefs expressed by my interviewees. As music attorney Gary Adelman, who formerly produced sample-based music and ran a techno music label called Liquid Sky, explained to me, purely sample-based works such as techno songs and mash-ups have historically been denied copyright, the legal marker of authorship:

> *Gary:* Under the copyright law of 1976, he who creates owns. That's the basic premise of copyright law. Copyright is an expression. And if you create it, you own it . . . when a copyright is generated, the author or the creator is the owner [unless they waive that right, as is the case with many recording contracts].
>
> *Aram:* So is there an example of the Court assigning a new copyright to a sample-based work?
>
> *Gary:* No. Not that I'm aware of.[52]

Law professor Jennifer Urban, taking a different tack, told me that, theoretically, copyright protection could be applied not just to sample-based music, but to the entire range of gray area between musical production and consumption. This is because a special subclass of copyright exists for the *creative selection and arrangement* of preexisting materials, in addition to the production of works from (putatively) raw materials:

> *Aram:* Is a person who creates an iPod playlist an artist or not?
>
> *Jennifer:* Sure. If it's a creative selection and arrangement. Yeah.
>
> *Aram:* From a legal standpoint?
>
> *Jennifer:* Yeah . . . I mean I've never heard of anybody trying to enforce a copyright on a playlist, but I know of lots of books that are made up of chapters by lots of other people, right? And the book is held to be separately copyrightable as a compilation.[53]

Attorney Bob Clarida made a similar observation, telling me that in a recent case, *Caffey v. Cook*,[54] "the Court held that the selection and arrangement of songs in a musical revue was protectable, even though the plaintiff had no copyright in the songs . . . [therefore] I think it's not a stretch to say that selection and arrangement of samples within a hip-hop track should be protectable."[55]

If we recall that, for DJ Earworm, skill in producing mash-ups is defined in part by "knowing how to choose" and "knowing how to arrange" source materials,[56] Urban's and Clarida's arguments for the application of "selection and arrangement" protection to configurable musical practices appear to be supportable.

Even if the Court were to agree, and grant copyright protection (and, therefore, institutional acknowledgment of artist status) to configurable music practitioners on this basis, they would still enjoy an inferior level of protection (and therefore inferior status) to traditional composers and instrumental performers. This is because, as Clarida explained to me, copyrights granted on the basis of selection and arrangement enjoy the "thinnest" possible copyright protection: "you basically have only a protection against, you know, actual literal copying of your selection and arrangement."[57] In other words, even a trivial change in the placement of a single sample within a work (for instance, if a mash-up producer were to switch the places of song fragments 100 and 101 in Osymyso's "Intro Inspection") would theoretically be enough to destroy copyright protection.

"Some Kid in His Bedroom"

One of the most interesting aspects of my discussions with musicians and executives about the borderline separating artist from audience was the frequency with which interviewees resorted to a single rhetorical device to justify their arguments. This device centered around a fictitious straw man, generally referred to as "some kid," and usually located either in his bedroom or in his basement. Whatever credits, qualifications, or accolades were being extended to a given configurable music practice or producer, they were simultaneously denied to "some kid" on the basis of his amateurism, inexperience, or isolation.

The prevalence of the "some kid" argument was especially high among music industry executives. For instance, DJ Paul V (who straddles the professional fence, as both a radio DJ and an active mash-up producer), in extolling the virtues of Go Home Productions, argued that GHP warrants being called a "musician" because "he knows how to play an instrument" in addition to simply DJing. This affects the quality of GHP's sample-based work, he told me, because "I think a musician's head obviously has a different approach because they create music themselves. So that has to have an effect on how you hear things and how you approach things. As opposed to some kid in his bedroom, who doesn't play an instrument."[58]

Similarly, Pete Ganbarg of Atlantic Records used the same straw man to champion the artistic exceptionality of certain configurable music practitioners: "The kid who is making a play list on his iPod is not nec-essarily a musician . . . I think that you've got the great DJ minds of this generation. They're artists in their own right for sure."[59] Hosh Gureli of Sony/BMG used this argument as well, telling me that "some-one in the basement putting two beats together, they could love it and to them it's art. But to the majority it might not be art."[60]

Although the "some kid" trope was most prevalent among industry executives, many configurable music practitioners used it as well. Dur-ing an interview with DJ Adrian and Mysterious D, the use of the term actually led to a lengthy discussion between the two of them about its meaning and significance within the context of the artist/audience bi-nary in configurable music, which bears repeating here in full:

Mysterious D: Mash-ups are so easy to make with software. You've got a kid in his room plopping an a cappella of any song over an instrumental of any song and it's a mash-up. But he's not an artist.

Aram: Why not?

Mysterious D: Because he's not really using it for an artistic form. He's just fucking around with software basically. Kind of like somebody who likes three chords on their guitar . . . do you call them a musician or are they not a musician? It's hard to say. You might call them a musician technically. But if you described to your friends, "This guy's a musician, but he only knew three chords and can't play anything else and doesn't choose to," I mean, then are you missing, you know–

DJ Adrian: But couldn't you say, couldn't you make a judgment call that was like, "Sure he's an artist but he's a bad artist." Just the same way you would say, "Yeah, he's a musician but just not a very good one."

Mysterious D: Good point. . . . So I use that because that's what the media tells everybody. That's not how we see it all, to be honest. I'm just used to using that because I'm gonna go with what most people believe. They call them "bedroom producers" and so on and so forth.

DJ Adrian: "Bedroom remixers."

Mysterious D: But we happen to know that a lot of the people that are involved in it [mash-ups] are either already doing [professional] remix work, they're DJs for X amount of years and a lot of them are ex-band members. So it's not just some kid in his bedroom. So I use that as cliché. Although there are that. There are kids–

DJ Adrian: And they're amazing.

Mysterious D: So, and I refuse to call that "less than," even though it gets implied as that in the media. And it gets implied as if, "It's a kid in his bedroom—it couldn't possibly be as good." Again, going back to the DIY aesthetic of punk rock, which is why we think it's okay. Yeah, you're right, he didn't know how to play his instrument, and he still made some sort of brilliant world-changing music. So that kid in his bedroom isn't that big of a deal. I think that could actually be brilliant. It's not a negative or not a cutback.[61]

I believe that the deep ambivalence about nomenclature and categorization reflected in this exchange strikes at the heart of the larger sense of ontological uncertainty I have discussed throughout this work. And the curious admixture of pride and deprecation that inheres to the concept of the "bedroom producer" and to the double-consciousness of the DJ echoes the same uneasy balance that characterized the concept of double-consciousness for another liminal social group when W. E. B. Du Bois first coined the term, over a century ago, in *The Souls of Black Folk*.[62]

This becomes especially apparent when we look at the ways in which configurable music practitioners use the term in reference to themselves. DJ Axel, who has worked as a professional DJ on both a full-time and part-time basis for much of his adult life, told me that he considers himself a "bedroom producer," and that this appellation means that he is "part of a community of mash-up artists."[63] Tony Montana, one of the earliest mash-up practitioners, used the term as well when I interviewed him in 2003, associating it explicitly with mash-ups' illegality and outlaw image (an association reinforced by his choice of DJ name—Tony Montana was the name of the fictional Cuban crime lord played by Al Pacino in the 1983 film *Scarface*):

Tony Montana: only some of the stuff i do . . is "leagle"
Aram: what about the other stuff?
Tony Montana: its bedroom producing [sic][64]

DJ Danger Mouse, who is probably the best-known mash-up producer today due to the popularity of *The Grey Album*, appears to go out of his way to emphasize the bedroom as both his physical and spiritual location in interviews he grants to the press. In a 2006 profile in the *New York Times* magazine section, for instance, the mash-up producer, whose given name is Brian Burton, told journalist Chuck Klosterman that the idea for the album-length mash-up came to him suddenly one day while he was cleaning his room. This moment of clarity becomes the turning point of the 5,000-word article, meriting an entire paragraph consisting solely of the sentence: "It was at this point that Burton decided to straighten up his bedroom."[65] Similarly, in a 2004 interview in *Remix* magazine, DJ Danger Mouse told interviewer Rob Kirby,

"I do almost all of my preproduction in my bedroom. I have to be working next to a bed when I'm coming up with new stuff."[66]

In its ability to communicate both deprecation and pride, both otherness and selfness, to suggest both the bonds of community and the exile of the outlaw, the term "bedroom producer" resembles nothing more than a well-known racial epithet that has been used against (and by) African Americans for centuries. The implications of this correlation, and of the articulation between DJ-consciousness and double-consciousness as we traditionally understand it, are complex, to say the least, and I attempt to unravel them more thoroughly at the conclusion of this book. For now, I simply observe that part of the significance of the bedroom as the locus of identification is its universality; we *all* have bedrooms, and in a configurable technological environment, we are *all* producers to some extent. In short, "some kid" isn't just a convenient rhetorical device; it's *us*.

Conclusion

As with the art/craft distinction, configurable technology and culture have made the line separating artist from audience far more difficult to police, or even to identify. Like earlier musical movements such as folk and punk, the configurable ethic appears to make membership in the creative class—or at least in the fuzzily defined intermediate class called "DJ"—more accessible. Yet, despite this openness, many people involved in sample-based music rely on a range of evaluative markers to distinguish between levels of expertise and/or quality, often echoing those used to distinguish between art and craft.

Musicians, industry executives, and the general public tend to differ radically in their views on configurable artistry—especially when it comes to the question of exceptionality, or genius. Nearly every configurable musician I spoke with rejected the concept of genius, opting instead to discuss "genius moments" or "genius works." The executives I interviewed were far more willing to accept and use this term—often in reference to musicians such as Sean "Diddy" Combs, whom (as I will discuss in the next chapter) is frequently cited as a negative example among some groups of sample-based musicians. On the other end of the spectrum, some survey respondents were unwilling to concede that configurable musicians can be artists at all, let alone geniuses.

Finally, much of the ambiguity and even resentment surrounding the question of configurable artistry can be seen in the commonly invoked trope of "some kid in his bedroom"—a cliché that, like some racial epithets, confronts categorical exclusion from the privileged class with a curious admixture of selfness and otherness, and of shame and pride.

6

Something Borrowed, Something New

The Original/Copy Binary

> Good artists copy. Great artists steal.
> Commonly attributed, in various forms, to T. S. Eliot,
> Pablo Picasso, and Igor Stravinksy

> I may be stealing a couple different songs but I'm still making a
> new song out of it.
> DJ Axel

The act of sampling, in which a bit of recorded sound or video is copied, transformed, and redeployed in a new setting and context, is still so strange and new that even the experts in the field can't find appropriate language to describe it. Questions of ethics, legality, and aesthetics aside, even the material and physical metaphors we use when discussing the subject seem to miss the mark. Sampling isn't "taking," because the source material is still available, intact, in its original form. It's not "borrowing," because the sampler doesn't ever return the work, except in a holistic sense. It's not "quoting," because (a) it's the mediated expression itself, not merely the ideas behind it, that's being used, and (b) the output often bears little or no resemblance to the input. Even the term "expression," which I use throughout this book, is something of a misnomer; etymologically, the word suggests the process of squeezing out something internal. Instead, sampling would more appropriately be termed "respiration"—the absorption, alteration, and exhalation of something external and ubiquitous.

These are not merely academic questions. How can we accuse or defend someone from a charge of theft, if we don't even know whether they've taken something? How can we make a claim to originality when we don't really know what constitutes copying? How can we understand what a DJ is saying if he or she is using someone else's voice? In short, questions of ethics, legality, and aesthetics hang on such definitional problems; we can't make sense of configurability without confronting them.

Unlike some of the modern framework's other binaries, which many of my interviewees had addressed only tacitly prior to our conversations, the original/copy binary has been a popular subject to address and debate among many DJs, producers, mashers, and remixers for years. And, as albums such as the X-Ecutioners' *Built from Scratch* (2002), the Kleptones' *Never Trust Originality* (2003), and the Streets' *Everything Is Borrowed* (2008) suggest, many musicians are well aware of the broader philosophical implications that come with the blurring and shading of the modern framework's lines.

This blurriness was evident in my interviews, as well. As Go Home Productions asked rhetorically, "What is theft, and what is borrowing? What is paying homage, and what is advancing? . . . I think I would find it hard to draw a definitive line."[1] Similarly, Matt Wand asked, "How far can you go with a quotation? Or can you just jump up in front of a Metallica gig, shout your name, and say, 'that was my gig'? . . . The problem is, it's hard to say where the line is, where it's the style of the person, and nothing to do with the samples."[2]

Echoing their comments about the other "gray areas" I discuss in previous chapters, many interviewees suggested that there are gradations of black and white separating the traditional binary between "original" and "copy." As Si Begg told me, "there's a scale, and on one end there's just ripping people off . . . then at the other end there is something that's such a creative use that you've moved a million miles away from it. . . . I guess most people are somewhere in the middle."[3] Yet, despite the many shades of gray they saw, many of the people I spoke with felt compelled to draw a "line in the sand," developing new discriminatory criteria to reinforce the eroding border between original and copy.

Configurability and Style

One of the most prevalent evaluative mechanisms I encountered was the notion that, through sheer force of will, a musician may inject enough of his or her own personality and vision into sample-based material to complete the alchemical transformation from "taking" to "making." This concept was reflected in the notion of personal "style" that Wand mentioned above, and in Go Home Productions' assertion that "personally, I try to add as much of myself as possible into the final thing that I do."[4]

Several interviewees made comparisons to stylistic originality in tactile arts or instrumental music. Tony Zeoli, for example, told me that a remix producer can have a "signature sound" that's so identifiable it's "like their handwriting."[5] Similarly, Strictly Kev told me that, among configurable musicians, "people have styles in the way they do things, in the same way that a guitarist would have. They've got something that's identifiable."[6] And Eric Kleptone told me, "you can recognize people's style [the same way you would] recognize someone's style on a saxophone or on a piano."[7]

But of what, exactly, does this elusive concept of style consist? In a context where most or all of the sonic material being employed originates in the work of another author and/or performer, how and when does a new voice emerge? In a context where conversations between the hand and the ear are mediated by conversion to machine language and back again, how can gesture or nuance remain?

Some interviewees cited the "selection and arrangement" processes I refer to in chapter 5 as the distinguishing factor between configurable musicians. In Si Begg's words, "which bits you use, how you arrange them, that's gonna be a personal style."[8] Similarly, DJ Adrian told me that an original stylist can be identified in part because he uses "source material that no one else touches." For instance, he said, "there's a new guy on the scene . . . and he's not all that great, you know, production-wise, yet. But he has been using crazy things like Klaus Nomi and Sigue Sigue Sputnik and things like that" as mash-up ingredients, which makes him instantly recognizable despite his relative inexperience and obscurity.[9]

In addition to selection and arrangement of materials, some configurable musicians I spoke with discussed specific production techniques, the resulting sonic artifacts, and the other ways in which a producer underscores the *transformation of the sample* as markers of personal style. For Jesse Gilbert, a Los Angeles-based sound designer, software developer, and sample-based experimental musician, the most important production element is the spatialization of sound: "Foregrounding and backgrounding and how you position the samples becomes all-important,

I think. How you create texture, how you create depth. How you understand something about the musicality of the sample."[10] Similarly, for DJ Paul V, stylistic originality lies in "the production value or what they were able to do maybe through filters or through processing, EQing, whatever, to alter the source material. . . . I think nuance is what the best mash-makers are able to have in their mixes."[11]

According to DJ Earworm, the *relationship between source materials* is the primary locus of stylistic originality for mash-ups, and this may relate to selection, arrangement, production, and even lyrical considerations:

> [Stylistic originality can reside] in the way that they think about words, or maybe the interplay of the words. You might recognize it in the song choices. The relationships between the songs. Some people prefer ironic relationships. Some people like puns, you know. Some people just want to have genre clash. The way that the arrangement might build or flow over time. You know, some people might bring in the instrumental as the vocal. . . . People might like echoes or cleansers or, you know, there's all these signatures where you can often hear the voice of the mash-up artist. . . . One thing is that the mash-up community isn't so large, that sometimes you can recognize just by, you know, song choice, even.[12]

Thus, for configurable musicians, stylistic originality can reside in the selection of source materials, the selection of samples from those materials, the temporal and spatial arrangement of samples, the transformative techniques applied to those samples, or the hermeneutic interplay between samples and techniques that characterize the work as a whole. And, as Si Begg observed, the richness and subtlety of style are augmented by the archivability and accessibility of the configurable technological infrastructure: "If there wasn't so much music to choose from, it'd be much less creative, but because there's this enormous wealth of music out there, that's kind of what makes it interesting."[13]

Of course, the concept of stylistic originality requires the existence of its opposite: the concept of stylistic *un*originality, or derivativeness. While most of the musicians I spoke with were unwilling to mention specific examples of derivative sample-based work, many acknowledged that it can be just as common as stylistic derivativeness in a traditional, instrumental musical environment. If originality in configurable music resides in the factors I mentioned above, such as selection, arrangement, and production, derivativeness resides there as well. As Strictly Kev complained, "I've heard people copying mixes that I did . . . the same tracks, the same cuts, done the same way."[14] Go Home Productions echoed this assessment, telling me that derivativeness in the mash-up aesthetic is something "you can tell in the artists they use [as source materials] but certainly in the way they put two artists together."[15]

Not everyone I spoke with agreed that stylistic originality and derivativeness could be heard in the work of sample-based musicians. As Osymyso told me, mash-ups may already be reaching the point where stylistic innovation—and therefore artistry—is virtually impossible: "There's only a small percentage of people in electronic music who you could definitely recognize once you put a track on. Kid Koala, DJ Shadow. . . . When it started and it was fresh, I think the idea was so new that you could identify who did it, and it was art. But now, it's so common, that you're just using a technique that already exists."[16]

For TradeMark G, stylistic originality may exist, but on a subtle enough level to elude the detection of the untrained ear: "Negativland has come to a point where they've got a certain style of editing, an original approach to choosing material . . . [but] as far as a level of recognizability or derivativeness that's obvious to someone that doesn't have my ear, I don't think there are many examples."[17] Eric Kleptone agreed, framing his observation in terms of the influential impact of a select few stylists: "people like John Oswald and Negativland have considerable amount of impact on a lot of people. And you can hear that."[18]

Relationship to Source Materials

Another approach to the original/copy binary that emerged from my conversations with configurable music practitioners is rooted in a set of procedural questions regarding how much of the source materials are used whole-cloth in the new work, how recognizable or obscure the source materials are in the mix, and the nature and degree of transformation that should be applied to a given sample by a producer in the process of creating a new work. TradeMark G succinctly summarized many of these considerations:

> It's frustrating as an artist that in the end, people don't remember your work; it's the source work that they'll remember. Add to that the [legal] risk that you take by sampling something recognizable. Add to that the popularity that you'll hopefully receive by sampling something well known and doing it in a good way. You're starting to take a real risk. This is the conundrum: how recognizable things do you sample? How far do you go with it? Do you leave the sample unmolested so it has

more power as an original source, do you fragment it so it's unrecognizable, adding my value but decreasing the risk of recognizability? . . . as an artist, it's a sort of tightrope that you walk.[19]

While nearly all of the configurable music practitioners I interviewed shared these same questions, there was no consensus regarding their answers. Some musicians told me that they believed the key to originality lay in the size and nature of the samples taken from the source recordings. As Go Home Productions argued, "I think it depends how much of the sample you've used. If you're just using a backing melody, and you add fifteen layers that are complementary, you've created something original." On the other hand, "If you've just taken a sample of the middle eight [bars] of a Beatles song and you start manipulating that, you're using a lot of the original sample."[20]

Even among musicians who applied this standard, it was acknowledged that there was no obvious bright line separating original from copy. In Osymyso's words: "What the cut-off is, I have no idea. It's very difficult to say you've created a new composition when the chunks are so big of the one you've taken it from. So maybe it has something to do with chunk size as well. It's when it stops being about the song the chunks are from, and starts being about the new song."[21]

A separate, but related, issue, is the question of how central a sample is to the new work it helps to create. As Go Home Productions told me, "there's a lot of artists who use samples intelligently, in combination with instruments, so the sample just adds to what they're doing, rather than them adding to the original sample. . . . It's how you use that sample that should determine whether it's really your tune."[22] He then cited Madonna's unoriginal use of ABBA in the song "Hung Up" as a negative example (just as Si Begg does in chapter 4, in our discussion of "creativity" as a criterion in making art/craft distinctions). Osymyso echoed GHP's argument, telling me, "if you move away from the original core melody and song structure, then it's a new composition."[23]

Recognizability vs. Obscurity of Source Material

The question of recognizability raised above by TradeMark G was one of the most contentious among interviewees; everyone I spoke to had a different take on the subject, and the opinions varied widely. Some people told me that the key to originality in sampling is total obscurity.

Go Home Productions, for instance, told me that "the clever sampling is when they take something and you still don't recognize it, in its remix form. It's how you disguise it."[24]

The aesthetic of obscurity is partly rooted in resistance to musical regulation. As Marc Geiger of WMA told me, "if you cut up the samples fine enough—and many artists I know have done—[it's] not recognized as a sample, and they get all the money because it's masked."[25] Other sample-based musicians and IP attorneys confirmed this observation, telling me that obscurity in sampling was a necessary strategy to avoid paying royalties, not for the purposes of keeping "all the money," but in order to eschew the permissioning and market influence inherent in commercial music—in effect, to eliminate money's role in music entirely. As Fred von Lohmann, a senior intellectual property attorney for the Electronic Frontier Foundation (EFF) told me, "the nature of mash-ups is being influenced by RepliCheck technology," a commercial brand of production software that "checks" CDs before they're replicated to make sure they don't contain unlicensed copyrighted material. Von Lohmann explained that "certain kinds of things escape its attention—pitch-bending, shorter samples, et cetera," and therefore these aesthetic decisions have become more prevalent among mash-up producers.[26]

Many of my interviewees rejected the aesthetic of obscurity in sample-based music. Some opted for what might be called an aesthetic of quasi-recognizability, in which originality is gauged by the audible transformation of sonic materials from their source state. As Strictly Kev told me, there are many options regarding "how you manipulate that sample. Are you going to play it straight, keep it in its original context, completely take it out of context, chop it up, rearrange it, use it literally as sound, take the whole melody?" Ideally, he said, "you can chop something up to the point where you know what the original is, but the melody is different."[27] V/VM also told me he "used to love taking full tracks and absolutely twisting them beyond belief and putting them out." However, he emphasized, it's always important to keep your source materials audible to the listener: "I think if you flip something so much, it might be recognizable but it's still your own. I guess the tipping point is, even though it's still recognizable—you could listen to it and be like, 'Oh yeah, that's "The Lady in Red" [by Chris De Burgh]— but where someone listening would say, "What the hell's happened to it? It sounds decrepit. Something horrible's happened to this file."[28]

As mattcatt told me, the aesthetic of quasi-recognizability is not only preferable, it's definitive in the case of "glitch" music—a subgenre of electronica characterized by sonic distortions resembling the accidental artifacts produced by faulty recording media and playback equipment. In his words, "glitch relies on the base track being remotely recognisable in order to justify the annihilation!"[29] Steinski also praised the aesthetic of quasi-recognizability, telling me that for him, "original" configurable music is "still based in actual music—you can hear drummers drumming, bass players playing, people singing, but it's kind of altered—so it's not like techno, or something that's completely synthetically-based."[30] In other words, Steinski argues that larger, more recognizable samples actually produce *more original* music than songs based on smaller, less recognizable ones.

As with the aesthetic of obscurity, the aesthetic of semirecognizability has some roots in strategic necessity. As Osymyso explained to me, allowing listeners to recognize some or all of a work's source materials can make it more accessible to them, paradoxically allowing the producer to take greater aesthetic liberties: "If you want to get people to listen to something that's slightly more unusual, abstract or difficult, you put something recognizable that they like in there and you've kind of won half the battle—because it's instantly recognizable, they're going to like it."[31]

Interestingly, Hosh Gureli of Sony/BMG made an argument parallel to Osymyso's, but with a market-oriented twist. Recognizable samples are valuable tools in a commercial producer's arsenal, he told me, because they allow music sellers to take advantage of consumers' preexisting affinities with the source materials. In his words, "'when you try to make a hit record, you try to take—not in all cases, but in the rhythmic format, which is 'Top 40' right now, with few exceptions—that when you put samples into music, it insures more likelihood of a hit."[32] Similarly, Pete Ganbarg of Atlantic Records told me: "Certain artists are going to use samples, replays, interpolations, stuff like that to help gain a wider audience. . . . For me, sampling is a great way to take something familiar and create something new out of it because familiarity is something that people are comfortable with. So if you're able to take an older record and use it to create something new so that more people will listen to, enjoy and ultimately buy your music, I'm all for it. Why not?"[33]

Other interviewees told me they believe that sample recognizability isn't simply permissible in configurable music, it is positively paramount. As DJ Adrian explained, "I really appreciate the beauty—[Mysterious] D and I both do—of maintaining sort of the integrity of the original song and adding something brand new to it, i.e., a brand new vocal [sample], and manipulating it into a completely different song."[34] Some survey respondents shared this notion that sample-based music incurs an ethical debt to the sampler, on behalf of the sampled. As one New York man in his twenties wrote, "as long as you acknowledge the original creator of item and do justice to his work I think remixes and mashups should be acceptable [sic]."

This premise that originality can be achieved, not by obscuring a song's sources, but by celebrating them, is one aesthetic factor that sets mash-ups aside from most other forms of sample-based music. DJ Adrian consciously acknowledged this, telling me that "if it gets glitched out beyond belief, where it's unrecognizable from its source material, then you're starting to get more into a remix [than a mash-up style]."[35]

DJ Paul V echoed DJ Adrian's emphasis on recognizability as an essential element of the mash-up style, explaining that the aesthetic language of the mash-up is premised on the interplay between two or more known variables: "if I hear a new mash-up of two tracks I've never heard before, I'm less interested. Because that takes twice as much time to know what the tracks are. It kind of takes away the discovery of how it's different than how I knew it."[36]

Strictly Kev told me that this emphasis on recognizability was the very factor that interested him in mash-ups in the first place: "Stealing big samples, that was one of the things that attracted me to it, really. That was one of the things that amazed me about mash-ups, is that there were people who were so untouchable that were just being brazenly sampled."[37] In other words, the onus to protect the "integrity of the original," as described by DJ Adrian, is fundamentally inseparable from Strictly Kev's desire to touch the untouchable, erasing the boundaries dividing amateur from professional and producer from consumer, with one fell cut-and-paste.

Within the mash-up aesthetic, then, the only way to be original is to acknowledge one's debts to others. Furthermore, to *oppose* or *obscure* the sampling of a song is paradoxically tantamount to sullying its "integrity." The tacit assumption here is that the appearance of creation ex nihilo is a flat-out lie, by definition. As Matt Wand summed it up: "Everything is derivative. It's just, really, if you think something is stylistically original, you're not familiar with the sources of derivation. . . . It's really just a question of how many strands, how many layers there are to the derivation."[38]

Significantly, this celebration of "brazen" sampling, and elevation of sample recognizability to the level of moral necessity, do not constitute carte blanche for configurable music producers. If recognizability is essential to originality, it doesn't necessarily ensure it, either. In chapter 5, I quote Hosh Gureli and Pete Ganbarg of Pure Tone Music calling Sean "Diddy" Combs a "genius" of configurable music—in part, for the brazenness of his samples, especially in the case of "I'll Be Missing You," his tribute to the late Biggie Smalls, featuring samples from the Police.

Although I never mentioned Diddy in my questions, however, a number of the mash-up producers I interviewed cited him—and "I'll Be Missing You" in particular—as derivative or downright dishonest for, as Go Home Productions described it, simply "taking the opening riff from "Every Breath You Take" and slapping a hip-hop beat under it."[39] Osymyso put it the most concisely, explaining that "I'll Be Missing You" "isn't in any way a new song. You'd say, 'that is someone rapping over the Police.' It's a very difficult thing to define, but the Puff Daddy stuff is soulless. It's just not clever."[40]

Mash-ups' emphasis on recognizability of sources is not solely an aesthetic decision, nor one premised entirely on the ethic of acknowledging one's own influences. According to many of the producers I spoke to, mash-ups have an added function, analogous to the relationship of blogs to mainstream media: they keep commercial music honest, by exposing the aesthetic debts and appropriations of mainstream pop. As DJ Paul V told me, "people do that all the time. They'll make a mash-up out of someone being inspired by something that came before. I mean, the 'Dean Gray' album [a 2005 mash-up album by Party Ben and team9, mixing tracks from Green Day's American Idiot with classic songs by artists such as Smokey Robinson, Aerosmith, and U2] is twelve tracks of that."[41] DJ Adrian told me that such influence policing is one of the highest aims to which a mash-up producer can aspire: "A great mash-up . . . makes you realize that all Western music is kind of the same."[42]

This critical aspect of the mash-up aesthetic can sometimes be missed entirely by its own targets. As Matt Wand recounted to me, producer Soulwax created a mash-up of Kylie Minogue's contemporary club track "Can't Get You Out of My Head" with New Order's classic "Blue Monday" in 2002. The songs are sufficiently similar that the result sounded, in Wand's estimation, "kind of redundant." The track became popular, though, receiving widespread radio airplay, and Minogue eventually added a live version of the mash-up to her touring act. This poses a troubling challenge to the mash-up ethic, as Wand explained to me: "What happens when people don't pick up on pieces being totally derivative? The masher put them together to show that point, but she missed the critical point of it . . . it was just a superimposition to kind of show how derivative the thing was."[43]

Sampling, Ethics, and Copyright

The ambiguity of the original/copy binary in the context of configurable music also has significant implications for questions of ethics and law. What debt does a sample-based artist owe to those being sampled, and what mechanisms can we use to judge the relative claims each has to "ownership" of the resulting configurable music product? There are no clear answers to these questions, from either an ethical or legal vantage point.

Just as many of the survey respondents argued that configurable music is intrinsically unoriginal, many also suggested that it is intrinsically unethical. As one Alabama woman in her forties wrote, "I feel any original material belongs to owner and their rights. [sic] Anything copied from it is not right." Another respondent, a California man in his fifties, argued against the ethicality of sampling as a *social* mandate: "Artists should learn to create for themselves. We are in dire need of NEW music. Go to school and learn how to use YOUR brain to create something nEW [sic]." Another respondent from Texas in his forties argued that legal sanctions against sampling amount to a form of social sanctioning: "Let us praise the people that produce original material and make those who can't pay for there [sic] whimsy."

Interestingly, some configurable music practitioners—mostly those involved in the commercial music industry to some degree—echoed the notion that unpermissioned sampling amounts to a breach of ethics. DJ Axel (a record label executive by day), for instance, told me, "the original composition of actually coming up with an original bass line and an original drum beat and an original hook—I'm stealing that. . . . Somebody composed the song. And I stole it."[44] Similarly, Dan "The Automator" Nakamura, one of the world's most famous and successful commercial music producers, told an interviewer that sampling requires a stricter ethical code than quoting: "I would say, as a writer, if somebody quotes a couple of paragraphs of mine in the context of something larger, then I don't really have the right to say anything about it. All literature and all writing is built on that. . . . When it's a recording, [however], it could be the guy's voice. Maybe he doesn't want to lend his voice to this project, so I respect that side of it."[45] Interestingly, Nakamura's double standard is echoed in contemporary sampling case law, as I'll discuss further shortly.

If sampling was deemed unethical by many survey respondents and interviewees, it had its proponents as well. As one Connecticut man in his twenties argued, the development of configurable music is inevitable and therefore permissible: "remixes and mashups are part of evolution." Another Louisiana man in his thirties was so supportive of configurable music that he used all capitals in his written response: "I LOVE TO HEAR OLD MUSIC RE-USED. IT IS GREAT!" Of course, most of the configurable musicians I spoke with believed that their behavior was ethical. Si Begg echoed a common sentiment—that sample-based music is often *more original* than instrumental music, and that the law is unfair for failing to recognize this fact. As he lamented about contemporary pop band Franz Ferdinand, "they're very much copying the style, the sound, even the image of these bands [from the '80s], but you'll never get sued for doing that."[46]

Some people reported qualified support for the ethicality of configurable music. One idea that surfaced several times was the notion that, as a New Hampshire woman in her twenties wrote, "If you are going to create a remix it should be better than the original." A Minnesota man in his fifties echoed this sentiment, writing, "Sometimes remixes are better than the original." However, configurable musicians did not tend to share the belief that this should be an ethical threshold—mostly, because they believed the threshold was too high. As Strictly Kev told me, "occasionally, you'll get [a remix] that's better than the original, but that's pretty rare."[47]

Another ethical qualifier that emerged in my conversations with configurable musicians was the notion that sampling is ethical as long as the sampler acknowledges and pays his debt to the sampled artist. They reported that, paradoxically, current copyright laws *prevent* them from doing so, by forcing sample-based artists to choose between unaffordable, untenable, or unobtainable licenses and underground, noncommercial distribution. As DJ Earworm told me, "You know, I would love to give it, you know, to be able to sell my mash-ups. And get some money to the people who deserve it. I mean like the artists mashed up. And keep a little for myself."[48] Osymyso told me he accepts the notion of sample licensing in theory, but thinks it hasn't been successful in practice: "I think if you take something like that, you should come to an agreement with the person who owns the copyright, pay them their due. But I think the copyright owners have taken it way too far."[49] Significantly, payment was not the only kind of duty sample-based musicians reported having to their sources. As Si Begg told me, "I think it's important to give people credit. I think, in some ways, that's even more important than the money."[50]

The legal landscape for configurable music is no less murky than the ethical one; in fact, a comprehensive analysis of the situation would require a book-length treatment of its own.[51] I will, however, briefly review some of the legal concepts and decisions bearing on the question of originality.

Currently, one of the more ambiguous aspects of music copyright law regards the question of whether there should be a de minimis defense for sampling—in other words, whether samples can be small enough in size to no longer constitute copies, in the sense of violating the reproduction rights of the works they are taken from (and therefore, to qualify as new or original works). There is a common misperception—cited by some interviewees and survey respondents—that a "three-second law" (or a five- or ten-second law) sets a legal de minimis threshold. In actuality, there is no legislation addressing this question, and the most recent case law is confusing at best, and self-contradictory at worst.

Recorded music is accorded two copyrights: one for the sound recording (the "master" copyright), and one for the composition (the "publishing" copyright). According to two relatively recent court cases, there is a valid de minimis defense for samplers relating to the publishing copyright, but no de minimis protection relating to the master copyright.

In the first case, known as *Newton v. Diamond*, the hip-hop band Beastie Boys used a six-second sample of a James Newton song, consisting of three notes played on the flute using a distinctive "multiphonics" technique. Although they had obtained a license for the master copyright, they had failed to do so for the publishing right. Newton sued, claiming infringement, but the Court found for the defendants, arguing that "when viewed in relation to Newton's composition as a whole, the sampled portion is neither quantitatively nor qualitatively significant."[52]

In the second case, known as *Bridgeport v. Dimension*, hip-hop group N.W.A. sampled a two-second guitar riff from a Funkadelic song, putting it through many of the detuning and editing processes that I discuss above as marks of stylistic originality within the configurable music community. However, because they had not acquired a license from the owner of the master rights, N.W.A. were found guilty of infringement. As the Court wrote in its decision, de minimis standards did not apply;

instead, there was an absolute edict against unpermissioned use of a phono recording: "Get a license or do not sample. We do not see this as stifling creativity in any significant way."[53]

Several intellectual property attorneys told me they disagreed with the *Bridgeport* decision. In Jennifer Urban's words, it was "a whacked-out decision . . . because Congress is the body that is able to decide what the appropriate scope is. Not the Court."[54] Similarly, Bob Clarida told me that he thought the decision was just "flat out wrong. You know, the idea that the de minimis doctrine somehow does not apply to sound recordings I just think is flat wrong. . . . I think at that point, you're not copying somebody else's expression."[55] Ron Bienstock, on the other hand, supports the *Bridgeport* decision, arguing that sample length is not a sufficiently consistent gauge of originality to merit legal support for a de minimis standard. In his words, the most original part of a song "may just be a five, six note phrase. All of a sudden so you say you can take that? What becomes de minimis? I think once you've sampled you've sampled."[56] TradeMark G agreed with Bienstock's negative assessment of sample length as an arbiter of originality (if not necessarily with his support of *Bridgeport*'s conclusions): "The threshold [for originality] changes depending on what kind of sample you're talking about. Don't bother trying to put a time frame on to it . . . there's no point in trying to do that."[57]

Despite the legal implications of the *Bridgeport* ruling, several interviewees told me that de facto de minimis standards often apply. As I mention above, Marc Geiger told me, "if you cut of the samples fine enough—and many artists I know have done—[it's] not recognized as a sample and they get all the money."[58] Attorney and former techno producer Gary Adelman echoed Geiger's observation, but offered a more nuanced analysis of the pros and cons associated with this procedural loophole: "A lot of the elements of especially techno and electronic music are just, you know, you can't pinpoint where they came from. It's just too difficult. . . . If you know anything about electronic dance music, you know that they're the worst offenders of sampling that there is. So god knows where they got it from. Most electronic dance artists are happy just to get their music played and sold. They're not really worrying about, you know who's using it. 'Cause they're the worst offenders."[59]

In other words, configurable musicians who chop up their samples finely enough can elude regulatory oversight and associated expenses, but by the same token, it's harder to prevent other configurable musicians from using their work in an uncredited fashion, and nearly impossible to produce a commercially viable product.

Other legal opinions and concepts can be applied to the question of originality in the context of configurable music, as well. Bob Clarida cited three additional cases that bear directly on the subject: *Feist v. Rural Telephone Service*[60] (briefly discussed above), which "would elevate the appreciation of the level of authorship in a hip-hop record" because of its emphasis on the copyrightability of selection and arrangement; *Campbell v. Acuff Rose*,[61] which introduces the concept of "transformative use" as an element of "fair use" defenses against copyright infringement; and *Amsinck v. Columbia*,[62] which argues that the threshold for infringing use of a copyrighted work in another work should be market harm (e.g., diminished sales). Although all three of these decisions offer viable arguments recognizing the originality of *some* sample-based works, none of them loom nearly as large as *Bridgeport*'s absolute prohibition against unlicensed uses of recorded materials in influencing the decisions of artists, music distribution companies, and judges in the current sampling environment.[63]

Although this may seem like an intractable situation, Gary Adelman (who was forty years old at the time of our interview) told me that he feels the laws will eventually "evolve" to reflect the subtleties of perspective reflected in my interviews with configurable music practitioners—largely because of generational shifts in the composition of the judiciary. In his words:

> As [younger people] start becoming judges and understanding digital technology and understanding sampling in a different way than people that are fifty-five now do, I think that there's going to be more cases decided on the side of the sampler . . . and finding that there's more and more . . . for lack of a better word, "fair use" of these samples. Because, look, you can take three notes from anybody and you could twist it, turn it, reverse it, you know, and it doesn't sound a bit like the original. But if some forensic music guy can go in and undo it all and he can prove that that's sampling, well, why should that be sampling? The guy obviously created something out of something else. So why should that be sampling? And I think that people of my generation, when we become judges, are going to go in that direction and say that's not sampling. But currently it is.[64]

Can Configurable Music Be Unique?

A final aspect of the original/copy dichotomy that bears investigating in the context of configurable music practices is the question of uniqueness.

In the absence of a concrete original work, does digital reproduction still dilute the perception of a work's value? How is scarcity defined and interpreted in a medium based on a limitless stream of ones and zeroes? Does the increasing intangibility of expression continue to find its counterweight in the fetishization of the author or the physical object? Does the hierarchy of uniqueness still hold sway, in either its traditional or inverted form? As with my other questions, interviewees offered a range of reactions and responses on these subjects.

A significant number of interviewees told me that the concept of uniqueness couldn't—or shouldn't—be applied to configurable music. Eric Kleptone put it the most bluntly, telling me, "to hell with uniqueness."[65] Matt Wand told me that the concept of uniqueness doesn't make sense given the mechanics of configurable music: "I guess I'd have to say that uniqueness is irrelevant in terms of sampling . . . people have tried to impose uniqueness on it, but you kind of have to give up."[66] Similarly, Si Begg told me that, with digital music, "there's no real product. It's just a bunch of zeroes and ones at the end of the day, and [they're] infinitely reproduced." He added, however, "I don't view that as a problem, really. That's fine."[67]

Marc Geiger also linked configurable technologies to a shift in the value proposition associated with uniqueness—but from an economic, music industry perspective: "My take on [uniqueness] is that it's purely qualitative. If there's a degradation in quality or a bootleg album . . . that would be the corresponding drop in value. [But] the Internet blew it all apart [because] there's no degradation in quality."[68] In other words, Geiger argues that the entire conceit underpinning the hierarchy of uniqueness—and therefore the economics and regulation of music distribution—has become untenable in the age of "perfect,"[69] infinite reproduction of information.

Some configurable musicians offered more socially oriented analyses. Closely echoing Walter Benjamin's prizing of the democratization of aesthetics over "aura,"[70] V/VM told me: "I don't think it's very important for sample-based music to be unique. I think it's very important for a lot of people to be able to listen to it, because it's still very marginalized."[71] And echoing Thomas Jefferson's oft-quoted argument that "he who receives an idea from me, receives instruction himself without lessening mine,"[72] Osymyso told me that "the originality of something isn't diluted with copying."[73]

TradeMark G took a historical perspective, suggesting that configurable technologies are simply returning the status of music to its original, precommodified state. In his words, music is "a time-based art, which produces no original. Even back before computers, you still didn't have an original for a song you'd make—you could perform it, or write it out, but neither is *really* the original."[74] In other words, the notion of a unique musical product was simply a convenient fiction aiding commerce and abetted by the mechanics of preconfigurable capture, storage, and distribution technologies.

Despite the prevalence of the "to hell with uniqueness" sentiment among my interviewees, there was some ambivalence about relinquishing the concept altogether, and some interesting strategies for *preserving* uniqueness in the face of its obsolescence. These sentiments are reflected in Mysterious D's comment that "we're actually playing with stuff that's already reproduced a million times. And, again, that's where the live thing comes in handy . . . I do think that, you know, art in its original form should have more value, you know. And it should continue to be valuable."[75]

This notion that live performance "comes in handy" as a substitute for the uniqueness of a recorded music artifact, and helps to preserve the value of music as a product, was echoed by many of the configurable musicians I spoke with. As DJ Earworm told me, "I think the way that generally musicians capitalize on the uniqueness, not so much by autographs, you know, it's their concerts. . . . Many mash-up artists are DJs as well. And you go to the live performance and you get that uniqueness." However, this is not simply an abstract concern for sample-based musicians. If uniqueness is a component of value in a commercial context, then it is also a key to remuneration. As Earworm explained further, live performance is "the only way that a mash-up can really make money, unless they do [commercial] productions . . . the value's always in the uniqueness. So that's why I'm DJing."[76]

One of the challenges for configurable music in a live context is how to communicate the uniqueness of the event to an audience. This is a problem, because the practice of producing mash-ups or remixes can be less than dynamic to watch or to contemplate; as V/VM told me, "people think all you have to do is press buttons."[77] Consequently, configurable musicians must strategically emphasize the now-ness of their performances by altering their musical praxes. As Osymyso told me, he's "currently trying to figure out a way of creating a performance so when people are attending the performance they are aware that that moment is a one-off, that you can't download a performance. . . . It's a unique moment, and ideally you're doing something that happens only once."[78]

Figure 8: TradeMark G and his assistant spinning the "Wheel of Mash."

One of the most interesting strategies I encountered in my research was TradeMark G's. When he performs with the Evolution Control Committee, part of his act involves bringing audience members onstage to spin the "Wheel of Mash"—a ramshackle, six-foot device similar to the one spun by contestants on television's *Wheel of Fortune* (fig. 8). The device has an inner wheel and an outer wheel, both spinning on the same axis, each of which contains the names of six different recording artists. When the two wheels are spun, the pointer identifies one of thirty-six possible combinations, which TradeMark G then mashes together on the spot. Despite the somewhat contrived nature of this spectacle, he told me, it's a useful tool for communicating the value of live performances to an audience, because "the nuances of it are all unique. There will never be that combination again."[79]

Another strategy some configurable musicians reported for preserving the uniqueness of music in a configurable context was the notion of limited distribution—essentially, imposing artificial scarcity on an infinitely reproducible resource. Strictly Kev told me that, paradoxically, this strategy is inherent to much configurable music because it isn't released through mainstream channels, and addresses a niche audience. In fact, he argued, this is a fundamental aspect of the mash-up ethic: "You're taking something mass produced and boiling it down into something that's incredibly unique, that will then be redistributed to a smaller audience."[80]

DJ Adrian and Mysterious D echoed this sentiment, and debated its implications in greater detail:

> *DJ Adrian:* If it's harder to get ultimately—I mean, because there's a limited amount, then there's a more perceived value. And with mash-ups, because they're illegal, you can't go through your regular distribution channels . . .
>
> *Mysterious D:* Yeah, some songs are up for one day. And maybe only, let's say, ten people downloaded it. Probably more than that. But say a hundred or two hundred or five hundred out of a billion people. It becomes, then, that song becomes limited and a little bit of piece of artwork because you can't get it again.
>
> *DJ Adrian:* And maybe you assign more value to it because of that. You know, like for instance the *Dean Gray* album . . . it got a cease and desist order. . . . So, you know, does the value of it go up because it was harder to get?
>
> *Mysterious D:* Yeah.
>
> *DJ Adrian:* Even though it's free and it's there's a million copies of it. Yeah.[81]

In other words, according to DJ Adrian and Mysterious D, illegality produces scarcity, which produces perceived value. This suggests that the inverted hierarchy of uniqueness is actually created and sustained by musical regulation—specifically, by current copyright laws, which prevent most mash-ups from being distributed via mainstream commercial channels.

Not every configurable musician I spoke with agreed that artificially imposed scarcity is meaningful or even possible in a configurable music context. As Matt Wand told me, "if someone releases something that's an edition of fifty CD-Rs, it doesn't make that much difference, does it, because someone can easily copy that. . . . I don't really think very much about those kinds of things." Wand added that such matters had been more important to him "in the past, when I ran a label"[82]—further suggesting that questions of uniqueness and value are often primarily important for commercial, rather than aesthetic, reasons.

If limited distribution of the finished product was one strategy for uniqueness reported by configurable musicians, limited access to source materials was another. As Matt Wand told me, "that might be the answer to the question of finding something unique—is the land-rush for ancient, crusty 7-inches [a vinyl record format] or albums that there was just, like, 100 ever made, so no one else can have that sample. You're the first to the motherlode."[83] Similarly, Strictly Kev told me, "it's the essence of DJ culture really—finding things that no one else had . . . you're looking for that thing that's not mass-produced, that hardly anyone's got."[84] These sentiments reflect a long tradition in the hip-hop and DJ communities of "digging in the crates," which has been discussed extensively by J. G. Schloss[85] and others.

While this ethic of finding rare samples from dusty and discarded vinyl records makes sense in the context of configurable music genres such as hip-hop or techno, it makes less sense in the mash-up community. As I discuss above, mash-ups are premised on the notion of *recognizability* and *critique of pop culture*—there's no sense in mashing together samples no one's ever heard before. This hasn't stopped the mash-up community from reposing value in unique source materials; rather than rare vinyl samples, they have shifted their focus to original master recordings of popular songs.

Most mash-ups are made using instrumental tracks and a capella vocals digitally extracted from commercial releases; although the extraction techniques have become increasingly sophisticated, the results still typically bear the sonic artifacts of the process, diminishing the sound quality and marring the purity of aesthetic intent. Sometimes, as with the case of Jay-Z's *The Black Album*, which DJ Danger Mouse used to make the *The Grey Album*, a capella vocals are made available by the record label, but these are broadly accessible, and confer less value on the resulting mash-up than would a digitally extracted vocal.

On rare occasions, however, a mash-up producer may gain exclusive access to master recordings, with or without the permission of the recording artist or record label that owns them. In these cases, the masher is able to produce a mash-up that not only sounds *better* than anyone else's could, but may actually be *impossible to produce* without such access. As DJ Earworm explained it: "The material I'm using is, you know, these MP3s and even CDs and stuff that's just floating around everywhere. That doesn't have any uniqueness to it. I mean, if I was taking the master tapes, that's different. Because then I'd be able to create this amazing master that was, you know, beyond the quality that anyone else could do."[86]

Go Home Productions has actually obtained access to master tapes for some popular recordings, after the copyright owners heard his unlicensed, digitally extracted mash-ups and decided to allow him to reproduce his work in higher quality for commercial release. While this allowed him to realize his aesthetic vision more fully, it also posed something of a double-edged sword; the exchange typically involves a quid pro quo, in which the masher may be asked to make aesthetic decisions he wouldn't make on his own. In GHP's words: "When I did *Rapture Riders*—the Doors with Blondie—it was a vocal take that only had the drums in it, but they were low enough so I could disguise it. But it was so much easier when the Doors guys gave me the master tapes, so I could just have the vocals. But some of these record companies will not give you these parts unless you're working for them, so you have to do the best you can do, you know?"[87]

Similarly, Matt Wand told me that while he loves working with master tapes for aesthetic reasons, sanctioned access actually narrows the range of available aesthetic possibilities. In his words, "the problem with the sanctioned remix is it cuts off the idea that you can use anything else—the whole world of sampled music—because if you use other copyrighted material, the label that sanctioned the remix doesn't want to be sued by another group."[88]

This ambivalence about the benefits of label-sanctioned access to master tapes was echoed in my conversations with configurable musicians about the sanctioned or unsanctioned uses of samples in general. As Si Begg told me, "if I do sample something, I don't think 'Oh, am I allowed to use this or not?' But when I have the finished product, then, yeah, I do have to think, 'Is anyone going to want to release this . . . and does this render it unsalable in a way?'"[89]

Some configurable musicians told me that the unsanctioned nature of the idiom was part of what initially appealed to them—after all, terms like "bootleg" do carry an air of illegitimacy. This minor thrill of the forbidden is hardly enough of an incentive to keep producers engaged. As TradeMark G told me, "there is a certain fun of sampling something without permission, knowing that you could get in trouble for it. But that's a juvenile delinquent feeling that I got over a while ago."[90] Most of the musicians I spoke with reported a general lack of concern regarding the question of sanctioning, except as a practical matter related to aesthetic or remunerative opportunities, as discussed above. V/VM summed this attitude up best: "I've never had permission to remix anything. I've never looked to have permission. It's not important to me—if I want to do something, I'll do it."[91]

A concept closely associated with the strategies of limited distribution and rare source materials, and the question of sanctioned distribution, is the fetishization of the physical recording artifact itself. As Matt Wand told me, the time-honored strategy of limited physical releases has been employed successfully in some cases as an antidote to the loss of perceived market value associated with digitization: "I see people releasing DVD editions of five because they want a collector to pay £2,000. If the collector wants to pay for it, that's good. And if an artist needs to find some way to create a market for himself, it makes sense."[92] Recent market experiments have borne this out; for instance, despite releasing their 2008 album *Ghosts I–IV* freely and under a Creative Commons license, Nine Inch Nails sold out all 2,500 copies of an "Ultra-Deluxe Limited Edition" package of the same songs, priced at $300 apiece, in three days.[93]

Not all interviewees were so sanguine about this model—at least, over the longer term. Many predicted that the perceived uniqueness and value of such objects will continue to diminish as configurable culture becomes normative. As V/VM told me, "I like a physical object in addition to a virtual one. I'm still of that generation where I like to have something in my hand. But I think for younger people it's not as important—all they want is the music."[94] Hosh Gureli of Sony/BMG shared this sentiment: "I can touch it, I can feel it, I can listen to it, I can look at it, great. . . . But guess what—that paradigm is changing, too. Music now, there's only one thing you're going to be able to do with it—and that's listen to it." While he said he's resolved to adjusting to this change professionally, Gureli told me he also regrets it. In his words, "music is just files now. And that's a little sad, because . . . I don't want to use the word 'earthy-crunchy,' but you can smell vinyl. Even a CD, you can hold it in your hand."[95]

Not everyone bemoaned the waning of the fetishization of physical products. Echoing Pierre Bourdieu's argument about commodity consumption as a mark of class distinction,[96] Eric Kleptone told me, "I would be glad to see that go out the door. Because it's, I mean, it's incredibly fake. I don't think it adds any value other than a kind of fake social standing for people to collect these sorts of things." To Kleptone, the absence of uniqueness, and the resulting incapacity of music to be used as an instrument of commercialism, is one of the main benefits of working in the mash-up idiom. In his words:

> I think people are being fooled, for the most part. You know, they're getting a false sense of worth out of their art products. I think something that is given for free and is listened to as a free product or something, you know, there is no way that you can misinterpret the intentions behind it. And I think that is a really important facet, particularly, of the way the mash-ups and so forth [have] gone online—is, there is no commercial intent really behind it. Although, you know, we

all want to make a living. . . . I think that that's a very important factor in when the audience listens to it. They're not being sold something. So they listen to it with more open ears.[97]

Conclusion

Despite the many shades of gray emerging between the poles of the modern framework's original/copy binary, stylistic originality remains a vital concern for many configurable musicians. Markers of originality include selection and arrangement of source materials, temporal and spatial arrangement of sonic materials, transformative technique, and overarching compositional and organizational sensibility. Similarly, configurable music can be stylistically derivative if it fails to differentiate itself adequately according to any of these criteria.

Configurable musicians also invest a great deal of significance in the relationship of their work to the material they sample. Strategic recognizability, unrecognizability, and quasi-recognizability of source materials each carry generic, stylistic, aesthetic, ethical, legal, and economic concerns, and all of these factors are inextricably linked to one another. While standards differ broadly between configurable musicians, some concerns—such as doing justice to sources and the onus to innovate—remain fairly consistent among them.

Unfortunately, these rich emerging aesthetic and ethical conventions are not matched by any similar degree of subtlety in our legal treatment of sample-based production. Although some standards have emerged from case law that could theoretically be brought to bear on configurable production, concepts such as "transformative use" and "creative selection and arrangement" are likely to be overshadowed by the *Bridgeport* ruling, which asserted that there is no de minimis threshold for sample length, below which unsanctioned use is permissible. The net result is that much configurable music is structurally excluded from the marketplace, and many musicians are forced to violate their own ethical mandates to acknowledge their creative debts, for fear of incurring financial ones.

Finally, although some configurable musicians believe that concerns over uniqueness and the fetishization of material objects are a thing of the past, others have developed a range of novel solutions for reinjecting scarcity, materiality, and immediacy into their productions and performances. These strategies range from limited-edition downloads to live, onstage antics reminiscent of game shows and carnivals. And, as I discuss further in chapter 7, these questions take on an added dimension of significance when brought to bear on the fourth foundational principle of the modern framework—the composition/performance binary.

7

Live from a
Hard Drive

The Composition/Performance Binary

> "We're the only bar in the area, you know, has a strictly electronic music policy. Come on around Saturdays, starting midnight we have your Sinewave Session, that's a live get-together, fellas come in just to jam from all over the state, San Jose, Santa Barbara, San Diego—"
>
> "Live?" Metzger said, "Electronic music, live?"
>
> "They put it on the tape, here, live, fella . . ."
>
> Thomas Pynchon, *The Crying of Lot 49*

> I ain't fucking Beethoven, but I'm doing my thing.
>
> DJ Drama

As with the other foundations of the modern framework I have discussed, the distinction between composition and performance has never been much more than a convenient fiction, and an often uneasy one, at best. The requirement that copyrightable works be ensconced in a "fixed, tangible medium," for instance, summarily consigns collective and/or improvised music to the inferior sphere of mere performance, while elevating the Romantic ideal of the sole composer, laboring in solitude at his or her sheaf of staff paper.

As other scholars have observed, this inherent bias helps to reinforce existing social inequities, disenfranchising musicians in oral and communal music traditions from American blues to Melanesian folk songs.[1]

It also structurally excludes the majority of working musicians from economic or reputational ownership of the work they produce, by consigning them to the role of mere "sidemen," or "interpreters."[2] Occasionally, certain musical works are elevated from "performance" to "composition" status, as when Charlie Parker's saxophone improvisations are painstakingly notated, ghost note by ghost note, then arranged and performed by bands like Supersax. Yet these rare exceptions only underscore the general rule, namely, a legally enforced musical division of labor.

Flawed though it is, this system was easier to justify and police in an age when the mechanics of composition and performance were more obviously separate. Pen and paper bear little resemblance to bow and fiddle, and a printed score can be put into an envelope and mailed to the copyright registry, while mere sound waves cannot (especially before the 1972 introduction of phono recording copyrights).

This is precisely why the distinction between performance and composition has become increasingly ambiguous in the age of configurable music. Can composition precede expression when a DJ is juggling beats between two vinyl platters, or dropping samples and effects into Ableton Live or another software program? Does a sequencer constitute a score, or an instrument? What would it mean for one configurable musician to "cover" or "perform" the work of another? These concepts, so integral to our traditional understanding of the division of labor in musical production, become elusive and slippery when we try to apply them to sample-based musical practices.

Is DJing Composing or Performing?

Many of my interviewees acknowledged that they had difficulty making such distinctions in the context of their own behaviors. As Si Begg told me, "there's many tunes in which those kinds of rules just don't apply any more. And certainly with the performance side of things, it does get very blurry with computers. What's performance and what's just playing back stuff? It does get quite tricky."[3] Similarly, DJ Axel said he had trouble parsing performance from composition at all: "If we're gonna consider that using ProTools [sound editing and sequencing software] is a performance, and it's its own instrument, and you're manipulating samples to put them in a way that makes a song, that's the composition part of it. Then composition and performance are kind of the same thing. So, yeah, it's simultaneous."[4] Tony Zeoli shared this sentiment as well, telling me, "I don't think that you can separate the two. . . . If you're blending [tracks] or if you're mixing . . . then you're composing a whole new work at that time."[5]

This ambiguity makes it especially difficult for configurable music practitioners to describe their own roles within the process of music creation. Si Begg told me he's "sometimes a composer. Sometimes more of a producer than a composer. But that's all composition, really. It's just not always composing melodies. It's more arranging noise."[6] Similarly, in speaking of his well-known work "Raiding the 20th Century" (released under the name DJ Food), Strictly Kev told me: "I wouldn't say I composed it. I'd say I arranged it. I see myself as an editor. I don't see myself as a musician or composer. I collect things. I take them apart, and I put them back together. That's how I see my role. I would say I'm a producer or arranger. Maybe I am all of these things."[7]

When I asked DJ Axel how he would describe his role in musical creation, he initially resisted calling himself a composer as well—largely because, as a music industry executive in charge of licensing songs, he is legally and procedurally required to deny that appellation to other configurable musicians who lack copyright permission and control over their works. However, he eventually added it to his long list of self-applied titles:

> *DJ Axel:* Producer, engineer, arranger and performer, definitely. Conductor, like Quincy Jones, not actually playing an instrument. Conducting an orchestra definitely. It's the composer part [that's difficult to address] and it's hard to extract myself from the fact that I work in this industry. You know. It's hard to—because I deal with this stuff every day. So it's hard to, like, not think about that. The fact that it is already an existing composition that I'm using. Yeah, so I might draw the line there actually.
>
> *Aram:* And say what?
>
> *DJ Axel:* And say that I'm the director. Or I'm the performer, engineer, arranger, conductor. But the actual comp—you know, now we're just splitting hairs. Fuck it. I'm all of that. You know, I mean, again, we're dealing in semantics. Ultimately, I *am* making a song. Verse, bridge, chorus. I may be stealing stuff. I may play some stuff on my own. I may, like, play a little bass line in my ProTools or something to put it over the top. Yeah, I think mash-up artists are composing. Not composing new music, but composing remix music.[8]

As with the other gray areas configurable technologies have opened between the stark polarities of the modern framework, many of my interviewees told me they have developed some kind of criteria to draw new lines, reinforcing the eroding boundaries between composition and performance. DJ Earworm offered an interesting distinction: "if you do it in real time, it's called musicianship. And if you do it ahead of time, it's called composition." He acknowledged that new production techniques have even eroded the temporal distinctions between "now" and "later": "With Ableton Live, the lines are really blurring. And you're able to sort of arrange music just ahead of time, in a way. And you can kind of, looking at it and seeing what's gonna be playing. And then you make decisions." Naturally, this blurring of temporal lines renders Earworm's line in the sand blurry as well. As he concluded finally, "so DJs are sort of right in between, you know, composition and performance."[9]

Other interviewees suggested that the line between composition and performance may, like the distinction between original and copy, have something to do with the number and size of sonic elements being appropriated for the new work. As TradeMark G told me, "I look at this whole progression of samples in music as a linguistic thing. If a song is a sentence, made of up words and letters, if you're DJing, the samples are probably words. If I'm composing, the samples are probably letters."[10] Osymyso combines Trademark G's emphasis on sample size with DJ Earworm's temporal focus, suggesting a spectrum of distinction between composition and performance: "It's composition when you're taking a lot of elements and using them to create completely new song-based things. The far end of the scale is a performance, mixing one or two elements together in real time. That's what a DJ does. It goes right along the scale."[11]

Interestingly, both Osymyso and TradeMark G use the term "DJ" here as a proxy for "performer," or "performance," in contrast to "composer" or "composition"—even though they, like most of my interviewees, frequently used the term in a way that encompassed the entire spectrum of configurable music practices. The ambiguity and plasticity of this term further reinforces my observations in chapter 5 regarding the multifaceted nature of DJ consciousness. Like the term "bedroom producer," the term "DJ" often functions as a useful straw man, applied to behaviors and individuals that do not merit inclusion in a traditional, well-defined, or highly respected category. The term can also be self-applied, and used either as a mark of pride or as a means of self-deprecation.

Several mash-up producers told me they believe their work to be mostly or entirely composition, as opposed to performance. As Mysterious D told me, for mashers, "the performance isn't as important because what we're trying to showcase is production and the actually individual tracks."[12] Similarly, DJ Earworm told me he believes that "a good mash-up artist is a good composer. Because, you know, you're moving these parts around and giving it new form."[13]

The fact that mashers can emphasize composition over performance, despite their theoretical entanglement, suggests another common taxonomic strategy: for many configurable musicians, performance is *defined* by the existence of a live audience (much as the term "artist" may also be defined by the existence of a live or remote audience, as I have previously discussed). Strictly Kev put it most concisely: "I don't really think of myself as a performer, unless it's in the context of DJing in front of a crowd."[14] Tony Zeoli agreed, telling me that when "you're sitting in a studio and you're finding and tweaking sounds and you're creating a body of work, you're composing, right? And then when you're out on the live stage, performing that work, then you're performing."[15] Trademark G made the same argument, but emphasized that the distinction was really a subjective judgment: "There's an obvious division—when I do a live performance, the audience is witnessing the performative aspect and vaguely aware of the compositional aspect."[16]

The notion that performance of configurable music is defined by the presence of a live audience has its theoretical weaknesses, and its detractors. For one thing, traditional notions of performance don't require a live audience; for example, a solo musician in a recording studio is still said to be "performing," even if he or she is the only person within earshot. Given that a sample-based musician's instrument *is* the recording studio, this makes the distinction even cloudier. Mysterious D acknowledged that this presents some obstacles to drawing a clear line in the sand: "When you're, you know, rearranging the songs, are you a performer? It's a very interesting, complicated question. 'Cause you're not—and you are."[17]

Another theoretical problem with the live-audience definition of performance is that, according to some of my interviewees, having an audience is integral to the *compositional* process. DJ Axel, for instance, told me that "it's like a comedian trying out new material before they go on [Jimmy] Kimmel or something," meaning that his compositional methodology is an ongoing process of refinement before an audience. He explained how he composed a recent mash-up: "I had to try out something before I actually worked it out. So I had the composition. The concept of the composition. Very vague. Performed it a little bit to see what would work and what wouldn't work. Tested it out. And then when I got it I sat down and performed, engineered, arranged and composed it."[18]

In other words, for DJ Axel, the modern framework's assumption that composition precedes expression falls flat on its face, or is completely inverted. If any linear order exists in this process, expression precedes and constitutes composition. In fact, the reality appears to be far more cyclical than linear, consisting of a continuing dialogue between Axel and his audience—many of whom are mash-up producers, as well.

The difficulties parsing configurable music performance from composition, and the focus on live audience as a definitive constituent of performance, become even more troublesome in light of a problem I mention in chapter 6, that is, the uniqueness question. Most configurable music production techniques do not translate into scintillating stagecraft. These are not unrelated issues; the fact that configurable music uses recorded sound as its starting point, and studio equipment as its primary mechanism, means that the practice of creating it in front of a live audience can seem redundant, disingenuous, boring, or all three.

Go Home Productions explained the dilemma of using "preexisting material" as the basis of live performance: "I can reproduce this stuff and play it out to a club. But to me, it's not a performance at all . . . it's purely DJ. It's composition. . . . How am I to perform Michael Jackson mixed with the Beatles in front of 1,800 people? It's ludicrous."[19] Interestingly, in contrast to Osymyso's and TradeMark G's statements above, GHP uses the term "DJ" here to mean "composition," and *not* performance; yet, like the other two configurable musicians, he reflexively uses the term negatively, as a *counterexample:* "not X, but DJ."

But what's most interesting about GHP's description is the fact that he considers a live performance to be a "reproduction," suggesting that the recorded version of his work constitutes the original artifact. In other words, once again, expression is viewed as the initial step in configurable music production; composition in this case is merely an afterthought—a necessary conceit allowing the musician to reproduce his work for the purposes of audience appreciation, and commercial gain.

DJing in Theory and Practice

I have already discussed one technique configurable musicians use to cope with the problematic nature of live performance—creating configurable instruments that emphasize the physicality and ephemerality of the event through sheer spectacle. TradeMark G's "Wheel of Mash" (described in chapter 6) is one such example. Another is the DJ team of

Cut Chemist and DJ Shadow; on a recent tour, their set was preceded by an instructional video explaining to the crowd the mechanics of vinyl-based DJ techniques, and emphasizing that the two DJs would be using *only* original 45-rpm vinyl "singles" to make their music, because the smaller, faster-spinning, scarcer discs are a greater challenge to obtain and manipulate than LPs, let alone CD- or MP3-based turntables, which have recently gained popularity among DJs.

Another technique many configurable musicians have used is to turn the absurdity of the event into the *subject* of the event. As Matt Wand told me, it has become commonplace "for people with a laptop to just push a button and mime—and some people have turned that into an art form in itself—to perform theatrics to what is essentially a pre-recorded thing—which could be quite good."[20] V/VM told me he has used this technique extensively: "I perform a lot of these messed-up versions in a live sense, but obviously it's not live. It's playback. But I mime them so horribly, like the worst cabaret show you've ever seen."[21]

Ironically, then, performing an exaggerated or poorly executed simulation of studio techniques on stage may confer more legitimacy, authenticity, and/or showmanship on a musician than simply standing at a laptop or turntable and faithfully recreating the physical motions of actual sonic production. It should be noted that this performative strategy is not entirely unique to configurable musicians; it has been used in the past as an inoculation against the indignity of "lip-synching" by performing artists on television. Phil Lesh, the bass player for the Grateful Dead, once famously held a broomstick instead of his bass on a "live" television appearance that, to the band's chagrin, used a prerecorded music track rather than an actual microphone feed. More recently, during a "live" appearance in 2004 on NBC's sketch comedy show *Saturday Night Live*, pop singer Ashlee Simpson broke into a bizarre dance when the show's technicians played a different prerecorded track than the one she had initially expected to lip-synch to.

Methods of parsing the performance/composition dichotomy, and of addressing the problems of live performance in a configurable context, tend to differ depending on the style of music in question. There is a wide gulf, for instance, between the strategies of mash-up producers and those of turntablists. Turntablism is a variety of configurable music—often considered an offshoot of hip-hop—in which a DJ spinning vinyl emphasizes his skill through extended improvisation, using a rapid sequence of difficult techniques such as backspinning, cutting, scratching, and beat juggling. As Mysterious D explained to me, "turntablists are less interested in composition [than mash-up producers]. They're not writing the music; they're simply interested in the skill part."[22]

Clearly, the division between mashers and turntablists is preceded by centuries of musical rifts between composition-oriented and performance-oriented musicians; Mysterious D's claim that turntablists are not "writing the music" echoes arguments by proponents of European classical music against improvisation-based African American musical forms such as blues and jazz, or by pop singer-songwriters against heavy metal guitar virtuosos. In fact, this comparison was made explicitly by several of my interviewees. DJ Adrian, for instance, told me: "I think turntablism, in its purist sense, isn't really about music, so much as it's about skill and technique. You go and see a really amazing turntablist, that's kind of like the equivalent of going and seeing Yngwie Malmsteen. Do you see Yngwie Malmsteen because he writes great songs? No! You see him to play 5,000 notes a minute."[23]

For some reason, Malmsteen, the heavy metal guitarist known for his innovative "shredding" techniques, was often cited by interviewees as shorthand for "complexity/quality of technique surpassing complexity/quality of compositional material," generally in the context of discussions about turntablism. Like Sean "Diddy" Combs, Malmsteen seems to have acquired an iconic status as a negative example among many configurable musicians, rarely requiring further explanation. And, as with Combs, this antipathy is understandable; if Diddy can be seen as the poster child for the gulf separating big money from independent musicians, Malmsteen (like his stated idol, Niccolò Paganini) can be seen as the poster child for the chasm separating professional instrumentalists from amateurs. For musicians dedicated to blurring or eradicating such distinctions, the two are equally anathema.

Of course, like all the dynamics of configurable musicianship I have discussed, the turntablism/mash-up division is not nearly so neat and tidy as I have presented it. For instance, some musicians, such as DJ Z-Trip, could easily be categorized as *both* turntablists and mash-up artists. DJ Adrian would disagree with this statement; as he told me, "Z-Trip works my nerve, because he's erroneously comparing what he does, which is turntablism, and comparing it to mash-ups."[24] However, as TradeMark G, told me, the distinction is philosophical, not absolute: "By Adrian's definition, you compose a mash-up. By Z-Trip's definition, you perform a mash-up."[25]

Although most of the musicians I interviewed come from the mash-up, techno, and hip-hop communities, there are other vantage points on the performance/composition dichotomy, as well. For instance, Jesse Gilbert, whose work could be classified as more academic or experimental than most of my other interviewees, told me that he considers all work produced in a sequencing environment like ProTools—whether mash-ups, hip-hop, or techno—to be "arrangements," whereas his own work is "more of an instrument model, where you're creating a software which is doing sample manipulation live, in response to gestural input by a performer."[26] In other words, for Gilbert, software creation is composition, improvisation using this software constitutes performance, and most of the other musicians I interviewed are doing neither, but simply "arranging."

Composition, Performance, and Copyright

From a legal standpoint, the performance/composition dichotomy in configurable music is as confusing and unresolved as the other binaries I have discussed. As attorney Bob Clarida told me, when it comes to configurable music, the existing legal categories "don't do a very good job. They're not very flexible. They're not very well suited to other kinds of creative practices that people do."[27] The legal categories that do exist, law professor Jennifer Urban argued, suggest a "stark privileging of the act of composition over the act of performance"—a philosophy she explicitly linked to the notion of "the romantic composer who sat in his studio"[28]—in other words, to the modern framework.

Current American intellectual property law only grants copyright—the badge of authorship—to expressions in a fixed medium, such as a score or a recording. Therefore, musicians who perform in front of an audience, but don't record their shows or keep written records of their work, do not qualify for copyright protection, and are not credited as composers.

Configurable musicians are not granted new copyrights for their work either, unless they add "original" elements, such as new lyrics or instrumentation, to those works. This eliminates the great bulk of mash-up and techno music from consideration. Therefore, according to existing copyright law, and despite their own self-description to the contrary, mash-up and techno producers are not legally considered composers. And to the extent that the recording industry accounts for them at all, they are generally considered "producers"—a work-for-hire position with no ownership stake in the finished product.

Some legal scholars have argued that, just as composition and performance are merging in a configurable context, the traditional legal divisions separating the two categories should be erased, and that new legal categories should be created, specifically to suit the mechanics of configurable music. Lawrence Lessig, for instance, asked and answered the following question on his blog, regarding *The Grey Album*: "Should the law give DJ Danger Mouse the right to remix without permission? I think so."[29] Similarly, attorney Gary Adelman told me that he favors "allowing artists to sample and to utilize master rights the same way they're allowed to use underlying compositions . . . I'm advocating a compulsory license."[30] Compulsory licenses, in which Congress and federal regulators mandate a set market rate for the use of copyrighted works in a given context, are essential to a variety of existing music industry economies, from radio to recordings, and allow anyone to use copyrighted materials at a fair and reasonable rate. Compulsory licenses, though, are generally an anathema to those within the industry; they would rather exert the power to withhold licenses in order to keep product scarce and prices high. In the case of sampling, which commands astronomical fees, this is certainly the prevailing opinion among rights holders.

Jennifer Urban told me she considers it "very unlikely that there will ever be a compulsory remix license"—in large part, due to successful lobbying by its opponents. Fortunately, this may not be the only route toward resolving the ambiguities and inconsistencies of configurable music law. Urban also told me she believes that "a voluntary collecting society license will happen as soon as labels make it to the realization that digital media is physically uncontrollable, but licensing will get everyone paid."[31] In other words, musical regulatory institutions will eventually be forced to accommodate the dynamics of configurable culture, by market pressures if not by statutory ones, as the modern framework inevitably continues to erode.

As I write this, Urban's prediction appears to be coming true. Warner Music Group recently announced that it is collaborating with other record labels to grant Internet service providers (ISPs) and their customers immunity from prosecution for certain kinds of copyright violation, in exchange for monthly fees to be collected by the ISPs. Although this arrangement amounts to a license in everything but name, the labels appear to be avoiding that terminology for legal and contractual reasons that are too complex to delve into here. According to a conversation I had with WMG executive Jack Foreman, this "covenant not to sue" will not only indemnify people for uploading and downloading copyrighted songs—it will also, to an extent, cover configurable practices such as remixes and mash-ups.³² While the complete details of this plan have yet to emerge, and the reports thus far provide more questions than answers, it appears that even the major labels are beginning to acknowledge that configurability demands a legal framework that encompasses a broader range of behaviors than simply "composition" and "performance."

Conclusion

The distinction between composing and performing, vague under the best of circumstances, has become nearly impossible to identify in a configurable context. Although musicians have developed a number of taxonomic criteria, such as time and location of sample manipulation, granularity of sample manipulation, presence or absence of an audience, and performativity (in the sense of spectacle) in response to this ambiguity, a great many of them simply argue that traditional definitions don't work. When pressed, most DJs claim to encompass the entire musical labor cycle (e.g., composition, performance, and production) within their configurable practices.

Unfortunately, our legal system has thus far taken the opposite tack: rather than applying the full range of relevant definitions to configurable production, DJs are most often considered neither composers nor performers, but rather producers, a technical role more akin to engineering than to artistry. Consequently, configurable musicians are structurally excluded from participating in the ownership of new cultural products and practices, and are typically denied the economic and legal benefits afforded to traditional composers.

While the law is unlikely to reflect these discursive changes any time soon, we are beginning to see music industry institutions make affordances in the marketplace for the widespread adoption of configurable music practices. As I discuss in the final section of this book, these nascent changes suggest a path for economic development after the collapse of the traditional "value chain," which is premised on an industrialized division of labor, and on the primacy of intellectual over material production. First, however, I address the role that configurability plays in undermining the final two elements of the modern framework: the figure/ground and materials/tools binaries.

8

Hooks and
Hearts
The Figure/Ground Binary

> Good evening, ladies and gentlemen, we'd like to remind you that
> we don't applaud here at the Showplace, or where we're working.
> So restrain your applause and, if you must applaud, wait till the end
> of the set—and it won't even matter then. The reason is that we are
> interrupted by your noise. In fact, don't even take any drinks, I want
> no cash register ringing.
> *Charles Mingus Presents Charles Mingus*
>
> If you're in a Jeep, and you dig what you're hearin', can I get a beep,
> and a side order of cheerin'?
> Q-Tip, *Push It Along*

Most of us can easily tell what constitutes the "figure" or "ground" of a
piece of music as soon as we hear it. Usually, the figure is the melody, or
sometimes, the "hook" of a song. Either way, it's generally the part we
find ourselves humming later on, or the snippet we sing when describing a song to a friend. The ground is simply everything else—the accompaniment, instrumentation, or supporting tracks. We don't pay as
much attention to it for the same reason we don't pay much attention
to the frame around a painting. In most cases, even if we're hearing a new
song, we instantly know what part to focus on and what part to ignore
because (as I discuss in chapter 2) figure/ground distinctions in Western instrumental music are fairly well delineated by an established

sonic symbolic language, and by the capabilities and limitations of traditional instrumentation.

Today, however, configurable music production technologies have enabled an unprecedented range and plasticity of aural expressive possibilities. With samplers, synthesizers, sequencers, and millions of possible digital filters and plug-ins, we can produce and reproduce virtually any sound that the human ear can distinguish. This opens an exciting new universe of possibility to musicians seeking to explore innovative expressions and ideas. On the other hand, this also means that musicians will have to reevaluate the meaning and function of figure/ground distinctions in their work.

First, this new universe of sounds—many of them lacking any perceivable melody and/or rhythm—must now be aesthetically codified and assigned contextual stylistic meanings in relation to one another. We need to make sense of them all, if we're going to use them as a form of communication. Second, many sounds previously considered external to music are now being appropriated within musical production, at the very moment that (thanks to iPods and other portable digital technologies) a nearly limitless library of recorded music is becoming instantaneously accessible to individual listeners in every conceivable locale. In other words, there is a greater interpenetration of musical and environmental sounds than at any other point in cultural history, and access to music is simultaneously becoming democratized (everyone can hear it) and individualized (we can each program our own personal "soundtrack" to life).

How can this new universe of musical possibility be integrated into a coherent stylistic system? How will the blending between musical and environmental sound influence our understanding of figure/ground relationships? If the melodic figure serves as an aesthetic proxy for the modern individual, what are the social ramifications of these formalistic changes? Among my interviewees, there was a broad range of engagement with these questions. Some told me that challenging the traditional figure/ground relationship was central to their work, others told me they preferred to use established figure/ground delineations, and still others told me that they rarely, if ever, considered the question.

"Mashing up Foregrounds and Backgrounds"

For some DJs, the modern framework's conventions are simply irrelevant in configurable music. As V/VM told me, digital production doesn't require him to engage with figure/ground distinctions at all, liberating him from the constraints of traditional composition: "I've never really thought about it in terms of foreground and background. For me, it's the whole thing, it's the end result. . . . I've never given much thought to melody, or to what people remember."[1] Similarly, Si Begg told me: "I don't think in terms of foreground and background. . . . I'm more interested in trying to make things a sonic whole, I suppose, without trying to break things down into traditional parts as such."[2]

Strictly Kev told me that, while he may not consider his music to be a "sonic whole" in the way that Begg does, he finds figure/ground distinctions difficult, given the multiplicity of elements he combines in his work. In his words, "you've got four backgrounds and four foregrounds. It's not clear cut any more."[3] Strictly Kev's work should not be confused with postmodern pastiche; although he combines a variety of elements into a new whole, it is anything but ahistorical. His "Raiding the 20th Century" release, for example, functions explicitly as a sonic history and genealogy of twentieth-century recorded music.

Steinski told me that traditional figure/ground relationships often don't play a role in his music either. But, he told me, this is neither because it constitutes a "sonic whole" nor because of the complexity and variety of its constituent elements. Rather, he rejects the Eurocentrism of the modern framework, and argues that hip-hop (his most frequent style of work) is Afro-diasporic, and follows a rival aesthetic tradition: "Depending on how deeply into hip-hop you are, you may not ever need a foreground. There are some guys, like me, who can sit around and listen to the same beat going around and around for twenty minutes. That takes it back to whatever valley humans existed in and sprang from in Africa, is drums. . . . The idea of melody and voice as foreground and bass and drums as background is kind of a Western concept. And hip-hop doesn't always conform to that." In his more market-oriented work, Steinski acknowledges he is more likely to follow traditional figure/ground distinctions: "Bass and drums are the background, and, if I'm going to do a piece of music for a film or commercial, where I have a guitar or a singer or piano, that's going to be the foreground."[4]

Mash-up producers were far more likely to acknowledge a traditional figure/ground relationship in their work than techno, hip-hop, or experimental musicians. This is because the relation between figure and ground is actually central to the aesthetic. As Eric Kleptone explained, "with mash-up, what you're actually doing is you're mashing up foregrounds and backgrounds. You're taking a foreground from one piece and you're putting it to a background on another piece."[5] Similarly, DJ Adrian told me: "for me, it's more like, 'hey, I like this rap and now I'm going to put it over music that I really like' . . . because, ultimately, the music is the bed."[6]

This willingness to take on traditional figure/ground dynamics could easily be misunderstood as a mere artifact of mash-up technique: if a musician is only using one vocal track and one instrumental track, how could he or she *avoid* replicating the modern framework's binary distinction? Further inspection reveals more at work here. DJ Earworm, whose work is known for incorporating a greater multiplicity of elements than the standard "A + B" mash-up template, agreed with Eric Kleptone and DJ Adrian, telling me, "vocals are almost always in the foreground. And so . . . usually the instrumentals become the background." He reconciles this precept with his omnivorous sampling habits by explaining that the mash-up aesthetic itself helps him to navigate between the many layers of sound competing for attention within his works: "There can only be one thing in the foreground at once. I mean, in a successful mash-up. You don't want to challenge people to pay attention to two things at once. It's just too hard. Unless one of them's been repeating for a while. . . . I definitely think about background, foreground, and make sure that there's only one voice expressing itself at a time."[7]

This process of negotiation, then, is the fundamental to the mash-up aesthetic. While the form may at first appear to take on the traditional figure/ground distinctions inherited from the modern framework in a direct and uncritical fashion, I would argue that it does so precisely *in order to examine those distinctions*, and by doing so, critiquing them as well.

We can observe this further in the way mash-up artists sometimes change the figural positioning of a sample as it travels from its original setting to its role in the configurable work. As TradeMark G told me, "In some cases, you'll have sampled materials that will already have been considered in a foreground/background kind of way. . . . But in other cases, you're sampling something more fragmented, and you do have to consider how that comes together [using] your artistic sensibility."[8]

Several mash-up producers explained to me how their own "artistic sensibilities" operate in this context. Osymyso (another mash-up producer known for expanding the form far beyond the A+B template) told me, "the roles are changed with sampling—what may have been just a little backing vocal may have been brought to the front."[9] Eric Kleptone gave me a concrete example of how he might take a Beatles sample out of its original figural context: "You can get hold of the drum track for "Strawberry Fields Forever," which is really quite crazy at the end . . . you can make that the foreground of a track . . . you can take background content and pull it into the foreground. You can manipulate the order of pieces."[10]

DJ Earworm offered an even more in-depth explanation of how figural recontextualization operates within his aesthetic: "You might have A express the verse and A-with-B expressing the chorus. And then C has been going on sort of unrecognizably as the instrumental. But then finally the bridge comes and then C becomes the foreground. And there's a certain amount of satisfaction from the tension of recognizing something's there and maybe the wanting to hear it, and then it finally comes to the foreground. . . . So, sort of playing with the foreground and background is a big part of the arrangement."[11]

For many mash-up artists, then, examining, critiquing, and playing with traditional figure/ground relationships is a central element of the process and the aesthetic, and even the raison d'etre of the style itself. It may be argued, therefore, that the true foreground of a mash-up isn't A or B or even C; it's the relationship and recontextualization between the constituent elements that identifies a work and makes it memorable—in other words, *the juxtaposition itself functions as the foreground.*

Several of my interviewees made this point explicitly. As Go Home Productions told me, "I don't think there's a foreground in a mash-up. It's a composite. It's the final results of the melding. . . . If you were going to describe Madonna's new single, you wouldn't sing the high part. You'd say, 'it samples ABBA.'"[12] TradeMark G made a similar observation: "Another element of it is juxtaposition. Recontextualizing something makes it stand out more. If I reuse that assertiveness training woman as a lead vocal in a new song, that's not where you'd usually hear her. That recontextualization makes things stand out."[13]

I don't mean to suggest that figural recontextualization is unique to mash-ups; in fact, the technique is common across the entire range of configurable musical styles. Mash-up producers simply use this technique to a slightly different effect, by putting it into conflict with the appearance of traditional figure/ground distinctions, which happens less often in other configurable styles.

The technique is so prevalent, in fact, that configurable musicians in each style claimed it as their own, sometimes to the exclusion of other styles. Jesse Gilbert told me that, in his work, "there is a constant morphing and foregrounding and backgrounding that can be done, so that there is no longer a kind of binary system, but that things can be moved in and out of foreground and background with a totally different kind of facility."[14] Similarly, Steinski told me he used the technique, as well: "Taking it from the background to the foreground is what rap did, with the drum. Taking it from the foreground to the background is what a lot of [other] people are doing. Using foreground as foreground and background as background is a mash-up."[15]

Remixing Public and Private

If, for many configurable musicians, the juxtaposition between constituent elements has become so central that, as Tony Zeoli put it, "whatever is in the music is all foreground to me,"[16] then what can be said to constitute the background? According to Si Begg, it depends on the context in which the music is heard. In a dance club, he told me, other pieces of recorded music constitute a form of background: "You have to take into account that quite possibly the first two minutes and the last two minutes [of your own song] might be mixed in with something else." He also, Begg adds, makes "music for a social environment. It's music that people can be talking over." In that context, "there's gonna be chatting and drinking and hanging out," and he accounts for those anticipated ambient noises within his aesthetic.[17] Matt Wand made a very similar observation: "with mobile phones, your conversations and your choice of music have suddenly become public. The private has become public. The music itself has become just a background."[18]

In other words, both Begg and Wand perceive an increasing erosion of the boundaries separating recorded music and the social environment in which it functions, and reflect those observations and expectations within the configurable aesthetic—although Wand characterizes his music as the background, rather than the foreground, relative to ambient social noise. Both Begg and Wand attribute this shift to the roles that configurable technologies now play in our lives, which are making recorded music a more pervasive element of our social environment, even as they conversely allow musicians to integrate environmental sounds into their work. This attitude is in stark contrast to modernist musicians—even those who used sampling techniques. Jazz bassist and composer Charles Mingus, for example, experimented many times with incorporating ambient and environmental sounds into his recordings. He was also infamous for admonishing audiences not to applaud, and commanding club owners and waiters not to ring up sales or even serve drinks while he was on the stage, because the clapping of hands, the clink of ice cubes, and the tinkle of cash register bells would sully the integrity of his performance.[19]

While some interviewees argued that configurable social practices are influencing the perception of figure and ground within their music, other musicians made the reverse argument: that figure/ground relations in their work may influence social formations. As Tony Montana explained to me, "a good mash up / bootleg is a culture clash . . . 2 styles that shouldnt work together but do [sic]."[20] V/VM said something similar: "I'm layering instruments which are never, ever layered together. [I like] to cross regions so you can have Chinese instruments playing with Indian instruments, with, like, bagpipes."[21]

The function of these sonic "culture clashes" is not solely textural, nor purely aesthetic. To the contrary, they often serve as models for the bridging of the social chasms characterized by those aesthetic divides. DJ Adrian told me, "that's definitely part of the appeal of mash-up culture, is the cross-pollination of scenes and culture."[22] And according to Mysterious D such cross-pollination is one of the primary purposes of Bootie, the multicity mash-up club that she and DJ Adrian jointly operate: "The audience in San Francisco is so mashed up, like the music, and that's one of our most—we're most proud of. Is actually to bring people that would never hang out together for a party night, for a fun night where they can all actually, like, have something in common. And have a good time. And be in the same place with people they would never even talk to. Or, you know, definitely clubs they wouldn't be in with the same people. You know, gay, straight, alternative, mainstream, you know, the whole everything."[23]

Recycling the "Hook"

Within the commercial music industry, people rarely, if ever, discuss the technical distinctions between figure and ground. There is an analogous concept, though: that of the "hook." True to its name, a hook is an element of a song that is intended to stick in people's minds, and to give the song its own identity. Typically, when songs are marketed via audio or video channels, the hook is excerpted as a stand-in for the song as a whole.

As veteran A&R executive Pete Ganbarg explained to me, the industry has come to view configurable technology as a boon in some respects, for its ability to recycle hooks from one song to another. In his words, his job "is to make commercial music that's going to sell as many copies as possible, and what sells commercial music? Hooks. So in sample-based music, if I'm able to use a sample which gives me another hook, I like as many hooks as I can fit in a tackle box."[24]

The relationship between hooks and configurable music is not always so straightforward. Strictly Kev told me an anecdote about a track he produced in 2000 that sampled Quincy Jones's song, "The Pawnbroker." In his words, he had "chopped it up and rearranged the rhythm section" in a way that made the song conspicuously different, but still quasi-recognizable, and then had "written a melody over the top, with horns." Because Kev wished to distribute the song commercially, he tried to license the samples from Jones. Jones agreed, but insisted on receiving 100 percent of the publishing royalties for the song—in essence, arguing that none of Kev's additions, including his new melody, constituted original composition. As Kev described it, he believes that he and Jones each believed their own contribution constituted the foreground of the work: "That [melody] to me was the hook of the song, but in his eyes, his sample was the hook."[25]

Copyright, Sampling, and the "Heart" of the Work

This subjectivity about the role of sampling in figure/ground relations, and vice versa, has added to the legal ambiguity surrounding configurable music practices. Typically, in music law, the melody of a song—traditionally considered the foreground, as I have discussed—earns a greater degree of copyright protection than other musical elements such as chord progressions or rhythm tracks. As several of my interviewees explained to me, this distinction is not written into the letter of the law; theoretically, every part of a song should be equally covered by copyright. In practice, the figure/ground distinction has become standard for a variety of reasons.

The first reason, as law professor Jennifer Urban explained to me, is that "copyright law tries to protect only things that are original, and a melody often seems more original." Another reason, attorney Bob Clarida told me, is that courts often tend to have "a sort of a notationalist bias. You know, if people say, 'Well, gee, it's not in the notation, so therefore it's not part of the composition.'"[26] A final reason, Urban says, is "because everybody on the jury and the judge have some exposure to the Western Romantic idea of how music is perceived, [so] there's probably going to be a trend toward privileging the foreground."[27] In other words, the modern framework, manifested in the concepts of originality, notational composition, and the Romantic ideal of the artist, is sufficiently powerful to provide a de facto legal distinction between figure and ground, despite the absence of any statutory justification.

Given that it's not always clear whether and when a sample qualifies as figure or ground, or whether configurable music even contains distinguishable figure and ground, this throws the copyrightability of sample-based works, and their relation to the works being sampled, deeper into legal limbo. As attorney Gary Adelman told me, "I don't think the law has addressed it all, actually."[28] In practice, this often means that configurable musicians are denied authorship and copyright protection.

The only case law bearing on figure/ground relations in a configurable context that any of the attorneys I spoke with could cite was *Harper & Row v. Nation Enterprises*,[29] a 1985 case regarding print publishing, in which the U.S. Supreme Court held that an excerpt of Gerald Ford's memoirs reprinted in *The Nation* magazine constituted copyright infringement because, although it was just a short passage, it constituted the "heart of the work." As Jennifer Urban explained to me, this concept has been applied to music-related cases as well, and she believes "you could fairly make some connection between the heart and the foreground."[30] I would argue that based on my discussion of the "hook" above, one could just as easily make a connection between the heart and the hook.

One of the few instances where the "heart of the work" argument has been applied to an actual configurable music work was the famous incident in which David Bowie and Freddie Mercury sued rapper Vanilla Ice for sampling the bass hook of their song "Under Pressure" in the rap tune "Ice Ice Baby." Though the suit was eventually settled out of court when Vanilla Ice agreed to share publishing royalties with Bowie and Mercury,[31] Urban told me that the sampling in this case "was seen as a copyright infringement because it was the heart of the work" that was taken, despite the brevity of the sample.[32]

This anecdote helps to exemplify some of the difficulties presented by the dissolution of the figure/ground distinction in a configurable context. Like Beethoven's "Moonlight" Sonata, in which the escalating series of three-note figures can be heard (or performed) as either figure or ground, the bass riff in "Under Pressure" constitutes both ground (as a rhythmic ostinato) and figure (as a hook). By sampling this segment,

Vanilla Ice unwittingly imported this ambiguity into his own song, where it was eventually resolved as figure.

This is partially because of the Western musical bias toward viewing melody as figural; as attorney Ronald Bienstock told me, because rapping is not typically melodic, "everything your ear is drawn to [in a rap song] on the melodic side will be the sample."[33] In other words, the bass riff became definitively melodic only when it was removed from its initial surroundings and placed in a context otherwise devoid of tonal information. But the outcome of this case is also evidence of an implicit bias against configurable culture within our musical regulatory institutions; if a dispute between a configurable musician and one operating within the traditional framework needs to be resolved, and it rests on an ambiguous question such as whether a sampled bass riff constitutes figure or ground, the institutional response will almost certainly be to side reflexively with the traditional musician.

Conclusion

Most configurable musicians agree that their musical practices and technologies problematize traditional figure/ground relationships in music. While some simply view themselves as liberated from old stylistic constraints, others actively engage in critiquing and renegotiating formalistic relationships within their work. For mash-up musicians especially, the juxtaposition of different sonic elements provides a map for the resolution of cultural divides, and the foregrounding of this aesthetic collision is a strategy for foregrounding the social imperative of this resolution.

Another aspect of figure/ground renegotiation in configurable music is its role in reimagining the relationship between public and private. Many sample-based musicians actively address the public/private divide in their work, either treating environmental sound and music as a background against which their own recordings stand as figure, or by acknowledging that their music is likely to be incorporated as a background into a larger sonic landscape. As I discuss in the concluding chapters, I believe these considerations are intimately linked to the emerging social reality of pervasive surveillance and digital "transparency."

Within the music industry, popular figures or "hooks" are often reappropriated through sampling to make a new song more marketable to the public. Our copyright and economic systems, however, tend to privilege figural musical components like melody, and so are currently incapable of encompassing the range of roles a sample may play in a new work; any ambiguity as to figure/ground relations tends to be resolved by according primacy to the work being sampled, rather than the work using the sample. This may lead to systemic inefficiency and underexploitation of creative resources, as when Quincy Jones and Strictly Kev disagreed about the degree to which Jones's samples were figural, and the two parties were not able to reach an agreement about how to bring the music to market. Ultimately, discussions about what constitutes the figure, the hook, or the heart of the work will have to follow emerging aesthetic and formal conventions; allowing law to dictate aesthetics will simply result in stalemate.

9

"He Plays Dictaphones, and She Plays Bricks"

The Materials/Tools Binary

> Sampling is never accidental. It is not like the case of a composer who has a melody in his head, perhaps not even realizing that the reason he hears this melody is that it is the work of another which he had heard before. When you sample a sound recording you know you are taking another's work product.
>
> Ralph B. Guy Jr., Circuit Judge, *Bridgeport v. Dimension Films*

> At the very least, you should be able to make some kind of use of somebody else's material as a building block. As a piece of raw material.
>
> Attorney Bob Clarida

In 1926, an American art collector purchased a new sculpture by the Romanian artist Constantin Brancusi, one of a limited edition of bronze casts titled *Bird in Space*.[1] The sculpture was barely representational, unlike most other contemporary works; lacking feathers, beak, or talons, it consisted of a graceful, 4.5-foot arc of smooth, gleaming metal standing vertically on a base. To an eye untrained in the latest principles of 1920s modern art, little about it would connote a bird, or even qualify it as a sculpture at all. Unfortunately for Brancusi and his patron, the U.S. customs officials lacked such training. Instead of allowing *Bird in Space* into the country under the duty-free exemption for works of art, they assessed a steep tariff, essentially treating the bronze as a chunk of nearly raw material or, in the words of customs inspector F. J. H. Kracke, who personally assessed it, "a manufacture of metal."[2] As he told the *New York Evening Post* during the court battles that ensued, his own judgment was supported by a panel of art experts retained by the government agency, one of whom opined that "if that's art, I'm a bricklayer."[3]

Although the Customs Court eventually found the sculpture to be "art"—and therefore exempt from import duty—the argument over *Bird in Space* has reverberated throughout the art world in the ensuing eight decades. As the prevailing aesthetics of the age moved further and further away from interpretive representation, and deeper into abstract, minimalist, and conceptual territory, it's become increasingly difficult for the untrained eye to spot the point at which a piece of raw material undergoes the alchemical transformation to artwork, or finished product.

Music has, to a certain degree, been spared much of this uncertainty besetting the visual and tactile arts. This is largely because the "raw material" from which it's made cannot be imported or even experienced in its untooled form. In today's cultural environment, a block of bronze or a surface with paint splashed on it could easily be classified as either artwork, material, or instrument, depending on the context; the annals of the art world are filled with cases of mistaken identity like *Bird in Space*. However, neither a saxophone nor the air it vibrates could possibly be mistaken for music itself, except in the most remote, conceptual sense of the term.

Once again, configurable technologies have disturbed this uneasy peace. By capturing sound in digital form, and making it as malleable to human will as a lump of clay, or an ingot of bronze, audio software finally introduces the same degree of ambiguity into musical production today that has marked material production in the past. A digital sound file may be a raw material (as a source for sampling), or a tool for production (as in the case of a sample bank), or a finished product (as a CD or MP3 sold in a store). Similarly, a computer itself may be used to quarry for material, to tool that material, and to distribute the finished product to a listener. No third-party observer could tell you which role a given piece of hardware or software plays in the production cycle, without more contextual information. And, for economic reasons such as market pricing and trade, as well as the broader social reasons I outline in chapters 2 and 3, the resolution of this ambiguity is vital to both musical and social evolution.

As with the other five elements of the modern framework discussed in the previous chapters, the sample-based musicians I interviewed told me they had a difficult time reconciling the materials/tools dichotomy with their own experiences. They offered a range of opinions regarding the new definitions of these terms in a configurable context.

Some told me flat out that the categories had no meaning in the context of their work. As V/VM put it, "I never think of it in that way."[4] Others didn't simply accept the existence of the traditional categories, but essentially restated the premises of the modern framework itself. DJ Paul V, for instance, told me that he considers mash-ups to be "art" because the process consists definitively in the application of tools to materials: "If art is basically taking elements that are at your fingertips, whether it's paint, dirt, cement, and being able to rearrange it and congeal it or whatever you want to call it, into something that's your own, that's art."[5] Similarly, TradeMark G echoed the modern framework's precept that tools impose order on materials: "There's a real feeling that you get after doing a piece of work, you sort of feel like you've championed the things that you've sampled. Like you have completely conquered something. . . . You really feel like you've cut down and reshaped your source into your own image. It gives you a godlike feeling."[6]

Although many of my interviewees told me they considered themselves to be using tools and materials in the production of configurable music, both terms were subject to a range of interpretations among the musicians I spoke with.

Configurable Music Materials

Some interviewees told me they considered songs—in the sense of a composition combined with a performance—to be their materials. DJ Adrian, for instance, told me that an essential question in mash-up construction is "how much source material is being used? How much of the original integrity of the song is maintained?" Later in the conversation, he used the same term again, telling me that "it's the right time and the right place for [mash-ups to emerge] in our culture, because we're being bombarded with so much source material."[7] Strictly Kev also focused on songs when I asked him about his methods, telling me, "as far as materials go, anything—any format, any genre, if something catches my ear."[8]

Other interviewees made a distinction at once subtle and significant, telling me that they considered phono recordings, rather than songs per se, to be their material. As DJ Earworm told me, "all sound is material. Any kind of digital sound that you can find . . . the materials are, you know, the music files that—my music collection, and the music that's available on the Internet. And, you know, just the world in general."[9] Similarly, Matt Wand told me that "the material is the recordings,"[10] and, for Go Home Productions, "the material is the record or the CD."[11] TradeMark G expanded on this point, discussing the aesthetic considerations of focusing on the recording, rather than the song: "Part of putting sample-based music together has to do with making do with what you've got . . . You don't approach it in terms of melody, harmony and so on, you approach it in terms of drums, instruments and vocal samples."[12] In other words, for TradeMark G, mash-ups are a form of *bricolage* that both exploit and comment on the unprecedented volume of recorded music and sound within our cultural environment.

As these comments suggest, many of the configurable musicians I spoke with maintain highly organized collections of materials they have culled from "raw" sources, such as CDs and MP3s. Typically, these collections take the form of a "sample library," stored on a digital medium, such as a hard drive. As Jesse Gilbert told me, "almost all of the stuff that I do in either performance or, like, sound design stuff, is made from preexisting samples. I tend to use them as kind of raw materials."[13] Similarly, Eric Kleptone told me, "I have hard drives full of samples. And you know, like, tapes and vinyl and stuff like that. But it's very much organized in the same manner that someone would organize, you know, raw materials. They're stacked up. They're in folders with labels. They get sifted. They get processed."[14]

Kleptone's portrait of digital and physical media coexisting side-by-side in neatly organized stacks is very much an image of our transitional moment. Many of the DJs and producers I spoke with reported using MP3s, CDs, and vinyl at various times and in various contexts, although there appears to be a strong trend away from the vinyl albums that defined DJ music at its outset, and toward purely digital materials. Ironically, the increasing fetishization of vinyl (such as the performance by Cut Chemist and DJ Shadow that I describe in chapter 7) only makes this more evident by contrast. As DJ Axel explained to me, he believes the evolution from physical to digital materials is both a natural and a necessary evolution: "Technology's moving pretty fast. And then, of course, there's all the purists who say it should be vinyl or nothing. And then what's funny is that I've run into CD purists. It's like, well, why pick *that* technology? . . . It's arbitrary. And it's like I always say, that there's no point in being a purist with turntablism, 'cause it was always technology-based. . . . What difference does it make? I mean, vinyl, sure it looks cooler. But it deteriorates in quality, it's heavy, it scratches, you know. I mean, yeah, I'm not a purist."[15]

Similarly, DJ Adrian told me that "our source material is usually digital," and that, if he found a vinyl record containing music that wasn't available in a digital format such as CD or MP3, he would immediately "rip that vinyl as an AIF file into my computer so I can start chopping it up."[16]

Configurable Music Tools

Naturally, as an increasing number of musicians report using digital materials, the tools are increasingly digital as well. As DJ Adrian told me, the growth of configurable music, and of mash-ups in particular, is fueled by the increasing accessibility of audio editing software: "The reason all of this is happening now isn't because people hadn't thought of it—it's because the tools are there and affordable. I mean, you couldn't do this ten years ago, because you didn't have cheap software that could do it."[17] Osymyso also told me he considered software to be his primary tool. Once you have your digital materials, he told me, "you do something to it with the tool, which is software."[18]

Go Home Productions told me that he considered hardware, rather than software, to be his instrument: "to me, the tool is the computer."[19] Strictly Kev echoed this sentiment, but emphasized that he still uses a vinyl rig sometimes as well: "All I need is a computer with a sampler, or a pair of turntables and a mixer as my tools."[20] DJ Earworm told me that the combination of hardware and software constituted his toolset: "the instrument is the computer. And the music production software."[21]

Still other interviewees cited a range of traditional and nontraditional instruments as elements in their toolboxes. Si Begg told me that, although he "come[s] from a techno background," he still integrates acoustic and electric instrumentation into his work: "I still play some instruments. Guitars and stuff. And then taking it to the computer. And then sampling it. So it was an instrument but now it's become a fragment of kind of a sample . . . you're using it as just this kind of chunk of audio."[22]

As Matt Wand told me, he and some of his colleagues have reached a bit farther afield: "The technology is the tool . . . the tools could be anything. I have a couple of friends—he plays Dictaphones, and she plays bricks. She's a classical flutist, but she's rejected it all, and now plays bricks."[23] Clearly, the use of everyday objects as musical instruments has a long and storied history predating configurability, but the philosophy that "the technology is the tool," so central to the configurable music ethic, makes such decisions both less philosophically alien and less awkward to accommodate mechanically. In other words, the difference between playing a guitar and a brick, so vast in the world of "live" acoustic performance, becomes trivial once they've both been digitized and imported into a sample-based sequencing or editing environment.

Thus, according to my interviewees, the tools for configurable music production may include software, computer hardware, audio production equipment, or traditional and nontraditional acoustic instrumentation. Several configurable musicians, however, noted that there is another important tool in the mix: their own minds and ideas. As DJ Adrian put it, "the tool is whatever software or, you know, equipment or gear that you're using to put it together—and your skill set of putting it together."[24] Similarly, Eric Kleptone told me that when samples "get processed," the process is "a combination of computer software and my brain."[25]

Strictly Kev told me he believes that the most important tool in creating configurable music is the mind of the maker—precisely because the other tools are so flexible and powerful. "You can pretty much do anything you want in terms of sampling technology these days," he told me, explaining that as a result, many people become gearheads—getting hung up on the latest and greatest equipment. But production equipment, he says, "doesn't have to be the best," and he adds, "It's what you're putting in that should be the priority. It's the imagination, not the hardware."[26]

While these earnest appraisals of the value of the human factor in configurable music may at first glance seem trite, I believe they offer a significant confirmation of a point I argue earlier in this book: that one of the ways in which configurability departs from earlier modes of cultural production is that it makes cognition socially transparent in a way it's never been before. The "black box" of the human mind merges with the fully auditable and visible interface of the computer, and the result is that we may witness the acts of reception, interpretation, reinterpolation, and response—the entire cycle of cultural participation—reflected through a monitor and a pair of speakers. When Kleptone uses the word "process," therefore, it has a double meaning—the sample is being processed by a computer in a mechanical sense, but it is also being processed by his own mind in a cultural sense—and the two processes are inextricable from one another.

The (Un)Finished Product

Despite the many definitions of "tools" and "materials" within configurable music, most of my interviewees tended to agree with DJ Earworm's assessment that "the finished product in this case is, you know, the polished mash-up."[27] Even this relatively straightforward statement may be interpreted in two different ways. Some, such as Go Home Productions, pointed to the actual physical medium, or the digital files produced by the creative process: "The finished product is what comes out of my CD burner."[28] Others, such as TradeMark G, emphasized the abstract song itself: "The finished product is intellectual property, and you can't point to it."[29]

An even greater ambiguity presented by configurable music production is the fact that, for many musicians, finished products often constitute their materials, and vice versa. As DJ Earworm explained to me, "For a mash-up artist, the idea is: the material is usually finished, you know, finished material that is generally known to others . . . but the irony is that the materials are also finished products."[30]

Other musicians told me that not only do other people's finished products constitute their source materials—oftentimes, their *own* products do as well. As Si Begg told me, "what I've started doing more and more for stuff I release is actually kind of sampling my own back catalog and messing about with my own stuff, which has been quite interesting."[31] Jesse Gilbert told me that he doesn't simply mine his catalog of finished work, but that like the mythical Ouroboros, which eats its own tail, he samples his own product as he's creating it—and that this process makes it very difficult for him to distinguish between the traditional categories: "Tools and materials don't apply [conceptually] because the software that I use can do live sampling, and I can live sample my output. So I can route the output back into the input and I can use that as a raw material. So maybe there's no difference between raw material and final product."[32]

There is also some ambiguity regarding the distinction between tools and products. This is partially because many of the configurable musicians I spoke with actually produce their own tools—including software, sample banks, and hardware. As DJ Earworm told me, "The tools are the software. And I've built some of the tools and I've borrowed other people's tools."[33] TradeMark G, who has built some of his own instruments mechanically (such as the Thimbletron, a sample-triggering rig in which wired thimbles glued to the fingers of gloves serve as contacts for electrical circuits) also incorporates a range of borrowed, built, and modified tools in his arsenal: "I could use someone else's tools, but it helps if I can add things like plug-ins into it to accentuate and influence it to do things it wouldn't do out of the box. Even better is if I write my own software, or create my own electronics. Creating my tools gives me a lot bigger ability. It's like [Marshall] McLuhan's quote: 'We create our tools, and thereafter, our tools shape us.' And that's what's happening here."[34]

At the heart of this ambiguity is the fact that the computer—the foundation of configurable music production—is such a multifaceted machine that it can constitute material, tool, and product simultaneously. TradeMark G observes, "computers have the benefit of being very flexible. . . . I see it as both: as not only a tool in and of itself, but as a tool that makes other tools, that can make other tools, and so on."[35] Similarly, Tony Zeoli told me that "if you're creating a sample bank, you're composing at the same time while you're creating a tool to use, which becomes a product that you embed in a final product."[36]

Materials, Tools, and Property

Intellectual property law does not address the erosion of the materials/ tools binary at all. In fact, it contains an interesting contradiction. As attorney Gary Adelman explained to me, when it comes to configurable music, "the tools are legal. But what you're creating is illegal."[37] In other words, people are allowed to possess computers and audio editing software, but they are not allowed to apply those tools to copyrighted materials owned by another party (except in the case of "fair use"—which is becoming increasingly hard to defend legally).

Within the modern framework, the definition of an artwork is the product created by the application of tools to materials. Therefore, if the law acknowledges that a configurable musician is doing so—by holding him liable for copyright infringement—it logically follows that he should also be accorded authorship status, and granted a copyright for the new work. But, as I have discussed, this is not the case. In other words, a configurable musician is legally held to be producing an artwork (tools applied to materials) to the extent that it constitutes theft, but not to the extent that it constitutes creation.

We can understand this policy—like the *Bridgeport* decision rejecting de minimis protection for sampling—as a categorical rejection of the configurable ethic, and an institutional bolstering of the materials/tools binary, in the face of the erosion I've described in this chapter. Whether this absolutist discursive inflexibility will lead to the preservation of the modern framework or its ultimate destruction is an interesting, and open, question, and one I address in the final section of this book.

Conclusion

As with the other foundational elements of the modern framework, the distinction between materials and tools has become significantly harder to conceptualize and police in a configurable musical context. While some of the DJs I interviewed understood their work structurally in traditional terms, there was no clear consensus concerning the exact definition of "tools" and "materials" for sample-based practices and aesthetics. Materials cited ranged from songs to recordings to collections of preselected samples. Tools included hardware, software, traditional instrumentation, and the human mind itself. And many interviewees conceded that the concept of a "finished product" has little or no meaning considering that the sonic material is likely to be chopped up and reconfigured yet again, either by themselves or by their peers.

Yet, as with the other binaries I discuss in previous chapters, my interviewees were neither uninterested nor pessimistic about resolving these ambiguities over the longer term. Although our language, our laws, and our cultural categories are not adequate to describe or analyze these behaviors, the ad hoc definitions and distinctions emerging within configurable musical communities offer many intriguing solutions on both practical and theoretical levels. In the final section of this book, I discuss the significance of these solutions, and attempt to weave the tactical approaches of the DJs I've interviewed into a broader strategic framework for understanding and accommodating the role that configurable technology and culture will play in the continuing evolution of our society at large.

III

THE LESSONS

Configurability and the New Framework

In the first part of this book, I argue that music is a powerful agent of social and political change, that a historical dialectic exists between musical regulation and resistance, and that this process is bounded by a discursive framework, which is strengthened by institutional bonds. In the second part, I suggest that the modern framework, which has reigned ascendant in Western culture for two centuries, is severely challenged by configurable technology and culture, and I discuss the ways in which musicians, executives, attorneys, and everyday people are trying to make sense of new musical codes and practices. In the final section, I address the following logical question: Is configurability actually capable of rendering the modern framework obsolete? And, if so, what kind of discursive regime is likely to replace it?

As with all forms of prognostication, especially on a grand scale such as this, my answers should be taken with a grain of salt. Society and culture are so vast and complex, the only development we can expect is the unexpected. However, given the historical and structural arguments I have made in the preceding chapters, I believe that a thorough analysis of the evolving musical discourse can tell us something useful we might not find in a saucer of tea leaves.

First, in order to examine the question of continuity versus rupture, I return to the taxonomy of resistance and regulation I lay out in chapter 1, and cite specific instances of ways in which configurable practices continue to conform to the historical dialectical process. Then, I address the question of co-optation. Modern institutions, and their discursive framework, would not have stood nearly so long if they didn't have an excellent immune system, capable of absorbing and rendering neutral (or positive) the many challenges that have arisen over the centuries. In order to gauge the music industry's prospects for successful containment of the configurability threat, I cite conversations with musicians and music industry executives explicitly addressing this subject.

In the final chapter, I discuss the potential grains of a new discursive framework lurking within the evolving language of configurability, and outline five specific social, cultural, and economic principles that I believe we may abstract from my interviews and analysis. These are Configurable Collectivism, the Reunion of Labor, the Collision of Public and Private, the Shift from Linearity to Recursion, and DJ Consciousness. These principles will, I hope, offer an indication of how our society will reorganize itself in the wake of configurability's disruptive power.

10
Critique and
Co-optation

There's a whole lot of stuff that's going to be changing in a mad
way, and the intersection of culture and law, which includes art,
is going to be writhing like a dying animal that's been hit by a car.
Steinski

In another campaign, "The Second Coming," Nike offers up a TV
[commercial] featuring 10 of its top NBA basketball stars for consumers
to mash up online. At the site, NikeMashUp.com, visitors can select a
soundtrack and short video clips and arrange them on a timeline.
All mash-ups, though, end with the tagline "The Second Coming"
and the Nike swoosh logo, and consumers can't add their own text
or pictures, allowing Nike to pre-empt the problems Chevrolet had
with a mash-up campaign last year in which its Tahoe SUV was
mocked by opportunistic users.
Media magazine

In the previous chapters, I argue that configurable music and technology challenge our discourse of music, and by extension, the entire modern framework. This process is somewhat inherent to the structure of
configurability; the conceits of modernity don't easily apply to a cultural system as radically different from the past as the one whose evolution we are now witnessing. But does this fact necessarily suggest
that configurability is fundamentally critical of what came before, or resistant to institutional power? Do configurable musicians view their
own work as critical? Does it even matter whether they do?

There is no single answer to any of these questions, but the question of configurability-as-critique appeared often in my conversations with musicians and executives, and was raised frequently by my interviewees.

Some people I spoke with told me that configurable music is a fundamentally critical cultural form, simply by virtue of the fact that it relies on preexisting expression as its genesis. As dance music industry veteran Tony Zeoli told me, "I think that definitely there is always some kind of critical [aspect]—whether it's humor, whether it's political, whether it's romance . . . even in the most blasé form." This is because he considers the remixer's contribution to be a "critical addition" to the work being remixed.[1] Others consider configurable music to be intrinsically resistant, by virtue of its often illicit nature. As music journalist Bill Werde told me, "mash-ups are an act of resistance, and inherently political, because they're illegal."[2] Not everyone shares these opinions. As Pete Ganbarg of Atlantic Records told me, "I think it's more of 'how can I best make my artistic statement' than it is a criticism about somebody's music."[3]

As I argue in chapter 1, one of the most interesting aspects of the regulation/resistance cycle is that neither regulators nor resisters must necessarily think of themselves as being engaged in any process larger than their own immediate needs and ambitions. "All politics is local," as Tip O'Neill famously said, and the same may be said of cultural politics as well. In my interviews with configurable music practitioners, executives, and attorneys, I found ample evidence that configurable music engenders resistance to musical regulation at every intersection of institutional site (legal, ideological, commercial) and community site (aesthetics, praxis, technology). But, while some of my interviewees viewed their struggles as skirmishes in a larger cultural war, others simply told me that their ambitions went no further than circumventing immediate obstacles erected by musical regulation of one kind or another.

Resistance to Regulation among Configurable Musicians

Clearly, as I discuss in my first chapter, it would be futile to argue that the entire universe of musical regulation and resistance fits neatly within the schematic boundaries of my or any other taxonomy. Aesthetics, praxis, and technology are as mutually dependent and deeply intertwined as are legal, ideological, and commercial institutions, and rarely could an act of regulation or resistance be characterized as solely belonging to one category, and not to another. For the sake of clarity and comprehensiveness, however, I will continue to use this taxonomy to discuss resistance within the configurable music community, and simply acknowledge at the outset that each categorization is fluid and debatable.

Several configurable musicians told me about aesthetic decisions they have made that may be understood as Aesthetic Resistance to Legal Regulation. Most common, of course, is the sample-based aesthetic itself, which typically bypasses the legal barriers erected by copyright law. V/VM made an interesting observation, telling me that he views the market saturation of commercial music as an aesthetic imposition, and that he feels it is within every person's rights to alter the sonic material within the public sphere to suit his or her needs and tastes. In his words, once commercial music has entered the marketplace, "it just becomes public domain to me. You just think, 'Why not? It's about time.' It's always there anyway; it may as well be anybody's track to do anything with. Hearing the same thing over and over again, it's like, 'I need to hear this in a different way.'"[4]

While V/VM is simply trying to alter his immediate environment to suit his individual tastes, Eric Kleptone told me that he conceives of his aesthetic as a kind of political statement against the legal strictures placed on music and culture. He doesn't "really want to be seen as a pirate" from a legal standpoint, he told me—in fact, the sonic material he uses "doesn't necessarily have to be stolen, that's not an essential-to-form part of the work." Rather, his group's name (the Kleptones) and high-profile sampling practices, featuring recent popular artists, are "just playing on public perception" of configurable musicians as thieves, in order to emphasize the injustice and absurdity of that characterization. As he explained, "activists have been getting themselves arrested on the street to publicize their causes. So getting cease-and-desist orders online is not really any different. It's a way to kind of publicize your cause."[5]

According to attorney Fred von Lohmann of the Electronic Frontier Foundation (EFF), this tension between legal regulation and aesthetic resistance has produced aesthetic changes in configurable music. As he explained to me, the legal prohibition against distribution of unlicensed samples "drives the entire music genre underground, which itself changes the nature of the enterprise through self-selection. The only people who make this kind of music are those who are willing to be renegades in the first place." Musicians less likely to challenge authority by nature, he told me, "will go make different kinds of music."[6]

Other interviewees discussed behaviors and strategies that may be categorized as Practical Resistance to Legal Regulation. According to Si Begg, many configurable musicians commit unintentional resistance, just by virtue of the fact that they are breaking the laws—even if their ambition is to celebrate unconditionally the music they are sampling. In his words, "people tend to see something they like, and they want to use it, so they take it. . . . You're breaking the law. But you're doing it anyway, so I guess that's kind of being a bit of a freedom fighter of sampling whether you like it or not."[7]

DJ Earworm told me that he consciously crosses legal boundaries— not to make a political statement, or to "stick it to the man"—but because it liberates him from many of the considerations that complicate aesthetic production within the sanctioned commercial sphere: "More than the fact that I'm willing to risk something by putting my stuff out there, I'm willing to invest all this time into something which has no legal mechanism to pay me back. And there's a certain purity in that, that everyone who's doing this is really doing it because they love doing it. And there's no one out there with the illusion that they're gonna become the next mash up star and be able to pay their mortgage."[8] As I discuss further on, Earworm may be wrong on this final point; many configurable music practitioners do see their work as a potential gateway to careers in commercial music. However, for Earworm, the principle applies: resisting legal sanctions against sampling is a way for him to achieve a greater "purity" in his work.

Due to the sweeping prohibitions against breaking the copy-protection technology found on all DVDs, many commercially available music downloads, and some CDs—even in the service of legally sanctioned "fair use," as I discuss in my first chapter—nearly every configurable musician engages in Technological Resistance to Legal Regulation at one point or another. In cases where musicians bypass the technological barriers to sampling copy-protected CDs, they aren't merely violating statutory law such as the Digital Millennium Copyright Act (DMCA); as the EFF's Fred von Lohmann told me, they are also contractually violating the end user license agreement (EULA) attached to these CDs, which "expressly ban remix culture as a question of contract law."[9]

Breaking copy-protection technology is hardly an arcane practice reserved for a doughty few sample-based musicians who wish to push legal and aesthetic boundaries. Nearly every configurable musical practice, from production-adjacent to consumption-adjacent, requires a degree of flexibility that digital rights management (DRM) and other technological impediments prohibit. As a result, there has been a steady demand for DRM-circumvention technology over the past decade. Such software, including PlayFair, later renamed HYMN (which bypasses Apple's FairPlay DRM software), and FairUse4WM (which bypasses Microsoft's Windows Media Audio DRM) has been available freely on the Internet for years, updated as quickly as the DRM software manufacturers could update their own encryption algorithms, and downloaded by untold millions of users. As I write this, in January 2009, Apple has just announced it will make its entire iTunes Music Store library available DRM-free; for the moment, the music industry tide appears to be turning against copy protection (not so for films, unfortunately). We may consider this development as a direct response to the years of direct and massive resistance I described above.

Several practices described by my interviewees may be categorized as Aesthetic Resistance to Ideological Regulation. Some configurable musicians directly integrate politically or ideologically oriented sonic materials into their work, in order to critique the individuals or ideological concepts contained in those materials. Tony Zeoli told me he "look[s] to remixers and producers to add elements of speeches and even Donald Rumsfeld or [George W.] Bush when they sound wack." This accomplishes three goals, he told me. First, it's a way to exert symbolic power over these subjects, in sonic effigy. Second, it's a form of ridicule; Bush's malapropisms, often hilarious even on first listen, can sound terrifying or absurd if looped over and over. Finally, he told me, it's a method of news dissemination and political advocacy. In his words, sampling a public figure in a dance-oriented track is "a way to key in people who aren't politically savvy or conscious, to hear something that they should be hearing, because they don't read the newspaper or whatever."[10]

Other interviewees told me that they view their work as a way to resist ideological regulation in the form of cultural hegemony or aesthetic strictures. DJ Adrian told me he views mash-ups as "culture jamming. It's total, it's really fucking with pop culture . . . you're subverting the dominant cultural paradigm, and turning it into something that you probably personally like. And that's what's really cool."[11] Similarly, V/VM told me that configurable music offers him a way to strip away what he views as the superficial sheen of institutionally sanctioned and industrially standardized beauty on popular music, revealing what he considers the ugliness and emptiness beneath it: "These days, a lot of the pop hits, the vocal is so processed. If you start messing around with it, it comes out sounding extremely horrible because it's already been processed in the first place, it's not a natural voice. Because obviously the person singing couldn't sing before. I think it's like removing the gloss from the top, stripping that layer of gloss paint from the top and revealing what's beneath. It's like peeling an apple and seeing the rotten core in the middle."[12]

Some configurable musicians told me they consider their work to constitute what we may categorize as Practical Resistance to Ideological Regulation. As Strictly Kev told me, he views his work as an act of resistance against the ideological premise that institutional sanctioning of musical praxis is morally right, or socially beneficial: "I think the whole bootleg/mash-up thing is flying in the face of all authority. Why should we let 'the man' stop us? . . . By the time it's officially sanctioned, it's dead and gone. People don't have time to wait these days."[13]

To Si Begg, resistance to ideological regulation of music is more personal than political. He told me that he resents the fact that the mass media are "pushing [music] into your intellectual head space, yet they're still saying it's theirs. Even when it's become part of the culture." Therefore, he told me, sampling is simply a way of reasserting control over one's own nervous system and cultural environment. The act of sampling, he told me, amounts to telling musical regulatory institutions: "You've been pushing this stuff down our throats for the last twenty, thirty years, and now we want to do something with it. Now you get upset about it. Saying it's yours."[14]

Interviewees also offered some interesting perspectives on Technological Resistance to Ideological Regulation. To DJ Adrian, the sudden accessibility of music production and distribution equipment within a configurable technological environment undermines the ethic of professional exceptionalism, the power of consolidated capital, and the mechanism of centralized control. As he explained to me, "ten years ago, to be a decent remix producer, you needed to have $30,000 worth of gear. Now, you can have free pirated software on a cheap computer and still make it sound damn good. . . . The mash-up community is Internet-based, which means that it's open source. It's global."[15]

To Jesse Gilbert, configurability offers the opportunity to resist another kind of ideological regulation of music technology. Specifically, he believes that traditional music editing software, which "sequences" audio clips along a strict timeline, represents an instrument of socially regulated timekeeping, and a continuation of the musical and temporal regulation presented by traditional Western scoring and orchestral organization. By building his own music processing software, Gilbert told me, he can harness the power of configurable technology without inheriting the constraints of the modern framework. In his words, "sequencers are all about this kind of regulated time-space. Everything is about accuracy. And there are all kinds of notions about rhythmic divisibility, about the imposition of the tempered scale onto synthesizers."

In Gilbert's opinion, the musical regulation represented by synthesizers and sequencers has a very pointed political purpose: to extend European cultural hegemony into the twenty-first century by creating tools that reify its logic and preclude alternative representations of time and space. As he told me, "my feeling is that it has to do with almost a reaction to the postcolonial moment."[16] He conceives of his work, therefore, as more than just an aesthetic exercise, but as a cultural intervention geared toward globalizing and democratizing the process of temporal and spatial organization.

One of the most frequent forms of resistance described by my interviewees was Aesthetic Resistance to Commercial Regulation. At the most local and immediate level, DJ Axel told me that his interest in mash-ups was born of the fact that, as a professional club DJ in Los Angeles, he was often required to play exactly the same popular hip-hop songs that the clubs' patrons were likely to have heard on commercial radio in their cars en route to the clubs. He told me he considered this requirement to be "artistically offensive and boring," so he decided he would play the popular music he was required to play, but would "mess with it" by mashing it up with other songs. Axel considers the mash-up aesthetic, therefore, to be a form of "protest" against the "mindless" conventions of the Los Angeles club scene.[17]

DJ Earworm considers the mash-up aesthetic to constitute protest on a larger scale. While he balks at the notion that he is somehow critiquing songs themselves by mashing them up, he feels that the music industry itself is generally the subject of critique within the aesthetic. Specifically, he rejects the industry's use of genre as an instrument of social distinction and market segmentation, and hopes to use mash-ups as a way to raise consciousness about these matters, and as a way to protest the industry's role in the process. In his words, mash-ups "let people enjoy stuff that they 'ought' to be critical of, and that their social cues tell them that they should be critical of. . . . I think most mash-up artists are critical of the music industry. But not the music." When I asked him what elements of the music industry he felt mash-up producers are reacting against, he told me, "the marketing muscle. The RIAA. The anti-piracy efforts."[18]

Matt Wand told me that his work constitutes aesthetic resistance against commercial regulation on an even larger scale; rather than reacting against individual employers, or even large-scale commercial institutions, his focus is on resisting capitalism itself. Echoing DJ Earworm's comments about the aesthetic "purity" that comes from eschewing commercialism, Wand told me that "you try to make a culture that's as abhorrent as possible, in order to keep people away from it, in order to keep it untainted by the money men and the powers that be, and to keep it from being dragged into the limelight and the mainstream."[19]

Several interviewees also told me that they believe the entire range of configurable music practices—from file sharing to remixing—represent a form of Practical Resistance to Commercial Regulation. Eric Kleptone told me he feels that the major record labels have stopped "trying to convince people that they're cool and hip," and have become more honest about their role as "the bad guys," by suing their own customers for file sharing, licensing their music at exorbitant rates, and sending cease-and-desist orders to configurable musicians that can't obtain or afford sampling licenses. Consequently, he told me, "I think a lot of the audience is gonna retaliate about, just the feeling that they are being conned by [the labels], that they have been conned in the past. So there's a kind of air of retribution there."[20]

Similarly, Go Home Productions pointed to the shift in cultural power engendered by configurable technologies as a genesis of practical resistance—not just against record labels, but against commercial recording artists, as well. In his words, commercial music "now is very much in the public's hands. And people can do what they want with it, and throw it back, and share it. And some artists like it, and some artists don't. And the record labels don't know what to do with it, that's for sure."[21]

Our final category, Technological Resistance to Commercial Regulation, can be seen in countless configurable music practices, including: the circumvention of DRM technologies, which I discuss above; the use of iPods, video game controllers, and other consumption-oriented devices as musical instruments (the iDJ, which allows iPod-based music to be manipulated like vinyl, has become an increasingly frequent weapon in the modern DJ's arsenal); and, of course, in the act of sampling itself—whether the source of the sample resides on vinyl, optical disc, or hard drive.

Configurable musicians are, for the most part, keenly aware that they are flouting the intentions of musical regulatory institutions when they engage in such behaviors—and, for many, this is part of the attraction. As DJ Earworm told me, "it's fun and naughty. It's always fun to be naughty. Especially when . . . there's DRM and they pipe down on, you know, all the music companies are not even selling us music any more. They're licensing it, lending it to us."[22] In other words, Earworm conceives of his technological interventions as a way to reclaim ownership over the music file itself, and thereby, to reassert cultural power over musical production.

Configurability, Cooperation, and Co-optation

Of course, no underground or counterculture is purely resistant; as Thomas Frank so eloquently writes of the complex dance between cultural regulation and resistance since the 1960s in *The Conquest of Cool*, "hip is the cultural life-blood of the consumer society."[23] And today, there are not many ideas or trends hipper than remixes, mash-ups, and DJ culture. Shortly after DJ Danger Mouse's *The Grey Album* prompted millions of downloads in 2004, the idea of the mash-up became nearly ubiquitous in the popular press, with the *New York Times* even listing the "mainstream mash-up" in its annual roundup, "The Year in Ideas."[24] More recently, *Time* magazine conferred the ultimate mainstream bona fides on configurable culture, choosing "You" (the reader) as the magazine's annual "Person of the Year" in 2006 (fig. 9). Although there is something contradictory and even unnerving about the flagship of corporate-owned print media telling its readers, "You control the Information Age" (Is it a concession of defeat? Disingenuous pandering? Or merely standard journalistic overstatement?), the move signals a shift in mainstream mythology regardless of its motives.

Predictably, many configurable musicians are ambivalent about the recent commercial embrace of their subculture. DJ Adrian views the commercial intervention as regrettable, but par for the course: "We have seen, in the past few years . . . corporate America trying to co-opt it. 'Oh! Youth culture! What's hip and now! Mash-ups! Let's co-opt it!' That's the American way." He doesn't feel that co-optation poses a significant threat to configurable music's resistant potential, because musicians will continue to produce innovations more rapidly than commercial efforts can encompass them. In his words, "bootleggers will always be one step ahead. Because they're going to think of things that wouldn't be possible being put together in a corporate boardroom."[25]

Other configurable musicians have told me they are already seeing commercial influence on their practices and aesthetics. DJ Axel, for instance, told me that he switched his focus from hip-hop to rock-oriented mash-ups because "I noticed that they were getting more radio play."[26] DJ Paul V, who spins mash-ups for commercial radio broadcaster Indie 103.1 FM (KDLD in Santa Monica, California), confirmed Axel's hunch, telling me that the radio station executives won't allow him to air mash-ups that lack a rock element, despite the fact that this prevents many of DJ Paul V's top choices from getting airplay: "Well, they're not going to play a Missy Eliot vs. Beyoncé mash-up. Because in

Figure 9: *Time* magazine cover depicting "You" as the 2006 "Person of the Year."

their mind—we have a difference of opinion. In my mind, I think the whole point of a mash-up is to step outside of your preconceived, your locked-in. But I don't run the radio station, and they do have a format, obviously, which is indie, alternative, British, you know—guitar-based music. They don't play Missy Eliot, they don't play Beyoncé, whatever."[27]

From the music industry side, co-optation appears to be both a necessary and a successful strategy. As Hosh Gureli of Sony/BMG told me, he views the current commercial embrace of configurability to be completely consistent with the music industry's historical practice of co-opting youth culture: "Every generation, the kids liked something that goes against the establishment. That's why Napster, Kazaa, and all those things—who made those things happen? Kids. To beat the system. But the corporations are realizing, if you can't beat 'em—join 'em." According to Gureli, this thought process is the genesis for a rash of recent business agreements between record labels and online music distributors. As he told me, "that's why we're making deals with MySpace now—so we can get a piece of the action."[28]

Configurable musicians have reaped some benefits as well from the increased commercial interest in their work—namely, they're able to make some money, and in some cases, to bridge the gulf separating "amateur" from "professional," to the extent that the gulf still exists. As early as 2003, mattcatt was beginning to receive financial offers and free and legal access to a capellas from "publishers who recognise the value of being mashed."[29] Eric Kleptone, describing more recent occurrences, says "there's a couple of other things that I'm looking at doing. Maybe doing some commercial remix work. And also a couple of film soundtracks. So this has given me avenues into other things—the work I've done as a mash-up artist."[30] Similarly, Go Home Productions told me that he's willing to downplay the illicit nature of his work if it leads to commercial work: "I think in the early days, I felt like I was doing something naughty, but I've kind of looked beyond that, and thought 'What if I make something creative [that] the artist would actually want to use?' [Labels and artists are now saying] 'We appreciate the mash-up you've done, but how'd you like to do a remix?' Which I enjoy equally as well."[31]

DJ Earworm has discovered that his fame as a DJ has led to opportunities a bit farther afield. In 2006, Wiley published a how-to book that he penned, called *Mashup Construction Kit*.[32] Earworm is quick to emphasize, however, that despite the money and fame he's received in the wake of the book's publication, he still barely makes enough from music and publishing combined to cover his basic expenses: "I'm pretty well known, but I don't make good money. You know, I'm really poor. I'm struggling."[33]

In short, configurable music characterizes both critique and resistance for a great many musicians, and appears in every category of our regulation/resistance matrix. There have also been considerable efforts at containment and exploitation by regulatory institutions, and, judging by the changes many musicians have made to their practices, these efforts have, to a degree, been successful. The question that remains is whether this push-and-pull amounts to the same dialectical process that has characterized the last two hundred years of musical and social history, or whether configurability's disruptive potential is great enough to tip the balance toward wholesale discursive and social realignment. This is the question I address in the next, and final, chapter.

11

"Plus Ça Change" or Paradigm Shift?

Obama's election as president is a beautiful testament to the
American collective consciousness that is flowering.
Russell Simmons

In my opinion, what we were doing was beneficial for the game . . .
DJ Drama

I have nearly reached the end of this book, and have yet to conclusively
answer my fundamental question. Does configurable music presage a
discursive break in our understanding of what music is and how it operates, and therefore portend a breakdown of the existing social order?
Or is the rise of the DJ simply one more development in an ongoing
dialectic between cultural regulation and resistance, as easily contained
within the strong yet flexible boundaries of the modern framework as
atonality, the birth of sound recording, and the electrification of blues
and rock music?

Clearly, the answer to this question is more one of judgment than of
empirical proof, and even historians of our era will differ regarding the
social significance of the striking changes we are currently witnessing
in the nature and capacity of communication media, and in the aesthetic codes and practices that exploit these media.

It would be easy to argue, conservatively, that despite the rise of configurable technologies, nothing much has changed in the cycle of cultural
production and consumption, and that our social institutions stand as
strong as ever, above the fray of petty fashion and the relentless churn

of musical style. As I describe in chapter 10, configurable music appears to be following a well-worn path from margin to mainstream—regulation, resistance, innovation, reification, co-optation, and ultimately cooperation, as practitioners and regulatory institutions seek their mutual benefit from the rising popularity of a new musical trend.

Of course, the process does have—and always has had—its detractors, but one could argue that their objections will recede into noise as the sound of configurability reaches its popular apex. How many now remember the stalwarts who complained that the Newport Folk Festival would overshadow and overexpose the burgeoning Greenwich Village folk revival movement, or the bebop aficionados who attempted to resist the migration of musicians like Charlie Parker, Dizzy Gillespie, and Thelonious Monk from Harlem after-hours clubs to glitzy midtown roosts? If these people are remembered at all, it is mostly as weathered talking heads in music documentaries, most likely portrayed as victims or cranks who suffered from trying to impede the inevitable.

On the other hand, there is much to suggest that a larger paradigmatic change is at hand. The unavoidable conclusion from my interviews is that each of the fundamental binaries that characterizes the modern framework is breaking down; again and again, interviewees described "blurriness," "gray areas," and "spectrums" emerging where clear lines once appeared to exist, and where our musical regulatory institutions still insist they do.

Though the configurable musicians I spoke with universally recognized this trend, their responses to it were understandably varied and ambivalent. Musicians tend to reflexively reinforce the boundaries of the modern framework, drawing lines in the sand, when the perceived legitimacy of their behavior or their ability to profit from it is at stake. Of *course* they have evaluative criteria distinguishing better from worse and original from derivative, they told me; otherwise, they are all in danger of being classified as derivative, uncreative, *not valuable*.

Similarly, many configurable musicians are perfectly willing to strive for uniqueness, or to draw lines in the sand separating composition from performance, in the context of remuneration. Because of the categorical rejection of configurable authorship by our legal institutions, and because our music industry is currently centered around controlling copyright, the range and number of wage-earning options open to configurable musicians is extremely limited. Consequently, they are much less likely to reject stark categorization when a paycheck depends on it.

Outside these exigencies, most configurable musicians tend not only to acknowledge the erosion of the modern framework's boundaries, but to welcome and even to celebrate it. Throughout my interviews, configurable musicians consistently distanced themselves from the binary categories of the modern framework, or sought to encompass them within a new, unified categorization: they are neither fans nor artists, they are *both* fans and artists; they are neither performers nor composers, they are *both* performers and composers; their workstations are neither mere tools nor mere materials; they are tools, materials, and finished products all at once.

Music industry executives, by contrast, are equally cognizant of the changes wrought by configurability, but are generally much more emphatic about the need to shore up the modern framework against any challenges. They are willing to view configurable music as an art form, but only with the traditional rules intact: artist exceptionality (to the point of conferring genius status on individual artists—a step almost universally rejected by the musicians I spoke with), division of labor, and of course, the use of the bottom line as the ultimate evaluative mechanism. To these interviewees, configurability is primarily seen as just another fashionable new musical style (or group of styles) to be packaged, marketed, and sold, like any other.

Even some interviewees in the music industry acknowledged that configurability doesn't constitute business as usual, and that it poses fundamental challenges to the music industry's modus operandi. For instance, consider this brief exchange with WMA's Marc Geiger, regarding the sustainability of the original/copy binary:

Aram: Do you think that it is going to hold up in the age of sampled music?
    I mean, do you think that the industry will be able to continually—
Marc: I think I already answered it. I said the Internet blew it all apart.
Aram: Okay. So it's over?
Marc: It's over.[1]

If we accept the premise that configurability is undermining the modern framework, disrupting the historical cycle of musical regulation and resistance, what conclusions can we draw from this realization? What assumptions or values will replace the ones codified by Kant and elevated to the level of dogma by the Romantics? And what may be the social consequences of the newly emergent framework? Again, there is no empirical method to answer this question; we are still in configurability's infancy, and discursive frameworks emerge from a lengthy process of cultural negotiation and consensus. However, there are a few general premises we may abstract from my interviews, and these offer some promising indications of the cultural logic of configurability.

Premise: Configurable Collectivism

First, there is an emerging value that we may call Configurable Collectivism (although the term Configurable Individualism would apply just as well). This represents a reorientation of the relationship between the individual and the collective. One of the strongest indications of this attitude is in configurable musicians' rejection of the premise of artistic exceptionality. Although my interviewees were willing and able to make value judgments, acknowledging relative degrees of artistic merit and disparate levels of cultural participation, they tended to reject the concept of the artist as a separate class of individual, or of art as a separate class of human endeavor. Furthermore, they soundly rejected the notion of artistic genius, opting to elevate individual works themselves to the level of exceptionality, rather than the individuals who produced them.

This ethic is also reflected in configurable musicians' emphasis on acknowledging sources, and on emphasizing the collective nature of cultural production. Nearly every style of configurable music has developed its own language of what is typically called "citation" in academic research and publication—rejecting the notion of creation ex nihilo that underpins the modern framework, and positing all cultural production as a collective enterprise. The variation between styles such as mash-ups, techno, and hip-hop seems to reside more in questions of sample size and recognizability than in disparate levels of dedication to the ethic of acknowledgment, which each shares in its own way. Ironically, as many of my interviewees told me, the greatest limit on their ability to share both reputational and monetary rewards with their sources and influences is the current copyright regime, which counterintuitively incentivizes musicians to claim the mantle of originality and individuality, disguising their creative debts for fear of incurring insurmountable legal and financial ones.

The social significance of configurable collectivism is potentially enormous. The individual represents the atomistic, indivisible unit of social policy and imagination within the modern framework, and the blurring of the lines between individual and collective endeavor is no less a threat to the modern framework than the quantum theory's blurring of the lines between wave and particle was to Newtonian physics. I don't mean to suggest that society is returning to some preindustrial state of absolute collectivism—such as the Tsarist Russian peasantry, who, as Richard Pipes relates, "had no opportunity to acquire a sense of individual identity" in relation to a collective that "submerged the individual in the group."[2] Nor am I predicting or advocating a society in which some institutional ideal of collectivism is enforced at gunpoint, as with the Soviet system that replaced the Tsarist one. It seems clear, though, that configurability engenders a more fluid distinction between individual and group than the modern framework can encompass, and that this must entail a renegotiation of the balance of cultural power and a reinvestigation of our atomistic social theories and the institutions that make them manifest.

Premise: The Reunion of Labor

The second general premise that emerges from my conversations with configurable musicians is the Reunion of Labor. As many of my interviewees told me, the erosion of the performance/composition and artist/audience binaries in configurable music makes it difficult or impossible for them to locate themselves within the modern framework's division of musical labor. The premise that composition, arrangement, production, performance, criticism, and appreciation are or should be conducted separately, by discrete individuals, simply does not jive with the experience of configurable music practitioners, who generally encompass all or most of those functions within a single, integrated process. This transformation is already so complete that the only definition of "performance" most configurable musicians can fathom requires the existence of an audience—a term that, by their own accounts, is becoming increasingly indistinct.

Moreover, the collapsing of the traditional orchestral or popular music group structure—both of which serve as models of social organization, as I have discussed—into the digital "one-man band" of the laptop or turntable rig further undermines the premise of the division of musical labor into categories such as "conductor" and "instrumentalist." In configurable music, all roles associated with musical production and consumption become contingent, fluid, and, in terms of the distribution of cultural power, equivalent.

Again, the social ramifications of this musical change are potentially significant. The division of labor has been a foundation of economic, cultural, and social organization for centuries, and is considered the sine qua non of the capitalist system in an industrialized society. At the very least, the reunion of labor in configurable music undermines an important ideological vector for this system, and helps to model an alternative system of social and economic organization. More radically, it may signal a shift away from the "alienation" of labor that Marx described, in which workers deprived of a stake in the goods they produce become disenfranchised and divested from cultural, political, and even interpersonal processes, as well.

This shift is arguably already underway in today's globalized labor market; as Manuel Castells[3] persuasively argues, labor in the "network society" has become increasingly "flexible," as the value and function of information has displaced other forms of capital in our economic system. This newly flexible workforce bears both the burden and the benefit of free agency; job security has diminished, even as labor's powers of self-determination and negotiation have increased. It is easy to see how, if the modern discursive framework reflected and amplified Fordist labor organization, the emerging configurable music framework similarly reflects and amplifies this new model of production. The DJ, like the knowledge worker, carries his capital with him—as a snail carries its shell. The old model of bosses, employees, and consolidated capital—like the old model of conductors, instrumentalists, and stable orchestras—is increasingly giving way to one of a network of peers, uniting and separating labor and capital on an ad hoc basis to achieve specific, targeted ends.

Premise: The Collision of Public and Private

The third general premise that emerges from my interviews is the Collision of Public and Private. This trend is evident in the way that many configurable musicians understand figure/ground relations in their work. Rather than viewing the musical recording as a self-contained and complete artifact, these musicians conceive of the audio they produce as part of a larger atmospheric soundscape, likely to interact with ambient social, industrial, and musical noises wherever and however it is audited. Likewise, they consider all of these sounds—from other recorded songs to the bleeps and bloops of electronic gadgets to the sound of bricks colliding—to be fair game as ingredients for their own work. As I quote Matt Wand in chapter 8, "The private has become public. The music itself has become just a background."[4]

This insertion of public noise into private, and vice versa, is even further exacerbated by another factor described by my interviewees: the fact that the creative process itself, once confined invisibly and inaudibly within the boundaries of the human skull, has suddenly become transparent and auditable, as the computer processor has increasingly become an extension (in a McLuhanist sense) of the human mind. To put this another way: at one time, creative processes were *defined* as internal, and cultural processes were *defined* as external. With the introduction of configurable technologies and practices, the line separating these levels of activity has blurred; the creative and the cultural are now one—and thus, what was once an exclusively private domain has now become public, and vice versa. This fact is part of my justification for merging psychological theories (e.g., the systems framework) and sociological theories (e.g., social network analysis) into a single, integrated model for understanding networked culture, as I outline in my first chapter.

As with my other general premises, the collision of public and private in configurable music suggests many social ramifications. As other writers and theorists have noted,[5] the traditional boundaries separating public from private in our society at large are rapidly eroding, as surveillance mechanisms pervade city streets; democratic governments rush to legislate away constitutionally protected rights prohibiting detainment, search, and seizure; mass media promote forms of entertainment, such as "reality television," normalizing the public judgment of private foibles and failures; and, most importantly, untold legions of Internet users post their names, photos, audio/video recordings, opinions, and predilections to social networking websites and blogs.

We have yet to understand the net effects of these rapid social and technological changes, but clearly they entail a shift of some kind in sociopolitical and cultural power relations. As Michel Foucault argues in *Discipline and Punish: The Birth of the Prison*, institutionalized surveillance of individuals (exemplified in Jeremy Bentham's model prison, the Panopticon) constitutes institutional control over individuals. This is because, in his famous equation, knowledge equals power, and more specifically, knowledge *of* is an instrument of power *over*: "power and knowledge directly imply one another . . . there is no power relation without the correlative constitution of a field of knowledge, nor any knowledge that does not presuppose and constitute at the same time power relations."[6]

Given the growing institutional surveillance over individuals, and the concomitant shift in power relations between institutions and individuals, there are essentially only three strategies an individual may undertake. One is to ignore the process completely—to think "I've got nothing to hide, ergo nothing to worry about," or to convince oneself that the benefits to our security represented by increased surveillance outweigh the detriments to our privacy. The second is to disappear as thoroughly as possible, by encrypting and obscuring the information we transact, and by refusing to use credit cards, mobile phones, ATMs, or any of the myriad points of surveillance we now encounter in our daily lives. Gene Hackman's character in the 1998 film *Enemy of the State*, an ex-NSA operative named Brill, exemplified the extreme of this strategy, living within a self-constructed Faraday cage to shield him from electromagnetic detection.

The third strategy for coping with institutionalized surveillance— one that appears to be increasingly popular—is to participate in the surveillance processes (both as surveillant and object of surveillance) actively and transparently. By employing this strategy, which Steve Mann et al. have termed "sousveillance,"[7] individuals can both mediate and understand the personal information they are transacting, and mitigate the inequity of information flow (and therefore social power) by surveilling the institutions in return. This is exactly the strategy undertaken by the protagonists in Cory Doctorow's recent novel, *Little Brother*,[8] in which a group of teenage computer hackers, building a virtual *samizdat* network between the XBOX game consoles in thousands of teenagers' bedrooms, document and expose the abuses of power committed by the Department of Homeland Security after they have been unjustly detained and tortured in the wake of a terrorist attack.

Configurable music, which explicitly acknowledges the erosion of public/private boundaries, and strategically integrates the entirety of our public soundscape (including "private" property) into its aesthetic, may be understood as a form of sonic sousveillance. By actively transcending the boundaries of the modern framework, DJs model and promote forms of listening and information transaction that are tailored to undermine the power exerted by what we may call the "panaudicon" of musical regulatory institutions. In other words, configurable aesthetic codes serve as templates for active social participation in the redistribution of knowledge/power in a surveillance society.

Premise: The Shift from Linearity to Recursion

The fourth general premise that emerges from my interviews is the Shift from Linearity to Recursion. Several of the modern framework's fundamental binaries are characterized by linear processes and organizational precepts. The artist/audience and composition/performance binaries, for instance, both reflect and reinforce the logic of the "value chain" and the "supply chain," economic and business management concepts predicated on the assumption of a linear process in the production of anything, including cultural artifacts. The premise of these concepts is that music (like any product) is composed (designed), performed (manufactured), recorded (productized), distributed, and audited (consumed)—consistently flowing in one direction from genesis to completion.

As many of my interviewees informed me, this linear logic does not apply to their musical production processes. For many configurable musicians, creation begins with consumption, just as artistry begins with audition. Furthermore, as I described, the modern framework's assumption that composition invariably precedes performance is challenged by creative strategies such as DJ Axel's, in which a more subtle and complex process of experimentation and refinement, relying on both compositional and performative elements, characterize his workflow.

Other linear aspects of the modern framework are challenged by configurability, as well. The blurring of the original/copy distinction undermines the premise that copies are *defined* by their subsequence to originals. Similarly, the notion that tools may constitute products, and products may constitute materials, completely erodes the linear assumptions of the modern framework's materials/tools binary, in which production begins with materials and ends with a *finished* product. In each of these cases, linearity is replaced by recursion—in which any stage of the process may constitute beginning, middle or end, depending on the context and the vantage point of the observer.

The social significance of this shift goes far beyond the obvious challenge to linear models of economic production and consumption. As many theorists have argued, linear logic, narration, and argumentation are the hallmarks of Western culture, and have been for millennia. W. J. Ong, for instance, argues that linearity is a feature of literacy, and vice versa: "sparsely linear or analytic thought and speech are artificial creations, structured by the technology of writing."[9] Similarly, Neil Postman argues that "the resonances of the linear, analytical structure of print . . . could be felt everywhere"[10] in the early American republic, during the dawn of the modern framework.

The challenge to linearity posed by configurable culture, therefore, amounts to a challenge to the epistemological processes that characterize modernity, and that reach back to the dawn of literacy and rational discourse. I am hardly the first theorist to draw a connection between the introduction of networked communication technologies and the development of recursive modes of narration, analysis, or other epistemological processes; arguably, it is one of the central tenets of postmodernism. However, I feel that the recursive logic inherent in configurable music differs from some other recursive expressive forms, such as postmodern literature, in an important respect. Postmodern literature employs nonlinear narrative structures as a *strategic challenge* to the aesthetic strictures of conventional narrative, and as a *symbolic reflection* of the disjunctive consciousness that characterizes life in contemporary, postindustrial society. Configurable music, though it may do these as well, is primarily recursive because nonlinear logic is *inherent to the process itself*. Configurable musicians may be more or less inclined to view their work as a strategic intervention or as a comment on the state of our society, but they are bound to the logic of recursion simply by virtue of their choice of expressive media.

In a sense, then, configurable culture poses a greater challenge to the linear logic of modernity than postmodernism did—precisely because it is a reflexive movement, rather than a deliberate one, and therefore portends a shift in the epistemological habits of society at large, rather than just the avant garde or the intelligentsia. Put another way, configurability in practice lives up to many of the promises made—but never fully delivered on—by postmodern theory.

Premise: DJ Consciousness

The fifth and final general premise suggested by my interviews is the Emergence of DJ Consciousness. As I note in chapter 10, interviewees described a form of double-consciousness regarding their work and their lives—an onus to view configurable music practices both from within and from without—that closely echoes W. E. B. Du Bois's famous characterization of the African American experience. This can be witnessed in the ambiguous use of the term "bedroom producer," which can function as a straw man "other" one minute and as a proud or consciously pejorative self-appellation the next. Similarly, the term "DJ" itself often seems to operate linguistically as a category or symbol whose referent is simply "other than." This can be seen in the ways that interviewees used the term somewhat contradictorily to mean both "not performing" and "not composing" in their discussions of the composition/performance dichotomy. Despite this fact, a considerable number of the configurable musicians I spoke with (and thousands of others, if not more) chose a professional alias beginning with the letters "DJ" (DJ Axel, DJ Adrian, DJ Food, etc.). "It is a peculiar sensation, this double-consciousness, this sense of always looking at one's self through the eyes of others," Du Bois writes.[11] DJs, as I was told by many of my interviewees in many different ways, are always hearing themselves through the ears of others.

But what can it mean that a cultural strategy and state of consciousness typically associated with a historically marginalized and disenfranchised social group have also come to characterize the figure of the DJ? And what are the implications of the fact that configurability is now ascendant, and is coming to characterize American mainstream consciousness?

My interpretation—and this phenomenon is clearly open to others—is that the very act of engaging culture through a configurable lens entails a recognition that we are *all* marginalized and culturally disenfranchised by the principles of aesthetic exceptionalism, the division of musical labor, and the propertization of expression that characterize the modern framework. Conversely, we are empowered by the act of embracing both self-ness and other-ness simultaneously through reconfiguring and reimagining our cultural environments.

In fact, each of the other general principles I have outlined—configurable collectivism, the reunion of labor, the collision of public and private, and the shift from linearity to recursion—in some way bears on this fifth general principle. Configurable collectivism problematizes the stark contrast between "self" and "other" represented by the modern myth of the individual. The reunion of labor requires configurable musicians—like flexible laborers—to see themselves as commodities, in order to successfully transact their intellectual labor and capital with others. The collision of public and private has obvious consequences for DJ consciousness, exposing internal processes to the scrutiny of others, and allowing each of us to encompass the universe of cultural information within our communicative lexicons. And the shift from linearity to recursion means that, because there is no such thing as a finished product, each of us depends on others not just to interpret, but to extend the meanings of our own expressions.

The emergence of DJ consciousness, therefore, may be understood as a harbinger of the rise of a network consciousness, or network culture (the distinction, as I have discussed, becomes increasingly blurry), or what we may alternatively understand as the epistemological analog of Castells's "network society."[12] This emerging consciousness recognizes the inequities of the modern framework, and attempts to rectify them through the democratization of cultural power. This is not to suggest that everyone will somehow become equal participants in an economic, political, or social sense, but simply that a new fluidity exists, in which each of us—forced to confront our public selves through the monitor of a surveillance camera or a Facebook profile editor—will have the ability to retrieve, reconfigure, and redistribute such information, and in so doing, to participate in the production of shared meaning.

Gender, Race, and Configurability

Of course, it would be naive to expect or suggest that configurable culture and society does or will constitute some form of utopian free-for-all. The most obvious caveat is that the very technological changes precipitating these cultural and social ones are contributing to an accelerating threat of global ecological (and sociopolitical) catastrophe, burying poor and politically disenfranchised communities around the globe under mountains of toxic waste, and rapidly warming our atmosphere to levels previously unknown during humanity's brief tenure on this planet. Unless we address these problems immediately and comprehensively, not only will the emerging configurable technology infrastructure cease to be sustainable, but our species itself may face extinction as well.

On a less alarmist note, it is clear from my interviews that many of the social inequities and disjunctures that have plagued our society in the past will not be magically eradicated by the rise of configurable culture. One thing that struck me during my research is that nearly every configurable music practitioner I spoke with was male—and this wasn't for any lack of effort on my part to balance the scales. Of the dozens of people I interviewed, only two musicians—Vicki Bennett (who records under the name People Like Us) and Mysterious D—were women. According to my interviewees, this disparity reflects the actual makeup of practicing DJs. As Si Begg told me, "I think there definitely is a gender gap, yeah. You'd be lying to say there wasn't." He said he attributes it more to disparate cultural training than to active bias within the community: "I think it's just, traditionally, geeking out with a computer is seen as a men's kind of a boys' club thing. But I think it's changing . . . most people I know would certainly be more than happy to see more women doing it."[13]

Mysterious D agreed with Si Begg to an extent, telling me that she had never experienced any personal resistance to joining the mash-up community. She traced the roots of the imbalance to the traditional disparities—born of both explicit bias and cultural training—within musical culture and economies at large:

> The music industry in general is dominated by males. Even though girls play guitar. Girls DJ. Girls do all these things. It just seems to be a lot rarer. And do I know why that is? That's a much bigger conversation. I think that it has nothing to do with mash-up culture. I think it has to do with music culture in general. . . . And also, you know, I hate to generalize, but guys tend to like gear more than girls do, and mash-ups are a gear-based thing. It's all about production. And, again music does seem to be, like, a boy's world just in general. . . . The girls want to come dance to it, and the boys want to figure out how to make it. At Bootie [the mash-up club she co-founded].[14]

As Mysterious D notes, the gender gap in configurable music appears to be "all about production"—more specifically, explicit bias is not required, because men in general are culturally trained to feel more comfortable with the means of production than are women. Whether this will change as a result of the increasing accessibility of configurable technologies remains to be seen. The fact that my interviewees didn't report any explicit gender bias within their communities is promising, but as Eszter Hargittai and Steven Shafer have shown, women continue to perceive their technology skills to be inferior to those of men regardless of their actual skill level, and this may have an inhibiting effect on their participation in mash-ups and other configurable musical practices. In Hargittai and Shafer's words, "Women's lower self-assessment vis-à-vis Web-use ability may affect significantly the extent of their online behavior and the types of uses to which they put the medium."[15]

Another disparity that emerged from my interviews was racial and ethnic. Many of configurable music's foundational innovations were developed in the context of Afro-diasporic aesthetics, practices, and communities—from the dub versions of 1960s and 1970s Jamaica to the hip-hop and turntablism of 1970s and 1980s New York City. However, as I discovered, today's mash-up and techno musician communities are overwhelmingly white in their racial makeup,[16] while forms such as dub and hip-hop tend to be more diverse, with significant participation by black musicians.

Compounding and amplifying the disparities in the composition of configurable musician communities are disjunctures in the aesthetic and ethical codes that characterize the styles themselves. As I discussed in previous chapters, the aesthetic logic of configurability differs broadly from one style to another. While mash-ups tend to be song-oriented, focusing on the narrative arc connecting a song's verses, bridge, and chorus, and downplaying the performative aspects of the form, hip-hop and turntablism tend to be more loop-oriented, focusing on the variations and deviations from a repeated theme, and are thus more deeply tied to the processes of improvisation and performance. This is evident in the gap between Steinski's description of "guys like me who can sit around and listen to the same beat going around and around for twenty minutes,"[17] and DJ Adrian's insistence that, in his music, "there's a break that goes into a bridge, and then there's a chorus, whereas, it's not just the same loop over and over and over and over again."[18]

The difference, as Steinski observed explicitly, and as should be evident to even those without formal musicological training, is that mash-ups tend to follow a more traditional European structural logic, while hip-hop and turntablism tend to follow a more traditional Afro-diasporic structural logic. In a word, mash-ups are coded as "white," while hip-hop is coded as "black." The distinction is culturally significant in spite of the facts that (a) neither community is racially monolithic—especially accounting for people who primarily listen, rather than produce, (b) both styles abound in exceptions (i.e., song-oriented hip-hop and loop-oriented mash-ups), and (c) the characterization of European music as song oriented, and African music as loop oriented, is a drastic generalization that reduces millennia of tradition representing hundreds of cultures and thousands of styles into a stark and unforgiving binary. This is because, in contemporary American society, the black/white binary, which holds such a dominant role in our cultural mythology and collective imagination despite the presence of tens of millions of people who fall into neither category, has been reinforced by centuries of sonic codification, and is reified and reinforced, rather than undermined, by such marketing tactics and stylistic developments as "crossover" and "fusion," even when they are strategically used as musical models of social integration.

We are accustomed to hearing music through a racial lens, and have arguably reduced many of our contemporary popular musical styles to racial grotesques that emphasize these differences precisely in order to play on the semiotics of identity. Current African American musical styles such as mainstream hip-hop and R&B tend to exhibit a prioritization of rhythmic instrumentation and a focus on melismatic and nonmelodic vocal improvisation that vastly outstrip many of the African and Afro-diasporic styles that comprise their aesthetic lineage. In the meantime, current popular music coded as "white," such as rock and country, have shed much of the rhythmic drive and improvisatory performative and structural approaches that characterized their earlier incarnations, and increasingly emphasize the melodic and compositional aspects of the works.

Thus, the differences between configurable musical styles such as mash-ups and turntablism must not be understood as accidents of cultural history, the inevitable result of disparate racial and ethnic groups each bringing their own idiosyncratic musical aesthetic training to a new set of production tools. Rather, we must view these new stylistic precepts as definitive statements of social identity, formed by the anything-but-arbitrary transplanting of aesthetic codes from instrumental musical styles onto new configurable production technologies and practices. Significantly, this is happening *despite* the rhetoric of universalism and social integration that so many configurable musicians espouse. Mysterious D, for instance, exulted that "mash-up culture's open to everybody. That's what's really cool about it. There's definitely no whatsoever, like, bias on gay, straight, black, white, girl, boy." Yet, in the same interview, she told me that although she "like[s] a lot of turntablist stuff," she views mash-ups and turntablism as "doing two different things," and argues that "turntablists are less interested in composition. They're not writing the music. They're simply interested in the skill part."[19]

I would like to explore the intersection of configurable music and racial politics more thoroughly, by examining configurable musical styles that reflect ethnic categorizations beyond the black/white binary, such as reggaeton, bhangra, and karaoke. This will have to wait for another book. For now, I will simply observe that, as much as configurability offers hope for the reorganization of social and cultural institutions along more egalitarian precepts, it is hardly immune to the gender and race-related inequities and disjunctures that characterized preconfigurable culture.

Changing of the Guard?

Finally, I will observe that, as with all social and cultural transformations, there are many powerful individuals and institutions with a stake in the existing order of things, and they will not sit idly by as their power is diminished by changes of any kind, no matter how profound. I have already described many of the ways in which musical regulatory institutions are attempting to confine the scope of configurable music's resistant potential, through legal, ideological, and commercial means. There is also resistance to change at a higher level, in the form of backlash against the ethic of configurability in general.

This backlash is currently epitomized in the work of scholars such as Andrew Keen, whose recent book, *The Cult of the Amateur*, excoriates blogs, YouTube, and Wikipedia as examples of the ways in which democratized cultural production ostensibly impoverishes our culture at large. In his words, "democratization, despite its lofty idealization, is undermining truth, souring civic discourse, and belittling expertise, experience and talent [and thereby] threatening the very future of our cultural institutions."[20]

As I hope I have shown in this book, I disagree with Keen on every point but his last. Far from "truth" itself, what is actually being undermined is a discursive system that reserves the power to determine what is true and false for a privileged few. If civic discourse is under attack, it is only at the hands of Nancy Fraser's disenfranchised and disaffected "counterpublics,"[21] fighting for a voice despite historical exclusion from Jurgen Habermas's rarefied "public sphere."[22] And, as my extensive interviews show, expertise, experience, and talent are hardly "belittled" by configurable musicians; these terms continue to hold much value within the communities I surveyed. However, the concepts are being actively challenged and redefined, in a continuing effort to craft aesthetic and ethical codes that simultaneously encompass *both* evaluative criteria *and* social inclusion, *both* individual accomplishment *and* collective endeavor.

As to the fate of our cultural institutions, I have to agree with Keen. Their future is certainly in doubt. But institutions exist to serve the needs of the people that inhabit them, not vice versa. And if the people who create culture by participating in it daily—producing, consuming, and rushing to colonize the growing gray area in between—demand a new set of institutions to serve our needs, no force on Earth can stop us from building them.

Notes

Preface

1. The defining feature of configurable music styles is the integral role of preexisting sound recordings (e.g., samples) in the genesis of new musical expression. I discuss this concept in far greater detail throughout the book, especially in chapter 3.

2. My mother takes issue with this characterization; she claims that my sister and I actively prevented her from playing the piano in our presence. As the father of young children today, I am inclined to believe her. I believe, however, that had musical production been more thoroughly integrated into the fabric of my family culture (as it is today), our resistance would have been less significant, and permanent, in its effects.

Introduction: The Bust

1. This was the official number provided by the police. DJ Drama told me in an interview that the actual number was "closer to 20,000."

2. Jem Aswad, "RIAA Speaks on DJ Drama Raid: 'We Enforce Our Rights'," *MTV News,* January 17, 2007, www.mtv.com/news/articles/1550169/20070117/dj_drama.jhtml (accessed December 1, 2009).

3. Phone interview, August 6, 2008.

4. Samantha M. Shapiro, "Hip-Hop Outlaw (Industry Version)," *New York Times Magazine,* February 18, 2007, www.nytimes.com/2007/02/18/magazine/18djdrama.t.html (accessed December 1, 2009).

5. Cornelius Castoriadis, *The Imaginary Institution of Society* (Cambridge: MIT Press, 1987).

6. Siva Vaidhyanathan, "Afterword: Critical Information Studies. A Bibliographic Manifesto," *Cultural Studies* 20, nos. 2–3 (2006): 292–315.

7. Vaidhyanathan, "Afterword," 293.

8. Vaidhyanathan, "Afterword," 293.

9. Not all of the scholars I name here would necessarily identify themselves as part of the CIS project, but their work all demonstrably shares an interest in the fundamental set of questions and concerns I reference above.

10. R. D. G. Kelley, *Race Rebels: Culture, Politics, and the Black Working Class* (New York: Free Press, 1994), 9–10.

11. Geoff Eley, "Labor History, Social History, *Alltagsgeschichte:* Experience, Culture, and the Politics of the Everyday—A New Direction for German Social History?" *Journal of Modern History* 61 (1989): 297–343.

12. Eva Illouz, *Consuming the Romantic Utopia: Love and the Cultural Contradictions of Capitalism* (Berkeley: University of California Press, 1997).

13. Illouz, *Consuming the Romantic Utopia,* 20.

14. Alan Lomax, "Song Structure and Social Structure," *Ethnology* 1, no. 1 (1962): 425–51.

15. Jacques Attali, *Noise: The Political Economy of Music,* trans. B. Massumi (Minneapolis: University of Minnesota Press, 1985) (original work published 1977).

16. Simon Frith, *Performing Rites: On the Value of Popular Music* (Cambridge: Harvard University Press, 1996).

17. Josh Kun, *Audiotopia: Music, Race and America* (Berkeley: University of California Press, 2005).

18. Lawrence Grossberg, *We Gotta Get Out of this Place: Popular Conservatism and Postmodern Culture* (New York: Routledge, 1992).

19. George Lipsitz, *Time Passages: Collective Memory and American Culture* (Minneapolis: University of Minnesota Press, 1990).

20. Lawrence Lessig, *Remix: Making Art and Commerce Thrive in the Hybrid Economy* (New York: Penguin, 2008).

21. Joanna Demers, *Steal this Music: How Intellectual Property Law Affects Musical Creativity* (Athens: University of Georgia Press, 2006).

22. J. G. Schloss, *Making Beats: The Art of Sample-Based Hip-Hop* (Middletown, CT: Wesleyan University Press, 2004).

23. Plato, *Republic,* trans. G. M. A. Grube, rev. C. D. C. Reeve.

24. Walter Benjamin, "The Work of Art in the Age of Mechanical Reproduction," in *Illuminations* (New York: Harcourt Brace, 1968).

25. W. E. B. Du Bois, *The Souls of Black Folk* (New York: Penguin, 1903/1989).

1. Music as a Controlled Substance

1. Plato, *Republic,* trans. G. M. A. Grube, rev. C. D. C. Reeve, books III, IV.

2. Fabre d'Olivet, *The Secret Lore of Music,* trans. J. Godwin (Rochester, VT: Inner Traditions, 1997).

3. This metaphor is still prevalent in modern China; contemporary Internet censorship laws are justified under the official slogan of "constructing a harmonious society."

4. M. H. Sommer, *Sex, Law and Society in Late Imperial China* (Stanford: Stanford University Press, 2000), 268–70.

5. E. J. Southern, *The Music of Black Americans* (New York: Norton, 1983), 182.

6. Paul Chevigny, *Gigs: Jazz and the Cabaret Laws in New York City* (New York: Routledge, 2005).

7. Chevigny, *Gigs: Jazz and the Cabaret Laws*, 4, 178.

8. Lawrence Lessig, *Free Culture: How Big Media Uses Technology and the Law to Lock Down Creativity* (New York: Penguin, 2004).

9. Siva Vaidhyanathan, *The Anarchist in the Library* (New York: Basic Books, 2004).

10. Anthony Giddens and Simon Griffiths, *Sociology*, 5th ed. (Cambridge, MA: Polity, 2006), 1,020.

11. D. J. Epstein, *Sinful Tunes and Spirituals: Black Folk Music to the Civil War* (Champaign: University of Illinois Press, 2003).

12. Penny von Eschen, *Satchmo Blows Up the World: Jazz Ambassadors Play the Cold War* (Cambridge: Harvard University Press, 2005).

13. Hildegard von Bingen, *The Letters of Hildegard of Bingen*, vol. 1, ed. and trans. J. L. Baird and R. K. Ehrman (New York: Oxford University Press, 1994), 79n1.

14. Fiona Maddock, *Hildegard of Bingen: The Woman of Her Age* (New York: Doubleday, 2003), 244.

15. E. R. Jorgensen, *Transforming Music Education* (Bloomington: Indiana University Press, 2002), xiii.

16. Thomas Kirchofer, "Stop the Music: Appeals Court Ruling Could Silence Napster," *Boston Herald*, February 15, 2001, 1.

17. IFPI, "Digital Music Report 2006," www.ifpi.org/content/library/digital-music-report-2006.pdf (accessed December 1, 2009).

18. Jacques Attali, *Noise: The Political Economy of Music*, trans. B. Massumi (Minneapolis: University of Minnesota Press, 1985) (original work published 1977), 15–18.

19. Aram Sinnreich and P. M. Monge, "The Role of Enforced Structural Holes in Independent Radio Promotion." Presented at the annual conference of the International Communication Association, New Orleans, 2004.

20. Aram Sinnreich, "Mash It Up!: Hearing a New Musical Form as an Aesthetic Resistance Movement." Presented at the annual conference of the National Communication Association, Chicago, 2004.

21. R. W. McChesney, *The Problem of the Media: U.S. Communication Politics in the 21st Century* (New York: Monthly Review, 2004), 10.

22. Until 2008, when it was eclipsed by Apple's iTunes Music Store, Wal-Mart was the largest domestic music retailer.

23. Neil Strauss, "Wal-Mart's CD Standards Are Changing Pop Music," *New York Times*, November 12, 1996, A1.

24. Originally, copyrights were granted for 14-year terms, with the potential for a single 14-year renewal. Currently, copyrights are granted for the life of the author plus 70 years—a potential term of 150 years or more.

25. David Bollier, *Brand Name Bullies: The Quest to Own and Control Culture* (Hoboken, NJ: Wiley, 2005).

26. The American Society of Composers and Publishers.

27. Bollier, *Brand Name Bullies*, 16–17.

28. Much as Motion Picture Association of America (MPAA) chief Jack Valenti testified to Congress in 1982 that "the VCR is to the American film producer and the American public as the Boston strangler is to the woman home alone."

29. For an in-depth review of technology's role in shaping music and vice versa, see: Mark Katz, *Capturing Sound: How Technology Has Changed Music* (Berkeley:

University of California Press, 2004); and Jonathan Sterne, *The Audible Past: Cultural Origins of Sound Reproduction* (Durham, NC: Duke University Press, 2003).

30. I acknowledge but decline to review here several branches of music technology that either died young or were stillborn (e.g., 8-track tapes and DATs).

31. Michel Foucault, in *Power/Knowledge—Selected Interviews and Other Writings 1972–1977*, ed. Colin Gordon (Brighton: Harvester, 1980), 142.

32. Megan Sullivan, "African-American Music as Rebellion: From Slavesong to Hip-Hop," *Discoveries* 3 (2001): 21–39; 22.

33. P. M. von Eschen, "The Real Ambassadors," in *Uptown Conversation: The New Jazz Studies*, ed. R. G. O'Meally, B. H. Edwards, and F. J. Griffin (New York: Columbia University Press, 2004), 189–203.

34. J. G. Schloss, *Making Beats: The Art of Sample-Based Hip-Hop* (Middletown, CT: Wesleyan University Press, 2004), 33.

35. John Cage, *Silence* (Middletown, CT: Wesleyan University Press, 1973).

36. Jeff Chang, *Can't Stop Won't Stop* (New York: St. Martin's, 2005), 122.

37. Douglas Thomas, *Hacker Culture* (Minneapolis: University of Minnesota Press, 2002), 131.

38. Anthony Giddens, *The Constitution of Society* (Berkeley: University of California Press, 1986).

39. J. D. Mayer, "A Tale of Two Visions: Can a New View of Personality Help Integrate Psychology?" *American Psychologist* 60, no. 4 (2005): 294–307; 296.

40. Figure is from Mayer, "A Tale of Two Visions," 297.

41. Mayer, "A Tale of Two Visions," 297.

42. P. M. Monge and Noshir Contractor, *Theories of Communication Networks* (New York: Oxford University Press, 2003), 11.

43. Monge and Contractor, *Theories of Communication Networks*, 69–70.

44. R. J. Herrnstein and Charles Murray, *The Bell Curve: Intelligence and Class Structure in American Life* (New York: Free Press, 1994).

45. D. J. Levitin, *This Is Your Brain on Music: The Science of a Human Obsession* (New York: Dutton, 2006).

46. Oliver Sacks, *Musicophilia: Tales of Music and the Brain* (New York: Knopf, 2007).

47. Sacks, *Musicophilia*, 247.

48. Ian Cross, "Music, Cognition, Culture and Evolution," *Annals of the New York Academy of Sciences* 930 (2001): 28–42; 31, emphasis in original.

49. Sacks, *Musicophilia*, 237.

50. Pierre Bourdieu, *Distinction: A Social Critique of the Judgement of Taste*, trans. R. Nice (Cambridge: Harvard University Press, 1984).

2. The Modern Framework

1. Hector Berlioz, *The Memoirs of Hector Berlioz*, trans. R. Holmes and E. Holmes (New York: Dover, 1966), 46, 59, 135.

2. Berlioz, *Memoirs*, 193, emphasis in original.

3. Berlioz, *Memoirs*, 194–95.

4. P. O. Kristeller, "The Modern System of the Arts: A Study in the History of Aesthetics," part I, *Journal of the History of Ideas* 12, no. 4 (1951): 496–527; 506.

5. Kristeller, "The Modern System of the Arts," part I, 506.

6. Woodmansee observes that Karl Philipp Moritz published an essay suggesting the centrality of disinterestedness to the enjoyment of art in 1785, five years before Kant's *Critique of Judgment* was published. See Martha Woodmansee, *The Author, Art and the Market* (New York: Columbia University Press, 1994).

7. James Trilling, "The Aesthetic of Process—and Beyond." Lecture delivered at Alfred University, November 3, 2005, ceramicsmuseum.alfred.edu/perkins_lect_series/trilling/ (accessed December 1, 2009).

8. J. A. Elias, *Plato's Defence of Poetry* (Albany: State University of New York Press, 1984), 2.

9. Fabre D'Olivet, *The Secret Lore of Music*, trans. J. Godwin (Rochester, VT: Inner Traditions, 1997).

10. P. O. Kristeller, "The Modern System of the Arts: A Study in the History of Aesthetics," part II, *Journal of the History of Ideas* 13, no. 1 (1952): 17–46.

11. Larry Gross, "Art and Artists on the Margins," in *On the Margins of Art Worlds*, ed. L. Gross (Boulder, CO: Westview, 1995).

12. This concept was championed by the Earl of Shaftesbury, around the turn of the eighteenth century.

13. Jacques Attali, *Noise: The Political Economy of Music*, trans. B. Massumi (Minneapolis: University of Minnesota Press, 1985) (original work published 1977), 15.

14. E. J. Southern, *The Music of Black Americans* (New York: Norton, 1983), 7.

15. Attali, *Noise*, 15.

16. John Blacking, *How Musical Is Man?* (Seattle: University of Washington Press, 1974).

17. K. A. Ericsson, N. Charness, R. R. Hoffman, and P. J. Feltovich, eds., *Cambridge Handbook of Expertise and Expert Performance* (Cambridge: Cambridge University Press, 2006).

18. Malcolm Gladwell, *Outliers: The Story of Success* (New York: Little, Brown, 2008), 38.

19. Kristeller, "The Modern System of the Arts," part I, 496–97.

20. Walter Benjamin, "The Work of Art in the Age of Mechanical Reproduction," in *Illuminations* (New York: Harcourt Brace, 1968).

21. E. E. Lowinsky, "Musical Genius—Evolution and Origins of a Concept—II," *The Musical Quarterly* 50, no. 4 (1964): 476–95; 479.

22. Lydia Goehr disagrees, arguing that the concept of "works as objectified expressions of composers, that prior to compositional activity did not exist" did not emerge until the end of the eighteenth century. See Lydia Goehr, *The Imaginary Museum of Musical Works: An Essay in the Philosophy of Music* (Oxford: Clarendon Press, 1992), 2.

23. Howard Becker, *Art Worlds* (Berkeley: University of California Press, 1982), 10.

24. Attali, *Noise*, 47.

25. Cited in Reuven Tsur, "Metaphor and Figure–Ground Relationship: Comparisons from Poetry, Music, and the Visual Arts," *PSYART: A Hyperlink Journal for the Psychological Study of the Arts* (2000): article 000201, www.clas.ufl.edu/ipsa/journal/2000_tsur03.shtml (accessed December 1. 2009).

26. L. B. Meyer, *Emotion and Meaning in Music* (Chicago: University of Chicago Press, 1961), 186.

27. Meyer, *Emotion and Meaning in Music*, 137.

28. Tsur, "Metaphor and Figure–Ground Relationship."

29. H. W. Janson and A. F. Janson, *History of Art: The Western Tradition*, 5th ed. (Englewood Cliffs, NJ: Prentice Hall, 2003), 25.

30. Meyer, *Emotion and Meaning in Music*, 60 (emphasis added).

31. Meyer, *Emotion and Meaning in Music*, 251–52 (emphasis added).

32. Becker, *Art Worlds*, 2.

33. Kristeller, "The Modern System of the Arts," part I.

34. Attali, *Noise*, 63.

35. Becker, *Art Worlds*, 16.

36. E. R. Jorgensen, *Transforming Music Education* (Bloomington: Indiana University Press, 2002), 146.

37. Gross, "Art and Artists on the Margins," 14.

38. For an in-depth discussion of the economic, social, and industrial factors underpinning this acceleration, see Wicke, Adorno, Paddison, or Caves.

39. Attali, *Noise*, 52.

40. 420 F.Supp 177 (S.D.N.Y., 1976).

41. M. William Krasilovsky and Sidney Shemel, *This Business of Music: The Definitive Guide to the Music Industry* (New York: Billboard Books, 1995), 243.

42. Gross, "Art and Artists on the Margins."

43. Pierre Bourdieu, *Distinction: A Social Critique of the Judgement of Taste*, trans. R. Nice (Cambridge: Harvard University Press, 1984).

44. Attali, *Noise*, 47.

45. Georges Charbonnier, *Conversations with Claude Levi-Strauss*, trans. J. Weightman and D. Weightman (London: Cape, 1969) (original work published 1961).

3. The Crisis of Configurability

1. Lawrence Lessig, *Free Culture: How Big Media Uses Technology and the Law to Lock Down Creativity* (New York: Penguin, 2004); Lessig, "Why Crush Them?" *Newsweek International*, November 28, 2005, 48; Lessig, "The People Own Ideas!" *Technology Review* 108, no. 6 (2005): 46–53; Lessig, *Remix: Making Art and Commerce Thrive in the Hybrid Economy* (New York: Penguin, 2008).

2. Raymond Williams, "Culture Is Ordinary," in *Studies in Culture: An Introductory Reader*, ed. A. Gray and J. McGuigan (London: Edward Arnold, 1997), 5–14.

3. Stuart Hall, "Encoding/Decoding, Encoding/Decoding," in *Media and Cultural Studies: Keyworks*, ed. M. G. Durham and D. M. Kellner (Malden, MA: Blackwell, 2001), 166–76.

4. Robin Dunbar, *Grooming, Gossip and the Evolution of Language* (Cambridge: Harvard University Press, 1998).

5. W. J. Ong, *Orality and Literacy* (New York: Routledge, 2002).

6. E. L. Eisenstein, *The Printing Press as an Agent of Change* (Cambridge: Cambridge University Press, 1979).

7. Marshall McLuhan, *Understanding Media* (London: Routledge, 2001).

8. Anthony Giddens, *The Consequences of Modernity* (Stanford: Stanford University Press, 1990).

9. Manuel Castells, *The Rise of the Network Society* (Oxford: Blackwell, 2000).

10. Leah Lievrouw and Sonia Livingstone, eds., *The Handbook of New Media: Social Shaping and Consequences of ICTs* (London: Sage, 2002); Donald Mackenzie, "Technological Determinism," in *Society on the Line: Information Politics in the Digital Age*, ed. W. H. Dutton (Oxford: Oxford University Press, 1999); Donald MacKenzie and Judy Wajcman, eds., *The Social Shaping of Technology* (Buckingham, UK: Open University Press, 1999); Robin Williams and David Edge, "The Social Shaping of Technology," *Research Policy* 25 (1996): 865–99.

11. Mary Madden and Susannah Fox, "Riding the Waves of 'Web 2.0': More Than a Buzzword, But Still Not Easily Defined," Pew Internet Project (2006), www .pewinternet.org/~/media/Files/Reports/2006/PIP_Web_2.0.pdf.pdf (accessed December 1, 2009); Tim O'Reilly, "Web 2.0 Compact Definition: Trying Again" (December 10, 2006), radar.oreilly.com/archives/2006/12/web-20-compact.html (accessed December 1, 2009).

12. Henry Jenkins, *Convergence Culture: Where Old and New Media Collide* (New York: New York University Press, 2006). For an in-depth critique of Jenkins' book, see Aram Sinnreich, "Come Together, Right Now: We Know Something's Happening, But We Don't Know What It Is," *International Journal of Communication* 1, no. 1 (2007): 44–47.

13. Søren M. Petersen, "Loser Generated Content: From Participation to Exploitation," *First Monday* 13, no. 3 (2008), www.uic.edu/htbin/cgiwrap/bin/ojs/index .php/fm/article/viewArticle/2141/1948 (accessed December 1, 2009); Trebor Scholz, "Market Ideology and the Myths of Web 2.0," *First Monday* 13, no. 3 (2008), www.uic .edu/htbin/cgiwrap/bin/ojs/index.php/fm/article/viewArticle/2138/1945 (accessed December 1, 2009).

14. Lessig, "Why Crush Them?"

15. Lev Manovich, "Remix and Remixability" (2005), rhizome.org/thread.rhiz? thread=19303&page=1 (accessed December 1, 2009).

16. I am not the only theorist to make a claim along these lines. Also see Axel Bruns, *Blogs, Wikipedia, Second Life, and Beyond: From Production to Produsage* (New York: Peter Lang, 2008).

17. Marshall Van Alstyne and Erik Brynjolfsson, "Global Village or Cyber-Balkans? Modeling and Measuring the Integrationof Electronic Communities," *Management Science* 51, no. 6 (June 2005): 851–68.

18. Douglas Thomas, *Hacker Culture* (Minneapolis: University of Minnesota Press, 2002), 147.

19. Alexander Galloway, *Protocol* (Cambridge: MIT Press, 2004).

20. Jeff Chang, *Can't Stop Won't Stop* (New York: St. Martin's, 2005); Dick Hebdige, *Cut 'n' Mix: Cultural Identity and Caribbean Music* (London: Comedia, 1987); M. A. Neal, *What the Music Said: Black Popular Music and Black Public Culture* (New York: Routledge, 1999).

21. D. J. Haraway, "Situated Knowledges: The Science Question in Feminism and the Privilege of Partial Perspective," in *Simians, Cyborgs and Women: The Reinvention of Nature* (New York: Routledge, 1991), 183–201.

22. Thomas Frank, *The Conquest of Cool* (Chicago: University of Chicago Press, 1997).

23. Chuck Klosterman, "The 'Snakes on a Plane' Problem," *Esquire*, August 2006, www.esquire.com/features/articles/2006/060706_mfe_August_06_Klosterman .html (accessed December 1, 2009).

24. "Steam Powered Game Statistics," www.steampowered.com/v/index.php ?area=stats (accessed August 4, 2008).

25. Canadian Broadcasting Company (CBC), www.cbc.ca/thering/remix.html (accessed August 11, 2006).

26. Bill Ivey and Steven Tepper, "Cultural Renaissance or Cultural Divide?" *Chronicle Review*, May 19, 2006, B6.

27. Steve Jones, "Money in the Mixtape; Rappers Build Street Cred, Sales via Underground," *USA Today*, April 21, 2006, 1E.

28. Theodore Gracyk, *Rhythm and Noise: An Aesthetics of Rock* (Durham: Duke University Press, 1996).

29. Nelson Goodman, *Languages of Art: An Approach to a Theory of Symbols*, 2nd ed. (Indianapolis: Hackett, 1976).

30. L. B. Meyer, *Emotion and Meaning in Music* (Chicago: University of Chicago Press, 1961), 186.

31. Some composers, such as Charles Ives and Charles Mingus, have more directly engaged such sounds within the context of their instrumental works, but they tend to be the exception rather than the rule.

32. J. K. Feibleman, "The Philosophy of Tools," *Social Forces* 45, no. 3 (1967): 329–37; 334.

Part II. Drawing Lines in the Sand

1. I offer only this single citation for the survey write-in responses, because I quote them so frequently, and because they share a single source. The citation is as follows: Radar Research/Intellisurvey Configurable Culture Survey (unpublished), July 2006 (n=1,779; population: U.S. Adults).

4. Yes, But Is It Art? The Art/Craft Binary

1. Karen Rosenberg, "Art in Review," *New York Times*, November 1, 2008, C27.
2. Phone interview, October 31, 2006.
3. Phone interview, October 4, 2006.
4. In-person interview, November 4, 2006.
5. Nicolas Slonimsky, *Lexicon of Musical Invective* (Seattle: University of Washington Press, 1965), 183.
6. Phone interview, October 2, 2006.
7. Phone interview, October 2, 2006.
8. In-person interview, November 17, 2006.
9. Phone interview, October 17, 2003.
10. Phone interview, October 6, 2006.
11. In-person interview, December 4, 2005.
12. In-person interview, November 4, 2006.
13. Phone interview, September 29, 2006.
14. Phone interview, November 29, 2006.

15. Larry Gross, "Art and Artists on the Margins," in *On the Margins of Art Worlds*, ed. L. Gross (Boulder, CO: Westview, 1995).

16. Phone interview, October 6, 2006.

17. Phone interview, October 31, 2006.

18. For a more in-depth analysis of the rhetorical approach to "legitimacy" among our survey respondents, see Aram Sinnreich, Mark Latonero, and Marissa Gluck, "Ethics Reconfigured: How Today's Media Consumers Evaluate the Role of Creative Reappropriation," *Information, Communication & Society* 12, no. 8 (2009): 1242–1260.

19. Phone interview, October 6, 2006.

20. Phone interview, October 31, 2006.

21. Phone interview, September 11, 2006.

22. 499 U.S. 340 (1991).

23. Phone interview, December 18, 2006.

24. Phone interview, September 14, 2007.

25. Phone interview, October 6, 2006.

26. In-person interview, September 8, 2006.

27. Phone interview, November 22, 2005.

28. Phone interview, October 6, 2006.

29. In-person interview, December 14, 2006.

30. Phone interview, September 25, 2006.

31. In-person interview, December 4, 2005.

32. Phone interview, October 19, 2006.

33. In-person interview, December 14, 2006.

34. Phone interview, September 11, 2006.

35. In-person interview, November 17, 2006.

36. Phone interview October 16, 2006; emphasis added.

5. Some Kid in His Bedroom: The Artist/Audience Binary

1. William Arnett and Paul Arnett, *The Quilts of Gee's Bend: Masterpieces from a Lost Place* (Atlanta, GA: Tinwood, 2007), 36 (emphasis in the original).

2. B. Johnson, "Suits Brought by Rural Alabama Quilters Resolved," ABCNews.com, August 25, 2008, abcnews.go.com/US/wireStory?id=5652373 (accessed June 12, 2009).

3. Phone interview, October 16, 2006.

4. In-person interview, November 13, 2006.

5. Phone interview, November 15, 2006.

6. Phone interview, November 15, 2006.

7. Bill Ivey and Steven Tepper, "Cultural Renaissance or Cultural Divide?" *Chronicle Review*, May 19, 2006, B6.

8. Phone interview, November 29, 2006.

9. Lawrence Lessig, "Why Crush Them?" *Newsweek International,* November 28, 2005, 48; Lessig, "The People Own Ideas!" *Technology Review* 108, no. 6 (2005): 46–53.

10. In-person interview, December 4, 2005.

11. In-person interview, September 8, 2006.

12. Phone interview, September 25, 2006.

13. In-person interview, November 4, 2006.

14. Phone interview, October 16, 2006.

15. Pierre Bourdieu, *Distinction: A Social Critique of the Judgement of Taste,* trans. R. Nice (Cambridge: Harvard University Press, 1984).

16. Phone interview, December 7, 2006.

17. In-person interview, December 4, 2005.

18. Phone interview, October 16, 2006.

19. E-mail interview, November 3, 2003.

20. In-person interview, December 4, 2005.

21. Phone interview, October 4, 2006.

22. Phone interview, November 29, 2006.

23. Phone interview, December 7, 2006.

24. Phone interview, December 5, 2006.

25. Phone interview, October 2, 2006.

26. Phone interview, September 25, 2006.

27. In-person interview, November 17, 2006.

28. Phone interview, October 19, 2006.

29. In-person interview, November 4, 2006.

30. Phone interview, October 4, 2006.

31. Phone interview, November 29, 2006.

32. Phone interview, October 6, 2006.

33. Phone interview, October 6, 2006.

34. Phone interview, September 11, 2006.

35. In-person interview, November 13, 2006.

36. Phone interview, December 7, 2006.

37. Phone interview, October 31, 2006.

38. Phone interview, September 29, 2006.

39. Phone interview, November 15, 2006.

40. In-person interview, November 4, 2006.

41. Phone interview, October 31, 2006.

42. Phone interview, October 6, 2006.

43. Phone interview, November 29, 2006.

44. Phone interview, November 15, 2006.

45. In-person interview, September 8, 2006.

46. Phone interview, August 6, 2008.

47. Phone interview, October 4, 2006.

48. Phone interview, September 25, 2006.

49. Phone interview, October 19, 2006.

50. Phone interview, November 28, 2006.

51. Phone interview, December 7, 2006.

52. Phone interview, December 13, 2006.

53. In-person interview, December 14, 2006.

54. 409 F. Supp. 2d 484 (S.D.N.Y. 2006).

55. Phone interview, December 18, 2006.

56. Phone interview, November 29, 2006.

57. Phone interview, December 18, 2006.

58. In-person interview, September 8, 2006.

59. Phone interview, November 28, 2006.
60. Phone interview, October 19, 2006.
61. In-person interview, November 4, 2006.
62. W. E. B. Du Bois, *The Souls of Black Folk* (New York: Penguin, 1903/1989).
63. In-person interview, November 30, 2005.
64. Instant message interview, November 3, 2003.
65. Chuck Klosterman, "The D.J. Auteur," *New York Times Magazine,* June 18, 2006, 40.
66. Rob Kirby, "Danger Mouse," *Remix*, July 1, 2004, remixmag.com/mag/remix_danger_mouse/ (accessed December 1, 2009).

6. Something Borrowed, Something New: The Original/Copy Binary

1. Phone interview, October 2, 2006.
2. Phone interview, October 16, 2006.
3. Phone interview, October 31, 2006.
4. Phone interview, October 2, 2006.
5. Phone interview, December 7, 2006.
6. Phone interview, September 11, 2006.
7. Phone interview, November 15, 2006.
8. Phone interview, October 31, 2006.
9. In-person interview, November 4, 2006.
10. In-person interview, November 13, 2006.
11. In-person interview, September 8, 2006.
12. Phone interview, November 29, 2006.
13. Phone interview, October 31, 2006.
14. Phone interview, September 11, 2006.
15. Phone interview, October 2, 2006.
16. Phone interview, October 6, 2006.
17. Phone interview. September 25, 2006.
18. Phone interview, November 15, 2006.
19. Phone interview, September 25, 2006.
20. Phone interview, October 2, 2006.
21. Phone interview, October 6, 2006.
22. Phone interview, October 2, 2006.
23. Phone interview, October 6, 2006.
24. Phone interview, October 2, 2006.
25. In-person interview, November 17, 2006.
26. Phone interview, November 9, 2005.
27. Phone interview, September 11, 2006.
28. Phone interview, October 4, 2006.
29. Email interview, November 3, 2003.
30. Phone interview, September 29, 2006.
31. Phone interview, October 6, 2006.
32. Phone interview, October 19, 2006.
33. Phone interview, November 28, 2006.
34. In-person interview, December 4, 2005.

35. In-person interview, December 4, 2005.

36. In-person interview, September 8, 2006.

37. Phone interview, September 11, 2006.

38. Phone interview, October 16, 2006.

39. Phone interview, October 2, 2006.

40. Phone interview October 6, 2006.

41. In-person interview, September 8, 2006.

42. In-person interview, December 4, 2005.

43. Phone interview, October 16, 2006.

44. In-person interview, November 13, 2006.

45. RU SIRIUS (2006), show #69 (Interview): Dan The Automator, 2006, www .rusiriusradio.com/2006/10/10/show-69-dan-the-automator/ (accessed December 1, 2009).

46. Phone interview, October 31, 2006.

47. Phone interview, September 11, 2006.

48. Phone interview, November 29, 2006.

49. Phone interview, October 6, 2006.

50. Phone interview, October 31, 2006.

51. For an excellent example, see Joanna Demers, *Steal This Music: How Intellectual Property Law Affects Musical Creativity* (Athens: University of Georgia Press, 2006).

52. 388 F. 3d 1189 (9th Cir. 2003).

53. 410 F. 3d 792 (6th Cir. 2005).

54. In-person interview, December 14, 2006.

55. Phone interview, December 18, 2006.

56. Phone interview, December 5, 2006.

57. Phone interview, September 25, 2006.

58. In-person interview, November 17, 2006.

59. Phone interview, December 6, 2006.

60. 499 U.S. 340 (1991).

61. 510 U.S. 569 (1994).

62. 862 F. Supp. 1944 (S.D.N.Y. 1994).

63. Phone interviews, November 22, 2005; December 18, 2006.

64. Phone interview December 6, 2006.

65. Phone interview, November 15, 2006.

66. Phone interview, October 16, 2006.

67. Phone interview, November 6, 2006.

68. In-person interview, November 17, 2006.

69. In point of fact, most digitally reproduced music does not constitute a "perfect" copy, because popular encoding algorithms such as the MP3 are "lossy," and may permanently remove up to 90% of the information contained in the "original" file. Moreover, the sonic imperfection is compounded through each subsequent act of digital copying. Given the social and technical mechanics of sampling I discuss throughout this book, it is likely that the majority of configurable musical works produced contain numerous sonic elements that are far less than "perfect" reproductions of their sources.

70. Walter Benjamin, "The Work of Art in the Age of Mechanical Reproduction," in *Illuminations* (New York: Harcourt Brace, 1968).

71. Phone interview, October 4, 2006.

72. Letter to Isaac McPherson, August 13, 1813.

73. Phone interview, October 6, 2006.

74. Phone interview, September 25, 2006.

75. In-person interview, November 4, 2006.

76. Phone interview, November 29, 2006.

77. Phone interview, October 4, 2006.

78. Phone interview, October 6, 2006.

79. Phone interview, September 25, 2006.

80. Phone interview, September 11, 2006.

81. In-person interview, November 4, 2006.

82. Phone interview, October 16, 2006.

83. Phone interview, October 16, 2006.

84. Phone interview, September 11, 2006.

85. J. G. Schloss, *Making Beats: The Art of Sample-Based Hip-Hop* (Middletown, CT: Wesleyan University Press, 2004).

86. Phone interview, November 29, 2006.

87. Phone interview, October 2, 2006.

88. Phone interview, October 16, 2006.

89. Phone interview, November 6, 2006.

90. Phone interview, September 25, 2006.

91. Phone interview, January 4, 2006.

92. Phone interview, October 16, 2006.

93. K. C. Jones, "Nine Inch Nails Sells Out of $300 Album While Offering Free Music Online," *InformationWeek*, March 5, 2008, www.informationweek.com/news/internet/showArticle.jhtml?articleID=206901933 (accessed December 1, 2009).

94. Phone interview, October 4, 2006.

95. Phone interview, October 19, 2006.

96. Pierre Bourdieu, *Distinction: A Social Critique of the Judgement of Taste*, trans. R. Nice (Cambridge: Harvard University Press, 1984).

97. Phone interview, November 15, 2006.

7. Live from a Hard Drive: The Composition/Performance Binary

1. Kembrew McLeod, *Freedom of Expression: Overzealous Copyright Bozos and Other Enemies of Creativity* (New York: Doubleday, 2005); Anne Barron, "Introduction: Harmony or Dissonance? Copyright Concepts and Musical Practice," *Social Legal Studies* 15, no. 1 (2006): 25–51; Marc Perlman, "How a French Baroque Motet Is Like a Melanesian Folk Song," *Andante.com*, August 2005, www.andante.com/article/article.cfm?id=25873 (accessed December 1, 2009).

2. Gabriel Fleet, "What's in a Song? Copyright's Unfair Treatment of Record Producers and Side Musicians," *Vanderbilt Law Review* 61, no. 4 (2008): 1235–79.

3. Phone interview, October 31, 2006.

4. In-person interview, November 13, 2006.

5. Phone interview, December 7, 2006.

6. Phone interview, October 31, 2006.

7. Phone interview, September 11, 2006.

8. In-person interview, November 13, 2006.
9. Phone interview, November 29, 2006.
10. Phone interview, September 25, 2006.
11. Phone interview, October 6, 2006.
12. In-person interview, November 4, 2006.
13. Phone interview, November 29, 2006.
14. Phone interview, September 11, 2006.
15. Phone interview, December 7, 2006.
16. Phone interview, September 25, 2006.
17. In-person interview, November 4, 2006.
18. In-person interview, November 13, 2006.
19. Phone interview, October 2, 2006.
20. Phone interview, October 16, 2006.
21. Phone interview, October 4, 2006.
22. In-person interview, November 4, 2006.
23. In-person interview, December 4, 2005.
24. In-person interview, December 4, 2005.
25. Phone interview, September 25, 2006.
26. In-person interview, November 13, 2006.
27. Phone interview, December 18, 2006.
28. In-person interview, December 14, 2006.
29. Lawrence Lessig, "The Black and White about Grey Tuesday," blog post, February 24, 2004, lessig.org/blog/2004/02/the_black_and_white_about_grey.html (accessed December 1, 2009).
30. Phone interview, December 6, 2006.
31. E-mail interview, August 22, 2007.
32. In-person interview, November 13, 2008.

8. Hooks and Hearts: The Figure/Ground Binary

1. Phone interview, October 4, 2006.
2. Phone interview, October 31, 2006.
3. Phone interview, September 11, 2006.
4. Phone interview, September 29, 2006.
5. Phone interview, November 15, 2006.
6. In-person interview, December 4, 2005.
7. Phone interview, November 29, 2006.
8. Phone interview, September 25, 2006.
9. Phone interview, October 6, 2006.
10. Phone interview, November 15, 2006.
11. Phone interview, November 29, 2006.
12. Phone interview, October 2, 2006.
13. Phone interview, September 25, 2006.
14. In-person interview, November 13, 2006.
15. Phone interview, September 29, 2006.
16. Phone interview, December 7, 2006.
17. Phone interview, November 6, 2006.

18. Phone interview, October 16, 2006.

19. Brian Priestly, *Mingus: A Critical Biography* (Cambridge, MA: Da Capo, 1984).

20. Instant message interview, November 3, 2003.

21. Phone interview, October 4, 2006.

22. In-person interview, December 5, 2005.

23. In-person interview, November 4, 2006.

24. Phone interview, November 28, 2006.

25. Phone interview, September 11, 2006.

26. Phone interview, December 18, 2006.

27. In-person interview, December 14, 2006.

28. Phone interview, December 6, 2006.

29. 471 U.S. 539 (1985).

30. In-person interview, December 14, 2006.

31. Kembrew McLeod, *Owning Culture: Authorship, Ownership, and Intellectual Property Law* (New York: Peter Lang, 2001), 87.

32. In-person interview, December 14, 2006.

33. Phone interview, December 5, 2006.

9. "He Plays Dictaphones, and She Plays Bricks"

1. The sculpture is sometimes erroneously referred to as *Bird in Flight*.

2. *Time* Magazine, "Art: Custom House Esthetes," December 17, 1928, www.time.com/time/magazine/article/0,9171,928613,00.html (accessed December 1, 2009).

3. Quoted in Martin Gayford, "When Art Itself Went on Trial," *Daily Telegraph*, January 24, 2004, www.telegraph.co.uk/culture/art/3610769/When-art-itself-went-on-trial.html (accessed December 1, 2009).

4. Phone interview, October 4, 2006.

5. In-person interview, September 8, 2006.

6. Phone interview, September 25, 2006.

7. In-person interview, December 4, 2005.

8. Phone interview, September 11, 2006.

9. Phone interview, November 29, 2006.

10. Phone interview, October 16, 2006.

11. Phone interview, October 2, 2006.

12. Phone interview, September 25, 2006.

13. In-person interview, November 13, 2006.

14. Phone interview, November 15, 2006.

15. In-person interview, November 13, 2006.

16. In-person interview, December 4, 2005.

17. In-person interview, December 4, 2005.

18. Phone interview, October 6, 2006.

19. Phone interview, October 2, 2006.

20. Phone interview, September 11, 2006.

21. Phone interview, November 29, 2006.

22. Phone interview, November 6, 2006.

23. Phone interview, October 16, 2006.

24. In-person interview, November 4, 2006.

25. Phone interview, November 15, 2006.

26. Phone interview, September 11, 2006.

27. Phone interview, November 29, 2006.

28. Phone interview, October 2, 2006.

29. Phone interview, September 25, 2006.

30. Phone interview, November 29, 2006.

31. Phone interview, November 6, 2006.

32. In-person interview, November 13, 2006.

33. Phone interview, November 29, 2006.

34. Phone interview, September 25, 2006.

35. Phone interview, September 25, 2006.

36. Phone interview, December 7, 2006.

37. Phone interview, December 13, 2006.

10. Critique and Co-optation

1. Phone interview, December 7, 2006.

2. Phone interview, October 17, 2003.

3. Phone interview, November 28, 2006.

4. Phone interview, October 4, 2006.

5. Phone interview, November 15, 2006.

6. Phone interview, November 9, 2005.

7. Phone interview, October 3, 2006.

8. Phone interview, November 29, 2006.

9. Phone interview, November 9, 2005.

10. Phone interview, December 7, 2006.

11. In-person interview, December 4, 2005.

12. Phone interview, October 4, 2006.

13. Phone interview, September 11, 2006.

14. Phone interview, October 31, 2006.

15. In-person interview, November 4, 2006.

16. In-person interview, November 13, 2006.

17. In-person interview, November 30, 2006.

18. Phone interview, November 29, 2006.

19. Phone interview, October 16, 2006.

20. Phone interview, November 15, 2006.

21. Phone interview, October 2, 2006.

22. Phone interview, November 29, 2006.

23. Thomas Frank, *The Conquest of Cool* (Chicago: University of Chicago Press, 1997).

24. Wm. Ferguson, "The Mainstream Mash-up," *New York Times Magazine,* December 12, 2004, 82.

25. In-person interview, December 4, 2005.

26. In-person interview, November 13, 2006.

27. In-person interview, September 8, 2006.

28. Phone interview, October 19, 2006.

29. Email interview, November 3, 2003.

30. Phone interview, November 15, 2006.

31. Phone interview, October 2, 2006.

32. Jordan Roseman, *Mashup Construction Kit* (Indianapolis: Wiley, 2006).

33. Phone interview, November 29, 2006.

11. "Plus Ça Change" or Paradigm Shift?

1. In-person interview, November 17, 2006.

2. Richard Pipes, *The Russian Revolution* (New York: Alfred A. Knopf, 1990), 95.

3. Manuel Castells, *The Rise of the Network Society*, 2nd ed. (Oxford: Blackwell, 2000).

4. Phone interview, October 16, 2006.

5. See, for example, Tiziana Terranova, *Network Culture: Politics for the Information Age* (Ann Arbor: Pluto, 2004); Robert O'Harrow Jr., *No Place to Hide: Behind the Scenes of Our Emerging Surveillance Society* (New York: Free Press, 2005); Mark Andrejevic, *iSpy: Surveillance and Power in the Interactive Era* (Lawrence: University Press of Kansas, 2007).

6. Michel Foucault, *Discipline and Punish: The Birth of the Prison,* trans. A. Sheridan (New York: Vintage, 1995), 27.

7. Steve Mann, Jason Nolan, and Barry Wellman, "Sousveillance: Inventing and Using Wearable Computing Devices for Data Collection in Surveillance Environments," *Surveillance & Society* 1, no. 3 (2003): 331–55.

8. Cory Doctorow, *Little Brother* (New York: Tor, 2008).

9. W. J. Ong, *Orality and Literacy* (London: Routledge, 1988), 40.

10. Neil Postman, *Building a Bridge to the 18th Century: How the Past Can Improve Our Future* (New York: Vintage, 1999), 144.

11. W. E. B. Du Bois, *The Souls of Black Folk* (1903; New York: Penguin, 1989), 5.

12. Castells, *Rise of the Network Society.*

13. Phone interview, November 6, 2006.

14. In-person interview, November 4, 2006.

15. Eszter Hargittai and Steven Shafer, "Differences in Actual and Perceived Online Skills: The Role of Gender," *Social Science Quarterly* 87, no. 2 (2006): 432–48; 444.

16. This is not universally the case; the seminal Detroit techno scene, for instance, began as primarily African American, and continues to consist largely of black musicians.

17. Phone interview, September 29, 2006.

18. In-person interview, December 4, 2005.

19. In-person interview, November 4, 2006.

20. Andrew Keen, *The Cult of the Amateur: How Today's Internet Is Killing Our Culture* (New York: Doubleday, 2007), 15.

21. Nancy Fraser, "Rethinking the Public Sphere: A Contribution to the Critique of Actually Existing Democracy," in *Habermas and the Public Sphere,* ed. C. Calhoun (Cambridge: MIT Press, 1989), 109–42.

22. Jurgen Habermas, *The Structural Transformation of the Public Sphere: An Inquiry into a Category of Bourgeois Society,* trans. T. Burger and F. Lawrence (Cambridge: MIT Press, 1989) (original work published 1962).

Index

Page numbers in italics refer to illustrations.

artist/audience binary, 107–23; configurability as challenge to, 84–85; configurable musicians as both artists and fans, 195; conservatories in institutionalizing, 59; erosion of, 108–12; at live music events, 61; in modern discursive framework, 8, 43, 46–49; and Reunion of Labor principle, 197; and Shift from Linearity to Recursion principle, 201; social function of, 66–67; "some kid in his bedroom" argument, 119–22

artists: configurable artistry, 112–13; defining uniqueness in terms of, 51; exceptionality attributed to, 48, 49, 50, 62, 84, 98, 108, 195, 196; genius associated with, 48. *See also* artist/audience binary

Art of Noise, The, 116

ASCAP, 26, 64

Attali, Jacques, 6, 24, 48, 54, 59, 63, 66

audience: in compositional process, 152–53; in defining art, 113, 115; defining performance in terms of, 152; engaged, 110; informed, 111. *See also* artist/audience binary

audio editing software, 174, 177, 186

Audio Home Recording Act (AHRA), 20

aura, 50, 51, 85, 139

authenticity, 51, 85, 154

authority: configurability seen as threat to institutional, 77–78, 82; mash-ups fly in face of, 186; in mechanical reproduction, 53

authorship: categorical legal rejection of configurable, 178, 194; in copyright law, 102, 118, 138; defining "art" in context of configurability, 9, 100, 101–2, 106; fetishization of the author, 139; for mash-ups, 8, 113; and original/copy binary, 51, 63–64

avant-garde art, mainstream aesthetic conventions reinforced by, 95

avant-garde composers, configurable techniques used by, 81

Axelrad, Pete. *See* DJ Axel

Bach, J. S., 24, 50

Baird, J. L., 22

Bambaataa, Afrika, 115

bass riffs, 168

Bavan, Yolande, 29

Beach Boys, 86

Beastie Boys, 136

Beatles, the, 27, 79, 86, 117, 163

beauty, Kantian view of, 45

bebop, 194

Becker, Howard, 54, 58–59

Beethoven, Ludwig van, 41–43, 54, 56–57, 167

Begg, Si, 97, 101, 102, 115, 125, 126, 127, 129, 135, 136, 139, 144, 149, 150, 161, 164, 174, 176, 184, 186

Behind the Music (television program), 62

Benjamin, Walter: on artist/audience binary, 107; on aura of work of art, 50, 51, 85, 139; on uniqueness of work of art, 9, 50–51

Benkler, Yochai, 4

Bennett, Vicki (People Like Us), 204

Berlioz, Hector, 41–43, 53, 54, 59, 65

Bienstock, Ronald, 103, 112–13, 137, 168

Bird in Space (Brancusi), 170–71

Birmingham school, 21

Black Album, The (Jay-Z), 143

black Americans. *See* African Americans

Blacking, John, 49

black/white binary, 206–7

blues, 148, 155

BMI, 64

Bollier, David, 26

Bootie (club), 97, 99, 165

"bootlegs," 144, 186

Bourdieu, Pierre, 39, 66, 145

Bowie, David, 167–68

boyd, danah, 4

Brancusi, Constantin, 170–71

Brand Name Bullies (Bollier), 26

brands, 68

breakbeat, 87

bricolage, 173

Bridgeport v. Dimension, 136–37, 138, 146, 170, 178

Bright Tunes Music Corp. v. Harrisongs Music, LTD, 64

Brubeck, Dave, 21, 29

Brubeck, Iola, 29

Buckles, Brad, 2

Built from Scratch (X-Ecutioners), 125

Burton, Brian. *See* DJ Danger Mouse

Bush, George W., 185

cabaret licenses, 19–20

Caffey v. Cook, 118

Cage, John, 32, 81, 116

Cambridge Handbook of Expertise and Expert Performance, 49

Campbell v. Acuff Rose, 138

Canadian Broadcasting Corporation, 81–82

Cannon, Donald "Don," 1

cassette tape, 27

Castells, Manuel, 198, 204

Castoriadis, Cornelius, 3

CDs: CD purists, 173–74; copy protection on, 184; digital and physical media coexisting, 173; as material for configurable music, 173; production and playback reunited in, 27

Cee-Lo, 79

Chang, Jeff, 32

Cherry, Don, 29

Chevigny, Paul, 19–20

Chiffons, 64

chord structures, 65, 166

CIA, 21

citation, 196

Clarida, Bob, 102, 118–19, 137, 138, 156, 166, 170

classical music. *See* Western classical music

Classic of Filial Piety, 18

Cliffe, Jess, 80

cognitive–affective capital, 39, 88–89

Cohen, Ted, 2

Coldcut, 104, 116

Cold War, 21–22, 28–29

Coleman, Biella, 4

collage, 99, 106

collectivism, configurable, 10, 180, 196–97, 203

Collision of Public and Private principle, 10, 180, 198–200, 203

Coltrane, John, 29

Combs, Sean "Diddy": "brazen" sampling by, 117, 133; mixtapes in rise to prominence of, 2; as representative of big money versus independent musicians, 155; seen as genius, 116–17, 122

"comebacks," 62

commercial music: commercialization of composition and performance, 24; configurable music seen as gateway to, 184; co-optation of configurable music, 77, 189–92, 194; mash-ups' incapacity to be used commercially, 145–46; mash-ups keep it honest, 133; modern framework sustained by institutions of, 61–62

commercial regulation of music: of aesthetic codes, 24–25; aesthetic resistance to, 187–88; historical examples of musical regulation, 24–28; in matrix of musical regulation, 17; of musical praxis, 25–28; in music's discursive framework, 39; of music technology, 26–28; practical resistance to, 188; technological resistance to, 188–89

common culture, configurability seen as undermining, 76

composite digital photographs, 83

composition: African versus European aesthetic, 30; audience in compositional process, 152–53; certain works elevated from performance to, 149; commercial regulation of, 24, 25–26; copyright for, 63, 136; linear composition-expression model, 85–86, 149, 153; music theory contrasted with, 46; and original/copy binary, 63; rise of composer in musical labor hierarchy, 54, 65; seen as more fundamental, 86, 149. *See also* composition/performance binary; scores

composition/performance binary, 148–58; configurability and blurring of line in, 9, 85–87, 149, 158; configurable musicians accept, 194; configurable musicians as both composers and performers, 195; in copyright law, 64, 156–58; DJs and, 8, 149–53, 158, 202; in modern discursive framework, 8, 43, 53–54; pedagogical institutions reinforce, 60; quantitative dimension of, 151; and Reunion of Labor principle, 197; and Shift from Linearity to Recursion principle, 201; social function of, 68

computers: hacking, 32, 77, 82, 200; laptop seen as folkloric instrument, 69. *See also* hardware; software

conceptual art, 84

conductors, 197, 198

configurability, 69–89; Afro-diasporic origins of, 205; antecedents of, 71; art/craft binary challenged by, 83–84, 95–106; artist/audience binary challenged by, 84–85, 107–23; basic principles of, 10–11; can configurable music be unique, 138–46; categorical legal rejection of, 178, 194; commercial co-optation of, 77, 189–92, 194; communitarian ethic of, 111; configurable artistry, 112–13; configurable

culture, 199; and changing definitions of art and artistry, 9; configurability makes it more accessible, 122; in copyright law, 102, 104–5, 118; creative selection and arrangement subclass of copyright law, 118, 146; defining "art" in context of configurability, 100, 101–3; skill contrasted with, 114

critical information studies (CIS), 4–5

critics, professional, 61, 111

Critique of Judgment (Kant), 44–45, 47

Cross, Ian, 38

Cult of the Amateur, The (Keen), 208

cultural studies, 4, 5, 37

curatorial art, 84–85, 109, 112

Cut Chemist, 154, 173

dancing, 21, 22, 45, 61

"Dean Gray" (Party Ben and team9), 133, 142

Demers, Joanna, 6

de minimis defense, 136–37, 146, 178

democracy: configurability seen as threat to, 76, 78; democratized cultural production, 208; new cultural practices seen as democratizing, 74

derivativeness, 98, 103, 127–28, 132, 133

Digital Millennium Copyright Act (DMCA), 20, 26, 184

digital pastiche, 85

digital rights management (DRM) technology, 28, 184–85, 188, 189

directionality, of musical and social change, 33

"Discourse on Music" (Xunzi), 18

discursive frameworks, 39–40; influencing, 40; the newly emerging framework, 195–203; revisions of, 40, 69. *See also* modern discursive framework

division of labor, 9, 197–98, 203

DIY ethic, 9, 111, 112

DJ Adrian, 99, 104, 110, 111, 112, 114, 120, 126, 131–32, 133, 142, 155, 162, 165, 172, 174, 175, 185, 186, 189, 190–91, 203, 206

DJ Axel (Pete Axelrad), 109, 114, 121, 124, 134, 149, 150, 152–53, 173–74, 187, 190, 201, 203

DJ Consciousness principle, 10, 180, 202–4

DJ Danger Mouse, 79, 116, 117, 121–22, 143, 157, 189

DJ Drama, 1, 2, 116, 148, 193

DJ Earworm, 100, 109, 112, 114, 115, 116, 118, 127, 135, 140, 143, 151–52, 162, 163, 173, 174, 176, 184, 187, 188, 189, 191–92

DJ Food, 102, 150, 203

DJ Kool Herc, 30

DJ Paul V, 103, 110, 116, 119, 127, 132, 133, 172

DJs: ambiguity and plasticity of category, 151; and artist/audience binary, 109–13; carry their capital with them, 198; clearing copyrights as impractical for, 3–4; and composition/performance binary, 8, 9, 149–53, 158, 202; in curatorial art, 84–85, 109; "digging in the crates," 143; DJ Consciousness principle, 10, 180, 202–4; double-consciousness of, 110, 121, 122, 151, 202; fears of illegitimacy of, 9; female, 205; as hip, 189; make creativity more accessible, 122; mixtapes created by, 85; and original/copy binary, 125; as "other than," 202–3; performative aspects of, 86; as promoting undermining of power, 200; reclaim the turntable, 27, 29–30; rising profile and power of, 84; as talent, 115; in theory and practice, 153–56

DJ Shadow, 116, 128, 154, 173

DJ Z-Trip, 155

DMCA (Digital Millennium Copyright Act), 20, 26, 184

Doctorow, Cory, 200

Dodekachordon (Glareanus), 53

Don Giovanni (Mozart), 56

double consciousness, 10, 28, 110, 121, 122, 151, 202

DRM (digital rights management) technology, 28, 184–85, 188, 189

dub, 27, 205, 206

DuBois, W. E. B., 10, 121, 202, 203

Duchamp, Marcel, 95, 99, 100

education. *See* music education

effort, degree of, 103–4, 106

Ehrman, R. K., 22

electronic dance music, 137

Eley, Geoff, 5

Ellington, Duke, 21

Enemy of the State (film), 200

environmental catastrophe, 204

environmental sound, 87, 160, 164–65, 168, 198

jazz *(cont.)*
159, 164–65; Monk, 19, 194; Parker, 19, 149, 194
Jefferson, Thomas, 139
Jenkins, Henry, 4, 74
Jones, Quincy, 166, 169
Jorgensen, E. R., 22–23, 60
jukeboxes, 26, 67

Kant, Immanuel, 44–45, 47, 49, 84, 100, 104, 195
karaoke, 83, 207
Keen, Andrew, 208
Kelley, R. D. G., 5, 6
Kid Koala, 128
Kirby, James. *See* V/VM
Kirby, Ron, 121–22
Kleptone, Eric, 109, 115, 116, 125, 126, 128, 139, 145–46, 161–62, 173, 175–76, 183, 188, 191
Klosterman, Chuck, 121
Kracke, F. J. H., 171
Krasilovsky, M. William, 65
Kristeller, Paul Oskar, 41, 44, 50, 53, 59
Kun, Josh, 6

labor, division of, 9, 197–98, 203
Lacan, Jacques, 3, 37
Latonero, Mark, 4
law: "art world" legal institutions, 59; categorical rejection of configurable authorship by, 178, 194; enforcement of originality and uniqueness by, 61; as institutional bulwark against change, 6; lack of subtlety in treatment of sample-based production, 146, 158. *See also* legal regulation of music
Le, Minh, 80
legal regulation of music: of aesthetic codes, 17, 18–19; aesthetic resistance to, 183; historical examples of, 18–20; as method of musical regulation, 17; of musical technology, 20; in music's discursive framework, 39; practical resistance to, 184; of praxis, 19–20; technological resistance to, 184–85. *See also* copyright
Lélio (Berlioz), 42
Lesh, Phil, 154
Lessig, Lawrence, 4, 6, 20, 70, 74, 110, 157
levels of meaning, of musical and social change, 34, 38
Levi-Strauss, Claude, 57, 67, 88

Levitin, D. J., 37
liberal arts, 44, 46
licensing: in commercial regulation of music, 25–26; composition-performance binary in, 64; compulsory, 157; exorbitant rates for, 188; in legal regulation of praxis, 19–20; mixtapes eschew, 85; for sample-based music, 135–36; voluntary collecting society, 157–58
limited distribution strategy, 141–42, 146–47
limited editions, 52, 145, 146–47, 170
linearity: linear composition-performance model, 85–86, 149, 153; shift to recursion from, 10, 180, 201–2, 203
Lipsitz, George, 6
lip-synching, 154
Little Brother (Doctorow), 200
liturgical music, 24
live music: designated venues for, 61; mash-ups in context of, 140–41. *See also* performance
Lomax, Alan, 6
loop-oriented music, 206
Lowinsky, Edward E., 53
Lucas, George, 83
lyrics, 64

machinima: as "art," 96; as configurable culture example, 8; as production-adjacent, 75
Maddock, Fiona, 22
Madonna, 101, 129, 163
mainstream, configurability and the, 76–82, 189
Malmsteen, Yngwie, 155
Mann, Steve, 200
Manovich, Lev, 74
marketability, 104–5, 106
Marx, Karl, 198
Masekela, Hugh, 29
Mashup Construction Kit (DJ Earworm), 191–92
mash-ups: as acts of resistance, 182; in advertising, 181; as "arrangements," 156; and art/craft binary, 83, 97, 98, 102, 103; and artist/audience binary, 8, 84, 109–12; as bricolage, 173; and changing definitions of art and artistry, 9, 102; checking software for, 130; coded as white, 206; commercial music kept honest by, 133; as configurable culture example, 8; copyright

creates scarcity for, 142; copyright protection for, 105, 118–19, 156; as cultural jamming, 185; as culture clash, 165; and "digging in the crates," 143; emergence in age of iPod, 87; end product of, 176–77; ethics of, 135; European structural logic of, 206; figural recontextualization in, 163–64; figure/ground binary in, 160–64, 168; as flying in face of authority, 186; as hip, 189; incapacity to be used commercially, 145–46; as Internet-based, 186; juxtaposition of sonic elements in, 163, 168; licensing for, 157, 158; in live context, 140–41; materials of, 172–74; and materials/tools binary, 172–76; modern social institutions challenged by, 14; musician community as overwhelmingly white, 205; as new punk rock, 111; and original/copy binary, 126, 127, 128; original master recordings in, 143–44; outlaw image of, 121, 144; pastiche ethic of, 99; process of negotiation in, 162; as production-adjacent, 75; as protests against commercial music, 187; as replete in themselves, 86–87; as situated knowledge, 78; skill and talent for, 114–15; "some kid in his bedroom" argument against, 119–22; as song-oriented, 206; standard "A + B" template, 162, 163; as statement of social identity, 207; style in, 126, 127; as subjective distortion, 85; tools of, 174–76; turntablism contrasted with, 155, 207; universalistic rhetoric of, 207; variation between other styles of sample-based music, 196; "viral" circulation of, 76

mass production: aura of work of art destroyed by, 51; enforcement of originality and uniqueness in, 61; in hierarchy of uniqueness, 52; original/copy binary in, 63; in producer/consumer hierarchy, 68; of recordings, 24

master recordings, original, 143–44

materials/tools binary, 170–78; configurability as challenge to, 88; copyright and, 177–78; materials of configurable music, 172–74; in modern discursive framework, 43, 57–58; musicians produce their own tools, 176–77; pedagogical institutions reinforce, 60; and Shift from Linearity to Recursion principle, 201; social function

of, 68; tools of configurable music, 174–76; workstations as both, 195

mathematics, music's relationship to, 45, 46

Matrix, The (film), 78

mattcatt, 112, 130–31, 191

Mayer, J. D., 34–35

McChesney, Robert, 25

McLeod, Kembrew, 4

McLuhan, Marshall, 177, 199

mechanical arts, 44

mechanical reproduction: artist's authority bridges gulf created by, 52; "authentic reproductions," 52; Benjamin on uniqueness and, 50–51; copyright for, 25–26. *See also* recording industry

melody: copyright protection for, 64, 65, 166; as figure, 64, 68, 87, 159, 166, 168; as "hook," 159; new sounds lack, 160; Western bias toward, 168; in "white" musical styles, 207

Mercury, Freddie, 167–68

Meyer, Leonard B., 55–56, 58, 87

microphones, 61

Mingus, Charles, 159, 164–65

mixtapes: Aphilliates Music Group raid, 1–2; authenticity attributed to, 85

modern discursive framework, 41–68; can configurability be contained in, 193; configurability as challenge to, 82–89, 179, 195; creation ex nihilo doctrine underpins, 196; crisis confronting, 88–89; durability of, 58–59, 69; elements of, 8, 43–44; erosion of, 195; Eurocentrism of, 161; institutional foundations of, 58–65, 60; modernists call attention to limits of, 95; musicians reflexively reinforce, 194; music industry attempts to shore up, 195; origins of, 44–58; social functions of, 66–68, 69; technological change as undermining, 69–70

modernism, 95

Monge, P. M., 35

Monk, Thelonious, 19, 194

Montana, Tony, 121, 165

"Moonlight" Sonata (Beethoven), 56–57, 167

Moritz, Karl Philipp, 213n.6

movable type, 54

Mozart, Wolfgang Amadeus, 56, 67

MP3s: digital and physical media coexisting, 173; digital rights management (DRM) technology for, 28; as material for

MP3s (cont.)
    configurable music, 173; and materials/
    tools binary, 88, 171; playlists as "art," 83;
    production and playback reunited with,
    27; vilification of, 23
MTV, 62
Murray, Charles, 37
music: and art/craft binary, 45–46; as
    bastion of orality, 54; central conundrums
    regarding, 37–38; as cognitive–affective
    capital, 39, 40, 88–89; composition-
    oriented versus performance-oriented,
    155; discursive frameworks for, 39–40;
    and macrosocial structures, 6; as marker
    of identity, 67; mathematics' relationship
    to, 45, 46; modern discursive framework
    for, 7–8, 41–68; neuroscientific interest in,
    37; power over social imaginary, 3, 32–39,
    179; as prior to and independent of its
    expression, 52–53; professionalization of
    musicians, 24, 49, 53, 61; as site of
    contestation, 6, 13–14, 21; social category
    of "musician," 48–49; technology shapes
    musical aesthetics and practice, 6; as
    time-based art, 140; traditional group
    structure of, 197, 198; as vector of
    communication between individuals and
    society, 33–34; viewed as innocuous, 13.
    See also audience; composition; configu-
    rability; musical regulation; musical
    resistance; music education; music
    industry; performance
musical instruments, 58, 59, 149, 175, 178
musical notation. See notation
musical regulation, 15–89; bias against
    configurable music, 168; dialectic with
    musical resistance, 7, 30–31, 89, 179, 193,
    195; explicit and implicit, 3; extent of, 13,
    16–17; historical examples of, 18–28;
    innovation as consequence of resisting,
    28–32, 31; matrix of, 17–18; methods of,
    17; in music's discursive framework, 39;
    Plato on, 17, 18, 21; regulatory institutions
    on power of music, 32–33; sites of, 17–18;
    taxonomy of, 18. See also commercial
    regulation of music; ideological regulation
    of music; legal regulation of music
musical resistance: aesthetic resistance to
    commercial regulation, 187–88; aesthetic
    resistance to ideological regulation,
    185–86; aesthetic resistance to legal

regulation, 183; among configurable
    musicians, 182–89; configurable music
    seen as inherently resistant, 182; dialectic
    with musical regulation, 7, 30–31, 89, 179,
    193, 195; DJs as destabilizing, 3–4;
    innovation and, 28–32, 31; in music's
    discursive framework, 39; practical
    resistance to commercial regulation, 188;
    practical resistance to ideological
    regulation, 186; practical resistance to
    legal regulation, 184; technological
    resistance to commercial regulation,
    188–89; technological resistance to
    ideological regulation, 186–87; technologi-
    cal resistance to legal regulation, 184–85
music education: as "art world" institution,
    59–61; conservatories, 59, 60, 83; cultural
    debates over, 22–23
music industry: as centered around
    controlling copyright, 194; collapse of
    traditional value-chain in, 158; configu-
    rability as seen by, 195; genius equated
    with profitability in, 117, 195; ideological
    regulation used by, 23–24; modern
    discursive framework supported by, 195;
    on separation of production and playback
    technologies, 26, 27. See also commercial
    music; recording industry
music magazines, 62
music theory, 46
Mysterious D, 97, 99, 110, 115, 120–21, 131,
    140, 142, 151, 152, 154–55, 165, 204, 205, 207

Nakamura, Dan "the Automator," 83, 134–35
Napster, 23, 191
narratives of success, failure, and redemp-
    tion, 62
Negativland, 104, 116, 128
"Nel Cimitero Di Tuscon" (Reverberi and
    Reverberi), 79
Neptunes, the, 83
nested networks-within-networks model,
    34–37, 36
network consciousness, 204
Never Trust Originality (Kleptones), 125
New Line Cinema, 79–80
Newport Folk Festival, 194
Newton, James, 136
Newton v. Diamond, 136
New York City cabaret licenses, 19–20
New York Times, 189

Nicholson, Mark. *See* Osymyso
NikeMashUp.com, 181
Nine Inch Nails, 145
notation: as "art world" institution, 59; and figure/ground binary, 166, 167; introduction of standardized, 54
Nozze di Figaro, Le (Mozart), 67
N.W.A., 136-37

objective faithfulness in art, 48, 50
obscurity, aesthetic of, 129–34
O'Connor, Sandra Day, 102
Office to Harmonize Sounds (Qing Dynasty China), 18
Ong, W. J., 201
online music stores, 28, 191
online radio, 26
opera, 66
oral tradition, 148
O'Reilly, Bill, 76
original/copy binary, 124–47; art/craft binary and, 103; can configurable music be unique, 138–46; configurability and style, 125–28, 146; configurability as challenge to, 85; copyright law defines and polices, 63–64; enforcement in visual arts, 61; ethics of sampling, 134–35; gradations in, 125; in modern discursive framework, 43, 50–53; as popular subject of debate, 125; recognizability versus obscurity of source material, 129–34; relationship to source materials, 128–29, 146; and Shift from Linearity to Recursion principle, 201
originality: in Berlioz's model of music and society, 42; and changing definitions of art and artistry, 9; in copyright law, 52–53, 102, 156, 166, 167; genius associated with, 117; markers of in configurable music, 146; professional critics as arbiters of, 61; remuneration incentivizes musicians to claim, 196; sample-based music seen as more original than instrumental music, 135; stylistic, 125–28, 146. *See also* creativity; innovation; original/copy binary; uniqueness
original master recordings, 143–44
Oswald, John, 128
Osymyso (Mark Nicholson), 99, 100–101, 102, 103–4, 114, 115, 119, 128, 129, 131, 133, 135, 139, 140–41, 151, 153, 162, 174
Outliers: The Story of Success (Gladwell), 49

Paris Conservatory, 59
Parker, Charlie, 19, 149, 194
Party Ben, 133
pastiche-based music, 27, 161
pastiche ethic, 99
"Pawnbroker, The" (Jones), 166
peer-to-peer (P2P) file sharing: as agent of empowered consumption, 75; communitarian ethic of, 111; in paradigm shift in communication, 70; as practical resistance to commercial regulation, 188; vilification of, 23
People Like Us (Vicki Bennett), 204
performance: African versus European aesthetic, 30; certain works elevated to composition from, 149; commercial regulation of, 24, 25–26; configurable music in live context, 140–41; defining in terms of audience, 152; relegation to lesser sphere, 54; removal from public sphere, 54; uniqueness of, 63, 140. *See also* composition/performance binary
Perry, Lee "Scratch," 27
Pet Sounds (Beach Boys), 86
phonographs, 27
Photoshopping, 83
physical recording: fetishization of, 144–45, 146, 173. *See also* CDs; vinyl records
piano rolls, 25–26
Pipes, Richard, 197
piracy, 20, 23, 52, 63, 186
Plato: on musical and social and political change, 7, 15–16, 32; on musical regulation, 17, 18, 21
PlayFair, 185
politics, modern discursive framework reflects, 67
Pollock, Jackson, 57
Pontanus, Jacobus, 46, 53
pop art, 84, 106
Postman, Neil, 201–2
postmodern literature, 202
post-production-centric directing, 83
praxis: commercial regulation of, 25–28; community-driven, 77; ideological regulation of, 22–23; legal regulation of, 19–20; in music's discursive framework, 39; practical resistance to commercial regulation, 188; practical resistance to

Southern, Eileen, 48

Stein, Steve (Steinski), 100, 107, 111, 115, 116, 131, 161, 164, 181, 206

Strauss, Neil, 25

"Strawberry Fields Forever," 163

Streets, 125

Strictly Kev (Kevin Foakes; DJ Food), 102, 105, 114, 126, 127, 130, 132, 135, 141–42, 142–43, 150, 152, 161, 166, 169, 172, 174, 175, 186, 203

"Stroke of Genius, A" (Freelance Hellraiser), 101

structure versus agency, of musical and social change, 33–34

style: "black" versus "white," 207; configurability and, 125–28, 146; integrating new universe of sounds into stylistic system, 160; music industry sees configurability as just another, 195

subjective distortion in art, 48, 50, 85

Sullivan, M., 28

"superproducers," 83

surveillance, 199–200

synthesizers, 187

"systems framework" personality psychology, 34–35

talent: configurable music producers on, 114–15, 208; deliberate practice versus, 49; as increasingly amorphous concept, 84–85; in modern discursive framework, 47; teachable skill versus innate, 97. See also genius

taste: as marker of class, 66; in modern aesthetics, 50

team9, 133

techno: as "arrangements," 156; avant-garde composers use techniques of, 81; and changing definitions of art and artistry, 9; copyright protection for, 118, 156; difficulty in identifying sources in, 137; and "digging in the crates," 143; figure/ ground binary in, 161; mash-ups contrasted with, 131; variation between other styles of sample-based music, 196

technology: attributes of recent communications, 71–73; change fueled by accelerating innovation in, 3; commercial regulation of, 26–28; configurable, 8; evolution from physical to digital materials, 173–74; ideological regulation of, 23–24; legal regulation of, 20; at live music events, 61;

modern discursive framework changed by, 43; modern social institutions challenged by new, 14; in music's discursive framework, 39; new practices undermine distinction between categories of production, 10; new universe of sounds produced by, 160; paradigm shift in communication caused by rapid advances in, 70; production versus playback, 26–27, 30; reciprocal interdependence between culture and, 70; in resistance to musical regulation among configurable musicians, 182–83; as shaping musical aesthetics and practice, 6; as site of regulation of music, 17–18; technological resistance to commercial regulation, 188–89; technological resistance to ideological regulation, 186–87; technological resistance to legal regulation, 184–85; women and, 205. See also computers

tekhne, 44, 45

television: copyright of musical performance on, 26; music programs, 62; "reality," 199; TiVo, 70, 84

Tepper, Stephen J., 84, 109

theft, 23, 125, 177

Thimbletron, 177

"This Land Is Your Land" (song), 26

Thomas, Douglas, 32, 77

T.I., 2

Time magazine, 189, 190

TiVo, 70, 84

tools. See materials/tools binary

TradeMark G (Mark Gunderson), 104, 110, 113, 116, 128–29, 137, 139–40, 141, 141, 144, 151, 152, 153, 155, 162, 163, 172, 173, 176, 177

"transformative use" doctrine, 138, 146

Trilling, James, 45

Troupenas, Eugène Théodore, 41, 42

True Hollywood Story (television program), 62

Tsur, Reuven, 56–57

turntablism, 154–55; as Afro-diasporic, 205; as loop-oriented, 206; mash-ups contrasted with, 155, 207; purism regarding, 174

"Under Pressure" (Bowie and Mercury), 167–68

uniqueness: Benjamin on, 9, 50–51; can configurable music be unique, 138–46;

configurable musicians strive for, 194; copyright law defines and polices, 63; defining in terms of artist rather than work, 51; and fetishization of art object, 9; hierarchy of, 52, 63, 67, 85, 139, 142; as key to remuneration, 140; in modern discursive framework, 50; of performance, 63, 140. *See also* originality

Urban, Jennifer, 104–5, 118–19, 137, 156, 166–67

Vaidhyanathan, Siva, 4, 20
Valenti, Jack, 211n.28
Valve Corporation, 80
Van Gogh, Vincent, 50
Vanilla Ice, 167–68
video games: Arcangel's *Self Playing Sony Playstation 1 Bowling*, 96; configurable practices in, 80–81; controllers used as musical instruments, 188; game mods, 75; machinima, 8, 75, 96; "walkthroughs," 96
Vidler, Mark, 98
vinyl records: "digging in the crates" for, 143; digital and physical media coexisting, 173; DJs spin in performance, 86; fetishization of physical recording, 145, 146, 173; physical characteristics of, 174; sampling from, 188; singles, 154
virtuosity, 50, 51
visual arts: configurable music compared with, 98–100; figure/ground distinction in, 55; and materials/tools binary, 170–71; materials/tools binary in, 57; omitted from liberal arts, 44; original/copy distinction enforced in, 61; shift from community-based to academic pedagogical model in, 59
vocals, 162, 185–86, 206
von Eschen, Penny, 21–22

von Lohmann, Fred, 130, 183, 184
V/VM (James Kirby), 97, 112, 114, 116, 130, 139, 140, 144, 145, 154, 160–61, 165, 172, 183, 185

Wagner, Richard, 81
Wal-Mart, 25
Wand, Matt, 105, 108–9, 111, 125, 126, 132, 133–34, 139, 142, 144 45, 154, 164, 173, 174–75, 188, 198
Warhol, Andy, 98–99
Warner Music Group, 157
Web 2.0, 74
Werde, Bill, 99, 182
Western classical music: Bach, 24, 50; Beethoven, 41–43, 54, 56–57, 167; Berlioz, 41–43, 53, 54, 59, 65; bias toward melody in, 168, composition and performance as separate in, 54; figure/ground binary in, 56–57, 159–60; versus improvisation-based African-American forms, 155; Mozart, 56, 67; professionalization of musical production in, 61; remixing in, 81–82; tools/materials binary in, 58; traditional group structure of, 197; von Bingen, 22
"Wheel of Mash" (TradeMark G), 141, *141*, 153
White Album, The (the Beatles), 79, 117
Williams, Raymond, 70
women, configurable music and, 204–5

X-Ecutioners, 125
Xunzi, 18

Yellow Submarine (film), 15
Yongzheng Emperor, 18

Zeoli, Tony, 112, 114, 117, 126, 149–50, 152, 164, 177, 182, 185

ARAM SINNREICH is fascinated by music, technology, and human behavior. He has written for periodicals including the *New York Times*, *Billboard*, and *Wired News*, and has offered his insight and expertise as senior analyst at Jupiter Research, visiting professor at NYU Steinhardt, director at innovation lab OMD Ignition Factory, and assistant professor at Rutgers SC&I, where he is currently employed. He also writes and performs music, and has worked with groups and artists including legendary ska/punk band Agent 99, punky reggae queen Ari-Up, Tony Award–winning actress and playwright Trazana Beverley, and NYC progressive soul band Brave New Girl.

Sinnreich holds an M.S. in Journalism from Columbia University, and a Ph.D. in Communication from USC Annenberg. He lives in Brooklyn with his bandmate and wife, Dunia, their children Simon and Asha, and a cat named Monkey.

CPSIA information can be obtained at www.ICGtesting.com
229230LV00001B/9/P